Six Sigma Producibility Analysis and Process Characterization

IBM CANADA LTD.
M&D IRC • DEPT. 1F/835
1150 EGLINTON AVE. EAST
NORTH YORK, ONT.
CANADA M3C 1H7

Six Sigma Producibility Analysis and Process Characterization

Mikel J. Harry
J. Ronald Lawson

Addison-Wesley Publishing Company, Inc.
Reading, Massachusetts   Menlo Park, California   New York
Don Mills, Ontario   Wokingham, England   Amsterdam
Bonn   Paris   Milan   Madrid   Sydney   Singapore
Tokyo   Seoul   Taipei   Mexico City   San Juan

The publisher offers discounts on this book when ordered in quantity for special sales. For more information please contact:
    Corporate & Professional Publishing Group
    Addison-Wesley Publishing Company
    One Jacob Way
    Reading, Massachusetts 01867
Library of Congress Cataloging-in-Publication Data

Harry, Mikel J.
    Six sigma producibility analysis and process characterization /
  Mikel J. Harry and J. Ronald Lawson.
       p. cm.
    Includes bibliographical references.
    ISBN 0-201-63412-0
    1. Quality control--Statistical methods. 2. Production
management--Quality control.   I. Lawson, J. Ronald. II. Title.
TS156.H347   1992
658.5'62'015195--dc20   92-14457
                                          CIP

ISBN 0-201-63412-0

3 4 5 6 7 8 9 10 11 AL 9796959493
Third printing February 1993

TABLE OF CONTENTS

TABLE OF CONTENTS (CONT)

TABLE OF CONTENTS (CONT)

LIST OF ILLUSTRATIONS

LIST OF ILLUSTRATIONS (CONT)

LIST OF TABLES

LIST OF SYMBOLS

Roman Symbols

A = Some event

A_i = Weighting factor related to the ith dimension of a mechanical design circuit

ANOVA = Analysis of variance

B = Some event

B = Bilateral tolerance

B_i = Conversion or "correction" factor related to the ith dimension of a mechanical design circuit

b_0 = The intercept of a line in a regression equation

b_1 = The coefficient of the linear effect of the first variable in a regression equation

b_{11} = The coefficient of the quadratic (squared) term for the first variable in a regression equation

b_{12} = The coefficient of the cross-product term of the first and second variables in a regression equation

Cov = Covariance

C_p = Capability of an actual or postulated manufacturing parameter which only considers the process spread in relation to the engineering specification width

C_p^* = Dynamic long-term capability ratio

C_{pk} = Extension of C_p which considers central tendency in relation to the nominal specification

C_R = Index of parameter robustness

c = Inflation factor assigned to a particular standard deviation so as to reflect the effects of nonrandom perturbing influences emanating from the underlying cause system

DRSS = Dynamic Root-Sum-of-Squares

d = The number of defects

d_2 = Ratio of the expected value of $\overline{R}$ (in samples of size n) to the σ of the population

d_2^* = d_2 value from MIL-STD-414. Corrects d_2 when N is small

df = Degrees of freedom

dpmo = Defects per million opportunities

dpm = Defects per unit opportunity

dpu = defects per unit

E = Test efficiency. Recognize that $(1 - E)$ 100 is the percentage of nonconforming items which escape the test

e = Base of natural logarithm (e = 2.71828+)

e = Random error term

F = Variance ratio

F = Any given assembly gap constraint or limitation

F* = Decision criterion for comparing two population variances

f = Frequency; generally, the number of observed values in a given cell of a frequency distribution

f = Used to describe a function of. For example, A = f (B) is to say that variable A is a function of variable B

$f(x)$ = The probability density function of x

f_e = Expected frequency

f_o = Observed frequency

fx = The frequency of X

G = A rational subgroup

G_{max} = Maximum worst-case asembly gap

G_{min} = Minimum worst-case assembly gap

G_{nom} = Nominal gap value

G_{range} = Total range of an assembly gap

G_{tol} = Assembly gap tolerance

H_o = The null hypothesis

H_a = The alternative hypothesis

i = Used to describe the ith case or occurrence of a variable

k = Proportion of a tolerance zone consumed by a linear mean offset

k* = Proportion of mean variation due to dynamic mean behavior

LCL = Lower control limit on a control chart

LSL = Lower engineering specification limit

Mdn = Median

Mo = Mode

MS = Mean square; e.g., MS_E is the mean square for error

m = Used to describe the mth case or occurrence of a variable. Also used to describe complexity; e.g., the mth part, opportunity, element, etc

N	=	Number of cases in a population
N	=	Number of articles in a lot or population
N	=	Statistical (total) sample size; also, nominal dimension value
NID (μ,σ)	=	Normal independent distribution with the mean μ and standard deviation σ
NID $(0,1)$	=	Normal independent distribution with the parameters $\mu = 0$ and $\sigma = 1$
N_e	=	Nominal design value of an envelope
N_i	=	i^{th} nominal dimension within a design circuit
N_{p_i}	=	Nominal design value of the ith part
n	=	Number of cases in a sample
n	=	Number of articles or observed values in a sample or subgroup. Also, the number of trials of some event
$\bar{n}$	=	Average subgroup sample size
n_i	=	Number of cases in the ith subgroup
np	=	Number of defective articles in a sample of size n
P	=	Probability
PCB	=	Printed circuit board
p	=	Probability
p	=	Fraction defective; i.e., the ratio of the number of defective units to the total number of defective and nondefective units
$\bar{p}$	=	Average fraction defective; i.e., the total number of defective units found in a set of samples divided by the total number of units in the samples
$p(x > a)$	=	Probability that x is greater than a
ppm	=	Parts per million
ppmo	=	Parts-per-million opportunities
Q	=	Minimum assembly gap performance criterion
q	=	Yield in the binominal relation; e.g., q $= 1 - p$
R	=	Maximum assembly gap performance criterion
R	=	Range of a set of n numbers; i.e., the difference between the largest number and the smallest number
$\bar{R}$	=	Mean of two or more ranges

r	=	The number of occurrences of some event; e.g., the number of defectives in a sample. Often related to the Poisson relation
RSM	=	Response surface methodology, an experimental approach used to optimize many different kinds of industrial proceses and systems
S	=	Sample standard deviation
S^2	=	Sample estimate of σ^2 (variance of a population; e.g., s^2 is the sample estimate of the variance of individual values, s_x^2 is the sample estimate of the variance of sample means)
SL	=	Specification limit; e.g., upper or lower. Represents the limit of allowable unilateral variation
SPC	=	Statistical process control
SRSS	=	Static Root-Sum-of-Squares
SS	=	Sum of Squares
SS_{TOTAL}	=	Total sum of squares
T	=	Total of all values in a set of values
T	=	A dimensional semitolerance; also, target value used for C_{pk} calculations
T_e	=	Design envelope tolerance
T_{p_i}	=	Tolerance assigned to the ith nominal part
t	=	Random variable of the t distribution
t	=	t test, used to test for the difference from some hypothesized mean or for the difference between sampled means, when the variability in the population must be estimated
t_α	=	The t deviate associated with a given alpha error
t_β	=	The t deviate associated with a given beta error
U	=	Unilateral tolerance
UCL	=	Upper control limit on a control chart
USL	=	Upper engineering specification limit
u	=	The number of units

$\bar{u}$ = Total number of defects in all samples divided by the total number of units in all samples; i.e., the average defects per unit

Var = Variance

V_i = Vector associated with the ith nominal dimension

WC = Worst case

WC_{max} = Maximum worst case

WC_{min} = Minimum worst case

W_i = i^{th} mean shift vector

X = A continuous random variable

$\overline{X}$ = Sample mean

$X_1 \ldots X_N$ = The underlying cause system of a characteristic

$X_1 - X_2$ = An arithmetic deviation

$X_1, X_2, \ldots$ = Observed value of some variable, usually a quality characteristic or a designator of specific independent variables; e.g., independent variable number one and two

$\widetilde{X}$ = The median value in a set of values or in a subgroup

$\widetilde{\overline{X}}$ = The average of subgroup medians; the estimated process median

$\overline{X}$ = Arithmetic mean: e.g., the average of a set of numbers $X_1, X_2, X_3, \ldots, X_n$ is the sum of the numbers divided by n

$\overline{\overline{X}}$ = Mean of several $\overline{X}$ values. Often called the grand average

X_{MAX} = Maximum measurement related to the variabled called "X"

X_{MIN} = Minimum measurement related to the variabled called "X"

X = An independent variable or variate, depending upon context. Also referred to as a "casual factor," or "variable within a cause system"

Y = A dependent variable. Also referred to as a "response characteristic," or "outcome"

Y_{FT} = First-time yield

Y_{RT} = Rolled-throughput yield

$Y_{RT;N}$ = Normalized rolled-throughput yield

Z = Normal distribution coefficient. Also called a "standard normal deviate."

Z_α = Standard normal deviate associated with a type I decision error

Z_β = Standard normal deviate associated with a type II decision error

Z_{crit} = Critical Z value

Z_{EQ} = Equivalent limiting standard normal deviate

Z_F = Z value associated with any given assembly gap constraint

Z_{LSL} = Limiting standard normal deviate related to a lower specification limit

Z_{LT} = Long-term limiting standard normal deviate

Z_{MID} = Mid-term limiting standard normal deviate

Z_Q = Z value associated with the minimum assembly performance criterion

Z_R = Z value associated with the maximum assembly performance criterion

Z_{SL} = Limiting standard normal deviate of a given specification limit

Z_{ST} = Short-term limiting standard normal deviate

Z_{USL} = Limiting standard normal deviate related to a given upper specification limit

Greek Symbols

α = The risk of making an error of the first kind; that is, stating that the population mean is different than some number when, in fact, this statement is false. Probability of rejecting the hypothesis under test when it is true. (Called the Type I error or level of significance.) In acceptance sampling, α = the producer's risk

β = Probability of a Type II error. The risk of making an error of the second kind; that is, stating that the population mean is the same as some number when, in fact, this statement is false. In acceptance sampling, β = the consumer's risk.

$1 - \beta$ = Power of a test

$\delta\sigma$ = Separation between two population means or a mean and its corresponding target value (expressed in standard deviation units)

$\delta\sigma_{EQ}$ = Equivalent separation between two population means or a mean and its corresponding target value (expressed in standard deviation units)

$\delta\sigma*$ = A mean offset which has been intentionally induced (expressed in standard deviation units)

ε = A random error term of a linear function

μ = The population mean (average); e.g., the mean of a lot

$\hat{\mu}$ = Hypothesized value for the population mean

μ_G = Assembly gap mean

μ_o = A fixed number against which some population mean is compared

ν = Degrees of freedom

Π = The symbol for multiplication

ρ = Pearson's product moment correlation coefficient

Σ = A mathematical sign meaning "take the algebraic sum of the quantities which follow"

ΣX = The sum of all of the values in a set of values

$\displaystyle\sum_{i=1}^{k} X_i$ = The sum of values from $i = 1$ to k, which is equivalent to ΣX only when k equals the total number of values

σ = Standard deviation of a population

$\hat{\sigma}$ = Hypothesized value for the population standard deviation

σ_G = Standard deviation of an assembly gap

σ^2 = Variance of a population

σ^2_{adj} = Adjusted variance

σ^2_{pool} = Residual variance pool

σ^2_{RND} = Random error term

σ^2_{SYS} = Systematic error term, due to nonrandom effects

σ^2_{TOT} = Total variance. Also called total error term

$\sigma^2_{i_B}$ = Adjusted variance corresponding to the ith dimension of a baseline design analysis

χ^2 = Chi-square. Most often given as a value related to the chi-square distribution

LIST OF SYMBOLS (CONT)

Mathematical Symbols

|X| Absolute value of X. (If X is a negative number the sign is ignored)

$\approx$ Approximately equal to

! Factorial sign n! means "take the product of the integers from 1 through n." (Note: either 0! or 1! = 1)

n! n factorial, where n can be any integer. n! $= n \cdot (n-1) \cdot (n-2) \ldots 1$

0! Zero factorial, which is defined as 1

$\doteq$ Observed to be equal to (approaches). Equivalent to

$\sqrt{}$ Square root

$\sqrt[n]{}$ n^{th} root

log Common logarithm

ln Natural logarithm

f(x) Function of x

∞ Infinity

$>$ Mathematical symbol for "greater than"

$<$ Mathematical symbol for "less than"

$\geqslant$ Mathematical symbol for "equal to or greater than"

$\leqslant$ Mathematical symbol for "equal to or less than"

$\sim$ Distributed as; for example, $Z \sim N(0,1)$ means Z is distributed normally with mean 0 and variance 1

$-$ Low level of variable in matrix experiment designs

$+$ High level of variable in matrix experiment designs

$\bigcirc$ Middle level of variable in matrix experiment designs

$\int$ Integral of

$\int_a^b$ Integral between the limits a and b

$\dfrac{dy}{dx}$ Derivative of y = f(x) with respect to x

$|\ \ |$ Mathematical symbol for "absolute value of"

$\displaystyle\prod_{i=1}^{n}$ Mathematical symbol for multiplication of n terms

$\rightarrow$ Approaches

% Percent

SECTION 1
INTRODUCTION AND OVERVIEW

1.1 THE MOTIVATING FORCE FOR CHANGE

The customers that form the enormous base of today's world market are sending a clear and undeniable message to Corporate America. They are demanding, without compromise, higher levels of product quality, at a lower cost, greater responsiveness, and added value. It goes without saying that such a message marks a new chapter in the book on business survival. For many corporations, this message has profoundly affected their strategic goals and objectives, as well as day-to-day business practices.

Motorola, Inc. is a company that has heard the message and risen to the challenge. According to USA Today (1989), "Motorola engineered one of the most dramatic [business] comebacks of this decade." In the final analysis, such performance was, in great part, attributed to a corporate-wide crusade for quality, as evidenced by Figure 1-1. This accomplishment was formally acknowledged by President Reagan at the White House in 1988, when he presented the first *Malcolm Baldrige National Quality Award* to Motorola, Inc. Figure 1-2 displays the award.

Figure 1-2. The Malcolm Baldrige National Quality Award

At the heart of Motorola's success story is a single, overriding objective. That objective is CUSTOMER SATISFACTION. As may be apparent, such an objective connects all of the activities in which a modern manufacturing organization engages. In essence, it provides the guiding light for all of the activities that characterize Motorola's Six Sigma (6σ) Initiative.

But what does it mean to say that a customer is satisfied? In order to answer this question, we must consider the definition of each term. In this manner, we will be able to discover the unique elements that form the overall concept. The definitions are presented in Figure 1-3.

Figure 1-1. Illustration Relating Motorola's Financial Performance to Quality

> **cus′tom·ẽr**, n [O Fr. coustumier, LL. custumarius, custom.]
>
> 1. a *person* who buys, especially one who buys regularly.
>
> 2. a person with whom one has to deal.
>
> **sat·is·fac′tion**, n [O Fr., from L. satisfaction (-onis), from satisfactus, pp. of satisfacere, to satisfy.]
>
> 1. to gratify fully the wants or desires of; to supply to the full *extent*.
>
> 2. to free from doubt, suspense, or *uncertainty;* to give full assurance to.
>
> 3. to comply with (rules or *standards).*
>
> H89-88   92716-37

Figure 1-3.   Individual Definitions Relating to Customer Satisfaction

As you can see from Figure 1-3, the term "customer" relates to a person who buys, and the term "satisfaction" alludes to the absence of uncertainty associated with standards. A careful integration of these two definitions reveals that customer satisfaction is closely tied to the extent of certainty a customer (i.e., a person) has that his quality, cost, and delivery standards will be complied with. In other words, it is the degree of confidence a customer has that his product and service-related expectations will be met by the producer.

Of course, the flip side to this is the risk that the producer will not be able to meet the customer's expectations. So how can the producer minimize this risk? The answer is quite simple – producibility. When an organization's ability to replicate any given standard is high, the likelihood of customer satisfaction is high. The inverse of this also holds true, as we shall see later on in the discussion. Given this line of reasoning, we may now say that producibility is one of the major determinants of customer satisfaction and producer risk.

1.2   THE ISSUE OF PRODUCIBILITY

During the last several decades, we have experienced an enormous explosion of technology. Because of this explosion, we see products that operate faster, have more features, occupy less space, and, in some instances, even cost less than their predecessors. The overriding manufacturing implication of the so-called "technology boom" is quite clear – for every incremental increase in product complexity and sophistication there must be some relative increase in

producibility; otherwise, the manufacturer will not remain competitive. In many factories, producibility has become a major business issue. It is often the key to economic success or catastrophe.

As we all are aware, the notion of producibility encompasses a myriad of seemingly complex topics. However, before we venture into the forest of technical detail, so to speak, let us gain an overall picture of what the term "producibility" actually refers to.

The term "producibility" has been defined in numerous ways, from many different perspectives. For example, the Military Handbook on producibility (1984) defines the term as

> *. . . the combined effect of those elements or characteristics of a design and the production planning for it that enables the item, described by the design, to be produced and inspected in the quantity required and that permits a series of trade-offs to achieve the optimum of the least possible cost and the minimum time, while still meeting the necessary quality and performance requirements.*

From an industry perspective, Motorola Inc. (1986) expresses it as

> *. . . the ability to reproduce, identically and without waste, units of product so that they satisfy all customer physical and functional requirements (quality, reliability, performance, availability, and price) and also satisfy Motorola business goals.*[1]

An integration of the main concepts presented in the aforementioned definitions reveals that producibility is primarily concerned with how easily and economically a design concept can be taken from development on through the production of a high-quality product, with particular emphasis on quality.

In the following discussion, it will become apparent that the focus is on two fundamental issues – measurement and the viability of cost-effective manufacture. Let us now turn our attention to these two issues.

1.3   THE ISSUE OF MEASUREMENT

Perhaps the emphasis on measurement can be better understood by the message Lord Kelvin (1891) extended:

---

[1] Translating this into statistical terms, from a design engineering perspective, produces the definition given by Harry (1987):
. . . The ability to define and characterize the various product and process elements that exert undue influence on the key product response parameters and then optimize those parameters in such a manner that the critical product quality, reliability, and performance characteristics display a) robustness to random and systematic variations in the central tendency (μ) and variance (σ^2) of their physical elements, b) maximum tolerances related to the "trivial many" elements and optimum tolerances for the "vital few," c) minimum complexity in terms of product and process element count (fx), and d) optimum processing and assembly characteristics as measured by such indices as cycle time, rolled throughput yield, etc.

. . . When you can measure what you are speaking about and express it in numbers, you know something about it, but when you cannot express it in numbers, your knowledge is of a meagre and unsatisfactory kind.

Hence, we assert that the issue of producibility or "manufacturing ease" must be quantifiable – i.e., measurable – if it is to be satisfactorily studied and subsequently used as a basis for decision making and performance benchmarking. After all, if a producer cannot measure the extent to which a product can be transitioned from development on through production, it is virtually certain that their knowledge of producibility is of a "meagre and unsatisfactory kind." With this in mind, we say that:

- If the producer does not know much about producibility, it is likely the producer is not in control of it.

- If the producer is not in control, then the producer and customer are surely at the mercy of chance.

- If both the producer and customer are at the mercy of chance, it is likely neither will be satisfied.

- If the customer is not satisfied, it is virtually certain that the customer will seek satisfaction elsewhere.

As a consequence of this logic, we may conclude that the ability to measure producibility is a major business issue and perhaps, the "yellow brick road" to manufacturing success. However, before we can discuss the specific metrics used to study producibility, we must first articulate the second fundamental issue. In short, we must address the phrase "manufacturing viability."

1.4 THE ISSUE OF MANUFACTURING VIABILITY

In order to illuminate the issue of manufacturing viability, we must focus our discussion on product variation. To facilitate this, let us consider a certain critical product characteristic, say Y_1. In this instance, we can let Y_1 be whatever comes to mind: e.g., the length of a mechanical part, voltage in a circuit, resistance of a material, etc. Let us suppose that Y_1 exhibits a large amount of variation relative to its performance standard. Under this condition, we may say that "ease of manufacture" is low when compared to the situation when the variation in Y_1 is small.

Thus, as variation increases, producibility decreases because the probability of nonconformance increases. In turn, this forces additional rework, scrap, cycle time, cost, etc. As rework and scrap increase, direct labor increases. Obviously, this implies working harder, not smarter. Hence, the "ease" with which one can manufacture a product is diminished as variation increases. Therefore, we may conclude that

variation and producibility are inversely related. But where does such variation come from?

1.4.1 Sources of Product Variation

As many of us are all too aware, product variation emanates from the underlying network of causal variables. Analytically speaking, this understanding may be expressed as $Y = f(X_1, \ldots, X_N)$, where Y is some product characteristic, also called the dependent variable, and $(X_1, \ldots, X_N)$ describes all of the independent variables in the cause system. Thus, we may interpret this expression to mean the output variable (Y) is a function (f) of the input variables $(X_1, \ldots, X_N)$.

Interestingly, the many variables within any manufacturing cause system can be classified into three primary sources of causation. Those sources are (a) inadequate design margin, (b) insufficient process control, and (c) unstable material and components. The relationship among these three sources has been graphically summarized in Figure 1-4.

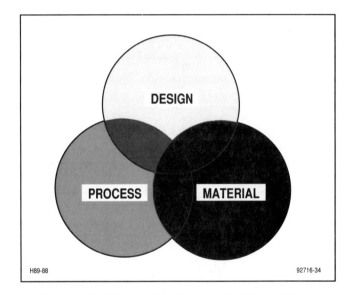

Figure 1-4. Relationship Between the Three Primary Sources of Variation

1.4.2 Quality and Producibility

It is apparent how the independent effects of the numerous design, process, and material/component variables and their combinative interactions form the foundation of product quality. When the "vital few" effects are controlled such that variation is minimized, product quality is improved. As quality is improved, producibility is enhanced, for the reasons given earlier. Hence, we can now better understand the interplay between product quality and producibility in the context of customer satisfaction. Along this same line of reasoning, Stoll, Kumar, and Maas (date unknown) stated:

. . . Producibility and quality are closely coupled because both are essentially the resultant or integrated effect of a myriad of diverse and complex interactions between the product and the manufacturing processes which produce it within a complex environment. These interactions involve all components of the manufacturing system. Inattention to these interactions during the design phase generally results in poor product quality, costly production problems, and a steady stream of engineering change notices (ECNs) during the production phase. Conversely, quality during the production phase is the result of a "producible design" created during the design phase. A producible design results from paying close attention to product/process interactions and seeking to minimize these interactions and their impact by designing the product and process as a coordinated system. In this sense, producibility can be thought of as "quality during the design phase."

1.5   THE ISSUE OF RELIABILITY

As previously indicated, producibility is inextricably linked to variation in a dynamic, synergistic fashion. From this vantage point, it is easy to see how variation is the principal determinant of product quality. In turn, the many facets of product quality either directly or indirectly contribute to the overall reliability of the end product. As a result of this domino relationship, we may say that the assurance of optimum product reliability is directly tied to an organization's ability to take a design concept from development on through production which, to a large extent, is tied to variation.

1.5.1   The Components of Product Reliability

In order to better grasp such interconnectivity, let us consider the classical "bathtub" reliability curve, as depicted in Figure 1-5. As you can see from this figure, the bathtub (upper graph) is formed by the blending of three different curves (lower graph). Now, let us individually consider each of the curves.

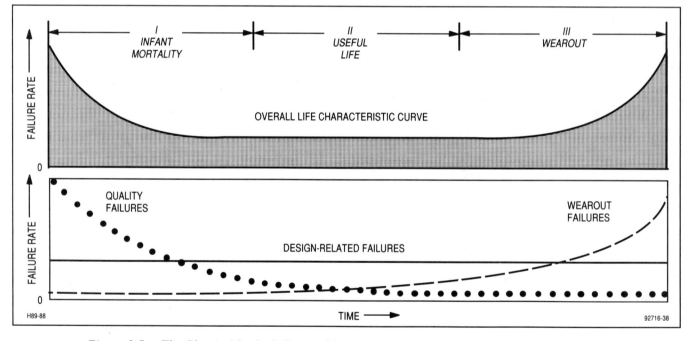

Figure 1-5.   The Classical Bathtub Curve of Product Reliability and its Underlying Components

First, there is the portion of the bathtub effect that is due to the inherent characteristics of the design. This is to say that the engineering specifications define the performance limits for each of the individual elements that comprise the entire product. Given this, we would expect any design-related stress to be a constant across many units of product. This holds because each and every unit of product is subject to the same "engineering-imposed" performance limits. Therefore, the product failure rate, attributable to the design, would tend to form as a straight line across the graph, thereby forming the floor of the bathtub curve.

The second curve is due to natural "wearout" of the individual elements that comprise the product. As one might expect, a part is more likely to display wear after an extended period of operation than after a short period; hence, the curve moves up across the graph. In short, the old saying "gravity prevails" holds true – all things eventually wear out.

The third and last curve on the graph is related to quality failures. Again, as one would expect, a newly manufactured unit of product is more likely to fail than a unit of product which has been operated for a moderate period of time. This phenomenon is primarily due to those defects that escape the manufacturing process. When a new unit of product fails after a short period of operation, we say that it was an "infant mortality," for obvious reasons. To avoid delivering such units to the customer, we perform what is typically called "burn-in." Each unit of product is tested, or otherwise "functionally exercised" for a period of time to get the "bad guys" out before delivery.

1.5.2 *Variation and Product Reliability*

Given that inspection and test efficiency are relatively constant from unit to unit, it is reasonable to assert that escaping defects will increase as manufacturing, component, and material variation increases. Whenever the rate of escaping defects increases, we can expect a higher field failure rate, due to the weakened condition of product as a function of increased variation. Hence, we may say that the need for burn-in increases as manufacturing capability diminishes. However, if the initial capability of the processes, components, and material is high enough to ensure that any given unit of product will not fail during initial operation, there would be little, if any, need for test, inspection, or burn-in. Thus, a product could be manufactured and shipped without unnecessary delay and cost.

Obviously, the production of an exceptionally high-quality product under such conditions significantly increases the likelihood of customer satisfaction and simultaneously decreases producer risk. At this point, the reader should fully recognize the synergistic link between process/component/material variation, design producibility, product reliability, and production costs. This synergistic relationship is graphically depicted in Figure 1-6.

1.6 SYNOPSIS OF THE ISSUES

Thus far, we have determined that variation is the primary enemy of customer satisfaction. We have also reasoned that we must describe variation numerically if we are to study and ultimately improve the ease by which products are manufactured. In particular, we must be able to quantitatively assess variation with respect to design margins, material/component specifications, and process control/capability. Only then can the issue of producibility be addressed in a practical and meaningful way. Again, if the producers cannot express what they know in numbers, control can not be exerted and, if control cannot be realized, the producer and customer are at the mercy of chance.

In light of the latter arguments, it may now be reasoned that the ability to forecast producibility, quality, and reliability is highly dependent upon a measure of the interplay within and between the three circles depicted in Figure 1-4. In addition, we may also say that the cost-effective optimization of producibility requires that we "design for producibility." This implies that the product designs will be relatively impervious or as some would say, "robust" to natural, unavoidable sources of process, component, and material variation. In turn, this assumes that we have a quantitative knowledge of process, component, and material capabilities.

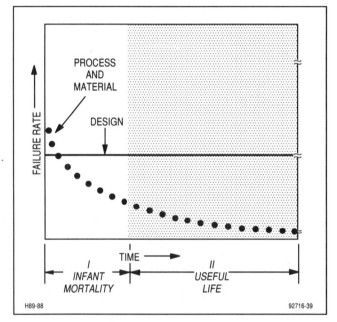

Figure 1-6.   The Window of Opportunity Related to Customer Satisfaction

As may be apparent, this suggests that we design products in the light of that variation which we know is inevitable rather than in the darkness of chance; hence, the need for the various 6σ initiatives presented in Figure 1-7. It should go without saying that the synergistic effects of these initiatives react in such a fashion that the whole is far greater than the sum of the parts – no pun intended. Figure 1-8 summarizes the net effect of the 6σ initiatives.

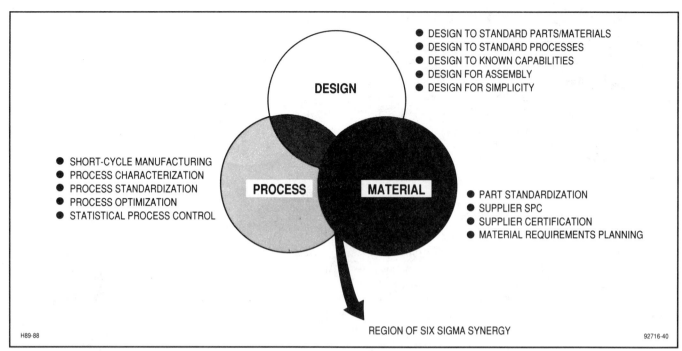

Figure 1-7. *The Six Sigma Initiatives that Underlie the Optimization of Producibility and Customer Satisfaction*

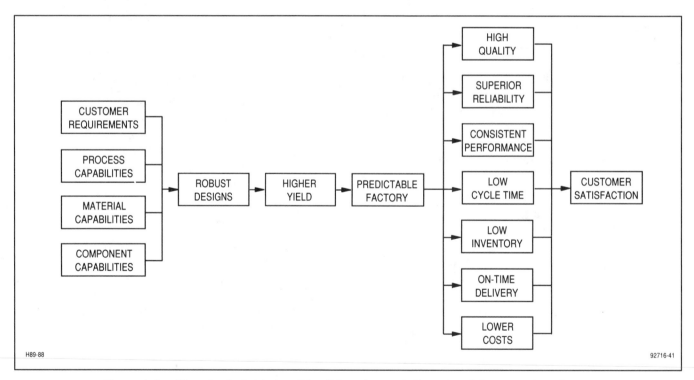

Figure 1-8. *How the 6σ Initiatives Blend Together to Achieve Total Customer Satisfaction*

SECTION 2
THE BASIS FOR PRODUCIBILITY METRICS

2.1 THE PRODUCIBILITY GAME

Since the issue of producibility involves the notions of manufacturing confidence and risk, it is reasonable to assert that the concepts underlying probability should serve as the foundation of any measurement scheme. To illustrate why this is so, let us consider an analogous example.

For the moment, we shall hypothesize a pair of "manufacturing dice" and a customer requirement that only allows those combinations that yield a 3, 4, 5, ... , or 11. In this instance, a 2 or 12 represents a nonconformance to standard, or as some would say, a quality defect. Thus, we may ask the question: "To what extent will the customer be satisfied?" In the language of statistics, the question would be, "What is the probability of not rolling a 2 or 12?" In order to answer the latter question, we must apply some fundamental probability theory.

2.1.1 The Concept of Joint Events

In statistical notation, the likelihood of some event A may be given by P(A). If some event A is independent of some other event, say B, the probability of both A and B occurring is P (A and B) = P(A) x P(B). In other words, the joint probability of A and B is multiplicative by nature.[1] Since a single die has six sides, the random chance probability that any given side will be face up is 1/6 = .1667 because (a) only one side can be up at any given time, (b) there are a total of six possibilities, and (c) each of the six possibilities has the same probability of occurrence. Of course, all of this assumes the die is unbiased. Thus, the random chance probability of nonconformance to standard may be given as 16.67 percent.

Extending this reasoning to a pair of dice, we may say that the probability of rolling two 1s would be .1667 x .1667 = .0278, or 2.78 percent. The same reasoning would also hold true for the possibility of two 6s. This may be directly verified by studying the exhaustive combinations given by a pair of dice, such as displayed in Figure 2-1.

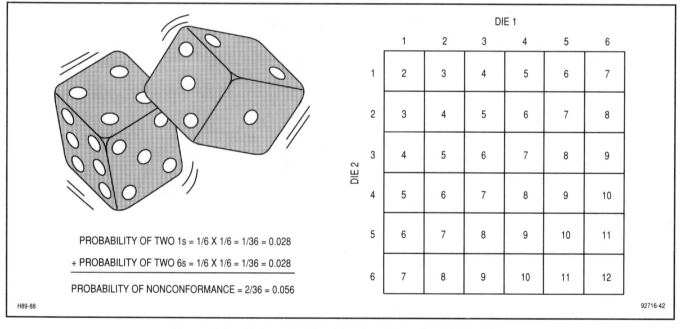

Figure 2-1.   Exhaustive Combinations Given by a Pair of Dice

---

[1] This is given by the multiplication theorem. This theorem states that the probability of several particular outcomes occurring jointly is the product of their separate probabilities, provided that the events that generate these outcomes are independent. Recognize that "independence" means that the outcome of one event must have no influence on and in no way be related to the outcome of the other event(s). If they are not independent, the joint occurrence of both A and B would be given by P(A B) = P(A) x P(B|A), where P(B|A) is equal to the probability that B will occur, assuming A has already occurred.

2.1.2 The Concept of Mutually Exclusive Events

Because the occurrence of a 2 or 12 cannot happen concurrently, we say that the two outcomes are mutually exclusive of each other. This is to say that a 2 and 12 cannot occur at the same time; i.e., they are restricted from occurring together.[2] Hence, the events of concern are mutually exclusive.

Any time that two events (say, A and B) are mutually exclusive, the probability of event A or B occurring may be given by summing their individual probabilities:[3] e.g., P (A or B) = P(A) + P(B). Thus, the total probability of not meeting the customer's standard, with respect to our manufacturing example, would be .0278 + .0278 = .0556, or 5.56 percent. This represents the risk of nonconformance.

2.1.3 Linking Probability and Manufacturing Yield

Given the risk of nonconformance, with respect to our dice example, we may intuitively reason that the probability of yielding a 3, 4, 5, ... , or 11 may be calculated as $1 - .0556 = .9444$. Thus, expected yield may be given by $P(Y) = 1 - [P(A) + P(B)]$. Hence, we may now say that the likelihood of customer satisfaction is 94.44 percent. Additional insight into these concepts may be realized by examining Figure 2-2, using Figure 2-1 as a frame of reference.

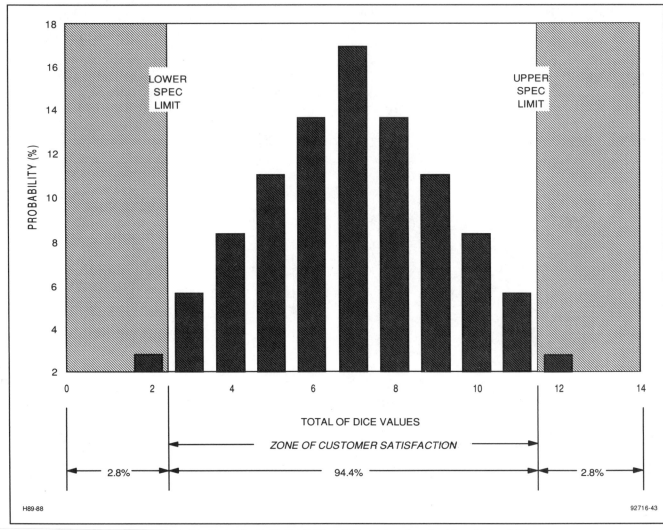

Figure 2-2.   Bar Chart of the Probabilities Associated with a Pair of Dice

---

[2] Such would be the case when considering a bilateral specification. A given measurement cannot be greater than the upper specification limit (USL) and less than the lower specification limit (LSL) at the same time. The measurement is nonconforming to the USL or the LSL, but not both.

[3] The uninformed reader is highly encouraged to gain additional knowledge concerning probability theory via almost any introductory textbook on mathematical statistics. Such knowledge is essential in order to progress beyond the elementary mathematical constructs presented in this booklet.

2.2 EXTENDING THE PRODUCIBILITY GAME

Now, let us suppose that we have two sets of dice. In this instance, we shall say that the first set of dice is the same gaming vehicle as used in the previously mentioned example (e.g., the customer has defined a 2 or 12 as a defect). As already indicated, the first-time yield (Y_{FT}) related to the first specification was determined to be 94.44 percent.

We shall now say that the second set of dice is related to a different specification. It shall also be known that the first specification is not related to the second. In this instance, the second specification is given by the combinative possibilities yielding a 4, 5, 6, ... , or 10; i.e., a 2, 3, 11, or 12 would be considered defective.

By the same statistical reasoning process applied earlier in the discussion, we could easily determine that Y_{FT}, as it relates to the second specification, would be 83.33 percent. Thus, we now have two independent opportunities for nonconformance, each with a different probability of success.

2.2.1   The Concept of Rolled-Throughput Yield

At this point, we could ask the question, "What is the probability of simultaneously meeting both specifications?" As you will recall, when two events are independent, the joint probability is multiplicative by nature. Notice that the joint yield is also called "rolled-throughput yield," and is designated as Y_{RT}. Hence, the likelihood of conformance to both specifications can be described by

$$Y_{RT} = \prod_{i=1}^{m} Y_{FT_i} \qquad \text{Eq. (2-1)}$$

where Y_{RT} is the rolled-throughput yield,[4] m is the total number of independent parameters, Y_{FT} is the first-time yield, and i is the ith parameter.[5] It is referred to as rolled-throughput yield because the first-time yield values are mathematically rolled into a single value, where that single value is indicative of the likelihood of nonincidental throughput. In other words, this metric is aimed at reporting the aggregate first-time yield for two or more independent response characteristics. The resulting yield value represents the likelihood of zero defects when considering each of the response characteristics simultaneously. In this sense, it is a direct measure of producibility. Let the reader clearly understand that the terminology does not imply manufacturing is one big crap shoot, although some may adamantly disagree.

Applying Eq. (2-1) to our dice example would reveal that the probability of picking up both sets of dice and rolling a "good" number would be .9444 x .8333 = .7870. This would be to say that there is a 78.70 percent chance of simultaneously producing numbers that conform to both specifications. In short, the simultaneous likelihood of success (Y_{RT}) is a direct measure of producibility – if the resultant is high, producibility is high; otherwise, producibility is less than desirable. The logic of this should be fairly intuitive.

2.2.2   The Concept of Normalized Rolled-Throughput Yield

Let us now turn our focus toward what is called "normalized rolled-throughput" yield ($Y_{RT:N}$). Essentially, such a yield represents the throughput-per-opportunity, where an opportunity may be given as a performance parameter, part, process step, etc. In this sense, $Y_{RT:N}$ may be thought of as the production capability of a "typical" opportunity within a system of opportunities.

Essentially, normalization neutralizes the influence of complexity. Because of this feature, it is possible to compare the producibility of one design alternative to another. In short, it gives us the ability to compare "apples and oranges," so to speak, irrespective of measurement units and complexity.

---

[4] Rolled-throughput yield is the product of all subordinate yields. For example, if there were three independent response parameters with respective yields of .999, .998, .990, the rolled-throughput yield would be .999 x .998 x .990 = .9870. The rolled-throughput yield represents the likelihood of zero nonconformities. In essence, it is the cumulative yield for m number of independent yield values. Of course, some people would argue that there are many instances in which the response characteristics are not independent of others and, as a consequence, the cumulative yield would be biased. While this is a true statement, we must recognize the balance between practical application and mathematical precision. In many instances, the covariance of two (or even three) events can easily be accounted for; however, if the number of covariates is large, due to the total number of events being considered, the task of computation can quickly overwhelm most practitioners. If one is concerned with "seven-digit precision," then the task of quantitative producibility analysis will be prolonged, and most likely prove to be a frustrating journey. Even if such precision is attainable, it is doubtful, in most instances, that the added value of precision in the final figures will justify such analytical concerns. While this certainly does not hold in all cases, it does hold in many. It is imperative to recognize that initial estimates of design producibility require only first-order approximations; therefore, as a general rule, the assumption of independence is reasonable unless the peculiarities of a situation indicate otherwise.

[5] Notice that m was previously defined as the total number of opportunities for nonconformance. In the instance of our dice example, there are m = 2 independent parameters, where a parameter constitutes a single categorical opportunity. The key is to recognize that m is a dynamic and flexible term. In some cases, m could be the number of independent assembly gaps in a mechanical loop analysis, the number of independent defect categories applied to a certain product, or even the number of parts called out in a set of engineering drawings. The use of m will take on greater relevance in subsequent discussions.

From a more technical frame of reference, we may say that this method considers the mth root of the rolled-throughput yield, where m is the number of independent opportunities being jointly considered. It may be expressed as

$$Y_{RT;N} = \sqrt[m]{\prod_{i=1}^{m} Y_{FT_i}} \qquad \text{Eq. (2-2)}$$

or, in equivalent form,

$$Y_{RT;N} = \left(\prod_{i=1}^{m} Y_{FT_i}\right)^{1/m} \qquad \text{Eq. (2-3)}$$

where $Y_{RT;N}$ is the normalized rolled-throughput yield.

2.2.3 The Application of Normalized Rolled-Throughput Yield

To better understand the importance of this metric, let us return to our dice example. As you will recall, Y_{RT} for both sets of dice was .7870. Applying Eq. (2-3) would reveal that the normalized rolled yield is $Y_{RT;N} = (.7870)^{1/2} = .8871$. This says that the normal or "average" first-time yield per specification would need to be 88.71 percent in order to achieve a composite throughput of 78.70 percent.

Expressed in different terms, it would be to say that one must average "good" numbers 88.71 percent of the time, with respect to each set of dice, in order to have "good" numbers on both sets of dice 78.70 percent of the time. This may be easily confirmed by reverse calculation: e.g., $Y_{RT}{}^m = .8871^2 = .7870$. Thus, we may now say, in the context of this booklet, $Y_{RT;N}$ represents the "uniform manufacturing capability" that must exist in order to achieve a certain aggregate yield.

2.3 TRANSLATING PROBABILITY THEORY TO PRODUCIBILITY METRICS

For the sake of discussion, let us suppose that a certain product design may be represented by the area of a rectangle. We shall also postulate that each rectangle contains 10 equal areas of opportunity for nonconformance to standard. Figure 2-3 illustrates this particular product concept.

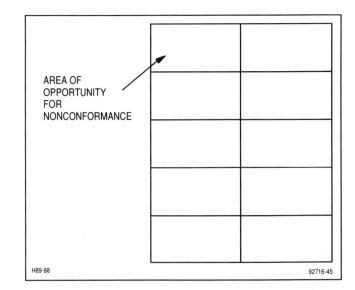

Figure 2-3. Abstract Unit of Product Consisting of 10 Equal Areas of Opportunity for Nonconformance

2.3.1 The Defects-Per-Unit Metric

Let us now suppose the quality records related to our example product indicate that, out of the last 1000 units manufactured, 1000 nonconformities were detected. For our example, we would compute

$$dpu = \frac{d}{u} \qquad \text{Eq. (2-4)}$$

where dpu is the defects per unit, d is the frequency or "number" of observed defects, and u is the number of units produced. In this instance, we would determine that dpu = 1000/1000 = 1.0. This means that, on the average, each unit of manufactured product will contain 1 such defect. Of course, this assumes the defects are randomly distributed.[6]

2.3.2 The Influence of Opportunity Count

We must also recognize, however, that within each unit of product there are 10 equal areas of opportunity for nonconformance to standard. Because of this, we may now calculate

$$dpm = \frac{dpu}{m} \qquad \text{Eq. (2-5)}$$

where dpm defines the defects-per-unit opportunity, and m is the number of independent opportunities for nonconformance per unit. In the instance of our abstract product, m = 10.

---

[6] In the context of this discussion, we may say that defects are distributed in a uniform or random manner. Since uniform defects are easily detected and quickly corrected, the assumption of a random model is often considered quite reasonable when considering a large amount of defect data gathered over an extended period of time.

Because m = 10 is given as a design constant, we may easily demonstrate that the probability of a nonconformance-per-unit area of opportunity is (1000/1000)/10 = .10, or 10 percent. Inversely, we may argue that there is a 100(1.00 − 0.10) = 90 percent chance of not encountering a nonconformance with respect to any given unit area of opportunity.

It is very interesting to note that the likelihood of a defect-free unit of product may be given by Eq. (2-1). In this instance, the probability of zero defects, for any given unit of product, would be $.90^{10} = .348678$, or 34.87 percent. This may be intuitively reasoned by studying Figure 2-4.

Now, if we increase the number of opportunities for nonconformance such that m = 100, it should be apparent that the probability of nonconformance-per-unit area of opportunity would be 1/100 = .01, or 1 percent. Consequently, the likelihood that any given unit of product will be defect free would be $(1-.01)^{100} = .99^{100} = .366032$, or 36.60 percent.

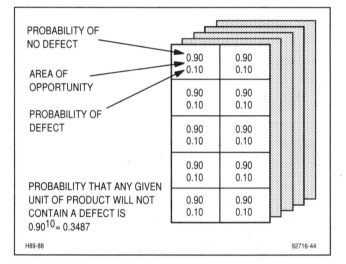

Figure 2-4. Probability of Zero Defects for the Abstract Product Example Under the Constraint m = 10 and dpu = 1.0

2.3.3 The Application of Defects Per Unit

At this point in the discussion, the reader is directed to Table 2-1. Notice that the table displays the effect of m on the likelihood of zero defects for any given unit of product, given dpu = 1.0. The reader should also notice that as m → ∞, the probability that any given unit of product will be defect free approaches e^{-1}. Further study shows that the probability that any given unit of product will be defect free may be approximated by e^{-dpu}. In this case, the probability of zero defects would be $e^{-dpu} = e^{-1} = .367879441$, or roughly 36.79 percent.

This point will be of immense importance to us in the following discussion concerning the Poisson distribution. As we shall see, this particular distribution is an invaluable tool when assessing producibility.

Table 2-1. Probability of Zero Defects as m Increases Under the Constraint dpu = 1.0

Number of Areas of Opportunity Per Unit of Product (m)	Confidence That Any Given Area Will Not Contain a Defect* (Y)	Probability That Any Given Unit of Product Will Not Contain a Defect Y^m
10	.9	.348678440
100	.99	.366032341
1000	.999	.367695425
10000	.9999	.367861050
100000	.99999	.367877601
1000000	.999999	.367879625
10000000	.9999999	.367879459

Observed dpu = 1.0

2.3.4 The Poisson Model

Keying off the latter arguments, we may now ask the question, "What is the probability that any given unit of manufactured product will contain two, three, or even more defects?" Well, when the probability of nonconformance per opportunity is less than 10 percent, but the overall likelihood of observing a defect is high, the Poisson distribution can be employed to answer such questions.[7] As may be apparent, these criteria seem applicable to our abstract product example.[8]

---

[7] Grant and Leavenworth (1980) indicated that the Poisson approximation may be applied when the number of opportunities for nonconformance (m) is large and the probability (p) of an event (r) is small. In fact, as m increases and r decreases, the approximation by the Poisson model improves. To further extend some of the criteria for applying the Poisson model, Juran (1979) stated that when the sample size is at least 16, the population size is at least 10 times that of the sample, and the probability of an event on each trial is less than 10 percent, the Poisson distribution can be used.

[8] In cases such as those discussed here, the Poisson model can be applied because there are many opportunities for defects; i.e., m is often quite large. In addition, the probability of nonconformance is low relative to each of the opportunities. Furthermore, the assumption of independence is reasonable, for the reasons given in the previous discussion. These factors, when taken together, satisfy the underlying assumptions of the Poisson distribution as applied to the abstract product example.

Given reasonable compliance to the underlying assumptions, we may calculate the probability (Y) by virtue of the Poisson relation. This particular relation is most often expressed as

$$Y = \frac{(np)^r e^{-np}}{r!} \qquad \text{Eq. (2-6)}$$

where n is the total number of independent trials, p is the probability of occurrence, and r is the number of occurrences of interest. Throughout the remainder of this booklet, the term "occurrences" can be used interchangeably with the word "defects."

2.3.5 The Application of Poisson

In most instances, the Poisson equation will allow us to avoid the burdensome calculations often associated with the binomial model, as will be discussed in greater detail later on. Such an approximation of the binomial is called "Poisson's Exponential Binomial Limit" or simply, "Poisson's Law."

To better relate the Poisson relation to our abstract product example, we may rewrite Eq. (2-6) as

$$Y = \frac{(d/u)^r e^{-d/u}}{r!} \qquad \text{Eq. (2-7)}$$

where d is the number of nonconformities or "defects," and u is the number of units produced. At this point in our discussion, the reader should recognize that d = np. Obviously, normalizing per unit of product reveals that d/u = np/u. Hence, a substitution of terms may be made for the normalized case where u = 1.

For the special case of r = 0 — i.e., zero defects — Eq. (2-7) reduces to

$$Y = e^{-d/u}. \qquad \text{Eq. (2-8)}$$

Thus, the relation described in Eq. (2-8) reflects first-time yield (Y_{FT}) for a specified d/u. Obviously, if Y_{FT} is known, or may be rationally postulated, we may solve for d/u by calculating

$$d/u = -\ln Y_{FT} \qquad \text{Eq. (2-9)}$$

where ln is the natural log. As we shall see, this is also a very useful tool when conducting a producibility analysis.

Through the application of Eq. (2-7), we may create a window from which to view the expected distribution of defects across u number of production units. It would reveal the theoretical number of production units expected to have 0, 1, 2, 3, ... , or more defects. For example, if we were to manufacture, say 1,000 units of product and subsequently discover d/u = 1.0, then we would expect the frequency distribution[9] given in Table 2-2.

Table 2-2. Poisson Distribution of Defects Under the Constraint that m is Large and dpu = 1.0

Number of Defects (r)	Probability of Exactly r Defects* p(r)	Number of Units With Exactly r Defects (u)	Total Number of Defects Contained Within u Units (d)	Expected Number of Escaping Defects** d(1-E)
0	.3679	368	0	0
1	.3679	368	368	4
2	.1839	184	368	4
3	.0613	61	183	2
4	.0153	15	60	0
5	.0031	3	15	0
6	.0005	1	6	0
7	.0001	0	0	0
8	.0000	0	0	0
TOTAL	1.0000	1000	1000	10

* Theoretically, r assumes values to infinity, but beyond r = 8, the resultant probability is so small it is negligible for the case dpu = 1.0.
** Assumed test/inspection efficiency (E) = 99%

---

[9] When applying the Poisson model, one may elect to conduct a post-hoc chi-square goodness-of-fit test, to directly verify appropriate application.

2.3.6   The Poisson Model and Rolled-Throughput Yield

Based on the Poisson model and our previous discussion concerning rolled-throughput yield, we may now generalize Eq. (2-1) and Eq. (2-8). This would entail rewriting Eq. (2-5) as d/u = m(dpm). Recognize that this expression holds only for the case $dpm_1 = dpm_2 = \ldots = dpm_m$; otherwise, we must calculate

$$d/u = \sum_{i=1}^{m} dpm_i. \qquad \text{Eq. (2-9a)}$$

Thus, we may rewrite Eq. (2-8) as

$$Y = e^{-\sum_{i=1}^{m} dpm_i} \qquad \text{Eq. (2-9b)}$$

Recognizing that the result of Eq. (2-9b) constitutes rolled-throughput yield (Y_{RT}), and based on a summation of exponents, we may alter Eq. (2-9b) to reflect

$$Y_{RT} = \prod_{i=1}^{m} e^{-dpm_i} \qquad \text{Eq. (2-10)}$$

Thus, the probability of zero defects for all independent product characteristics can be ascertained using discrete data.[10] In the instance of normalized rolled-throughput yield, the generalized relation would be given as

$$Y_{RT;N} = \sqrt[m]{\prod_{i=1}^{m} e^{-dpm_i}} \qquad \text{Eq. (2-11)}$$

In equivalent form, Eq. (2-11) may also be expressed as

$$Y_{RT;N} = \left(\prod_{i=1}^{m} e^{-dpm_i} \right)^{1/m}. \qquad \text{Eq. (2-12)}$$

In subsequent discussions within this booklet, we shall see why the integration of Poisson with the notion of normalized rolled-throughput yield is vital to the successful study of producibility.

2.3.7   The Estimation of Escaping Defects

If the manufacturing test efficiency is known, or can be rationally postulated, it would now be possible to estimate the number of escaping defects. To illustrate, let us postulate a combined test/inspection efficiency (E) such that E = .99. Under this constraint, we could easily determine that 100(1.0 – E) = 1.0 percent of the defects would escape the manufacturing process. In the instance of dpu = 1.0, we would expect $(1 - e^{-dpu})(1 - E) = (1 - .36788)(1 - .99) = .0063212$ escaping defects per unit of manufactured product. If we were to indicate that 1,000 units of such product were to be built, we would then expect one escaping defect per 1/.0063212 = 158.2 units of manufactured product.

---

[10] Two kinds of data can be used for measuring producibility. Parameters that describe characteristics of the product such as its size, weight, electrical properties, etc., are usually of a continuous nature; that is, the units of measure can be divided into finer and finer increments. The limitation of the extent of this division is determined only by the precision of the measuring instrument. For example, the length of a metal bar can be measured with different tools. A ruler marked in sixteenths of an inch would give precision to a sixteenth of an inch with the ability to estimate to a thirty-second of an inch. However, if a vernier caliper is used, the precision of the measurement may be moved to the thousandth-of-an-inch level. What has been described thus far is continuous data.

Another way to look at the data is to merely count the frequency of occurrence: e.g., the number of roles of the dice that fall between 3 and 11, without concern about the actual value of the dice combination rolled. Or one can count the number of 2s and 12s rolled. In the latter case, one is counting the number of times that the test is failed. Notice that such data is not capable of being subdivided into more precise increments and, therefore, is called discrete data. The Poisson and binomial models cited earlier are used in connection with such discrete data. Because of the inability to subdivide discrete data, inferences made from the data are limited by the number of observations made. In other words, the sample size required to characterize a parameter which is described by discrete data is much larger than that required when continuous data is used.

The tail area under the curve generated by a distribution of continuous data, where the tail boundary is defined by some limits set on the parameter in question, is representative of the number of units that have a parameter value outside those boundaries. If the boundaries determine which units pass or fail the test, then the tail areas represent the number of defective units. In the limits expressed earlier – i.e., large numbers of units and small probability of defect occurrence – the count of defects can be approximated by the properties of the Normal distribution. On the other hand, yield is a measure of the number of units which have fallen within the boundaries and, therefore, have passed the test.

The concept of yield, then, is useful not only in describing the producibility of a single parameter, but it can be applied across several types of products and processes. In the discussion to follow, it will be shown how data describing this variety of products and processes can be compared on a common plane, regardless of whether the data is continuous or discrete.

Now, if we were to further postulate that 20 percent of the defect categories have the potential to induce a functional failure during the useful life of the product, it would be reasonable to assert that the customer could expect to encounter about one field failure out of every 791 production units as a result of the existing production capability. Obviously, the engineering and business uses for such an approximation technique are many. While it is fully recognized to be a first-order model, it has a strong engineering appeal and a reasonable degree of analytical validity.

2.3.9 The Binomial Model

Should the assumptions surrounding the Poisson model prove to be unreasonable, we may turn to the binomial model.[11] This particular model may be given by

$$Y = \frac{m!}{r!(m-r)!} p^r q^{m-r} \qquad \text{Eq. (2-13)}$$

where p is the constant probability of an event and $q = 1 - p$. Interestingly, for the special case of $r = 0$, the binomial model reduces to

$$Y = (1-p)^m \quad . \qquad \text{Eq. (2-14)}$$

Because of this special case (i.e., $r = 0$), we conclude that the probability of zero defects, subject only to the assumptions of the binomial model, may be described by the first-time yield (Y_{FT}). At this point in the discussion, the reader is directed to Figure 2-5. Essentially, this figure contrasts the Poisson and binomial models.

For those cases where the underlying assumptions of the Poisson or binomial model cannot be met, the hypergeometric model may be employed. For additional information on this particular model, the reader is directed to the bibliography.

2.4 APPLICATION OF THE BASIC METRICS

At this point in our discussion, we may now generalize many of the previously mentioned concepts. To begin, let us suppose that we have before us a certain portion of a very simple electrical design. It shall also be understood that there are only three components applicable to this portion of the design. In this instance, we shall designate our components as

Y_1, Y_2, and Y_3, respectively. In addition, we shall say that the respective circuit design will function or "play" if all three parts are within tolerance.

To further set the stage, let us suppose that the three components are "standard" parts and have been used in other products. We shall also say that the historical first-time yield values associated with these parts were recorded in a manufacturing database. In this instance, the first-time yield for each part (Y_1, Y_2, and Y_3) was extracted from the database and determined to be .9995, .9987, and .9765, respectively.

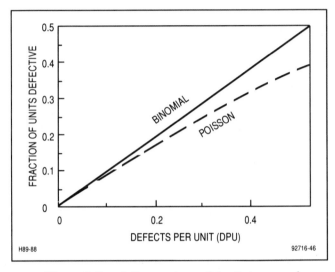

Figure 2-5. A Comparison of the Poisson and Binomial Models

Given the latter information, we may apply Eq. (2-1) to determine the rolled-throughput yield. In this case, $Y_{RT} = .9995 \times .9987 \times .9765 = .9747$. In short, we may say that the probability of simultaneous yield is 97.47 percent. In other words, there is a 97.47 percent likelihood that any given production unit, built in accordance to the previously mentioned circuit design, will "play" during first-time test. In short, it is the probability that any given manufactured circuit will not have an "out-of-spec" component. Expressed differently, it is the likelihood of not having a first-time electrical test failure. Of course, the rolled-throughput yield only applies to that portion of the overall design which we are discussing. As previously indicated, this is but one index of producibility.

---

[11] The reader should note that application of the binomial model requires the assumption of a constant probability of occurrence. This is considered sufficiently reasonable in most situations.

For the sake of furthering our discussion, suppose that Y_{RT} = .9747 was considered unsatisfactory. In this instance, we will say that the manufacturing objective required the first-time test circuit yield to be Y_{RT} = .9990 in order to meet certain higher-level production goals. Under this constraint, we may apply Eq. (2-2) to determine the normalized rolled-throughput yield. In this case, we would easily compute $Y_{RT:N}$ = .99967. This means that each part (Y_1, Y_2, and Y_3) would need to display a first-time component test yield of 99.967 percent in order to achieve the higher-order manufacturing goal. In turn, this would tend to suggest that the capability of each part would need to be upgraded, with the possible exception of Y_1. It might also indicate the need for product redesign, i.e., reconfiguring the circuit so as to reduce complexity and/or open tolerances. In any event, it is apparent that some form of action would be required before releasing the design for production. Hopefully, the reader would not consider "tightened" inspection as an optimization alternative.[12]

---

[12] It has been demonstrated by many highly experienced quality practitioners that "inspecting quality in" simply does not work, not to mention the fact that it is extremely cost prohibitive. The idea that additional testing, burn-in, inspection, etc., provides a viable means to improve product quality ignores the concepts underlying prevention. To embody this philosophy is to say that "we can sort our way to better performance and producibility." The caveat cannot be overemphasized. For additional information on this topic, the reader is directed to Grant and Leavenworth (1980) and Juran (1979).

SECTION 3
THE MODEL FOR PRODUCIBILITY ANALYSIS

Given the review of basic probability theory and its application to producibility, we may now immerse ourselves in a more advanced scenario that will better illustrate how the performance metrics and related methodology can be used.

3.1 ESTIMATING LONG-TERM PRODUCIBILITY

For purposes of discussion, let us consider the product illustrated in Figure 3-1. We can readily imagine that this particular product consists of several major assemblies, with each assembly comprised of several sub-assemblies. Specifically, our discussion will focus on the elements displayed in Figures 3-2 and 3-3. As may be apparent, only one chain in the total design hierarchy has been described and illustrated, simply to delimit the scope of discussion and presentation. With a little study, one can readily generalize the ensuing logic to any other chain in the design hierarchy, or any other product, for that matter.

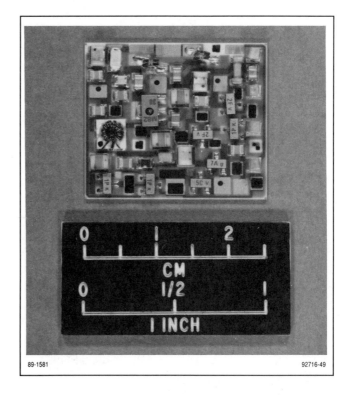

Figure 3-2. Selected PCB Contained within the AN/PRC-112(V) Radio Set

With respect to Figure 3-1, it will be known that there are i mechanical specifications: e.g., assembly tolerances, stress requirements, thermal limits, etc. In addition, we shall say that there are j electrical specifications: e.g., response time, circuit gain, etc. We shall also say that there are k other characteristics which must conform to specification: e.g., quality characteristics such as solder joint wetting, paint finish, etc. Thus, we may now say that there are $i + j$ number of test parameters and k number of inspection characteristics.

3.2 THE ROLE OF PARAMETER CAPABILITY DATA

Now, imagine that a data base of process, material, and component capability data (of a statistical nature) has been formed as the result of extensive characterization studies.[1]

Figure 3-1. Photo of the AN/PRC-112(V) Radio Set

---

[1] Such studies are conducted in order to derive statistical data relating to the various performance characteristics. In turn, the statistical data is used to project first-time yield. While this may seem somewhat benign, the reader must recognize there is "more to it than meets the eye." For example, only certain types of statistical information are useful in quantitative producibility analyses. If an engineer has the "wrong" type of characterization data, it is possible that the engineer could be precluded from conducting a meaningful analysis. In short, characterization data serves as a base for the producibility metrics given in this booklet. Therefore, we may say that the concepts and tools that underlie producibility analysis and parameter characterization form an interactive subsystem within the "design for manufacturability" strategy. Unless "data-tool alignment" is at hand, the likelihood of a thwarted analysis is high.

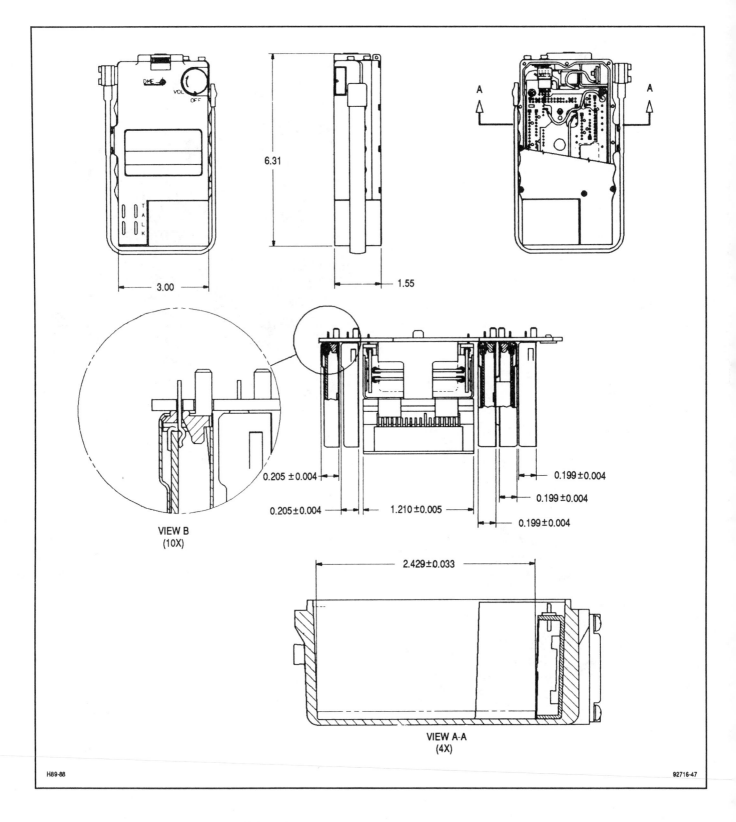

VIEW B
(10X)

VIEW A-A
(4X)

Figure 3-3. Selected Engineering Drawings of the AN/PRC-112(V) Radio Set

Let us further postulate that the aforementioned data is of two varieties: short-term and long-term.[2] Next, we shall say that various computer analyses and simulations were undertaken for each of the i and j parameters using the characterization data as a basis of simulation. Obviously, such an undertaking would produce more realistic short- and long-term, first-time parameter yield estimates simply because we would be working with known process, component, and material capabilities.

3.3 THE ROLE OF MECHANICAL ENGINEERING

Suppose that we select any one of the assembly gaps associated with Figure 3-2. If the process capabilities of the related parts are known or capable of rational estimation,[3] it would be possible to compute the probability of assembly using a statistically based methodology.[4] This would provide the expected first-time yield associated with each independent assembly gap.

If there was a total of m = 6 independent assembly gaps, and the long-term, first-time yield (Y_{FT}) projection for each gap was 99.73 percent, it is easy to see that the rolled-throughput assembly yield (Y_{RT}) for the product, over many manufacturing intervals, would be computed using Eq. (2-1). Doing so would reveal that $Y_{RT} = Y_{FT}^m = .9973^6 = .9839$, or 98.39 percent. This is to say that there would be a 98.39 percent likelihood that any given unit of product could be assembled without encountering an interference fit.

We can now see how it is possible to estimate the joint yield or "cumulative probability" of zero irregularities with respect to mechanical assemblies.[5] As may be apparent, our example excludes all other mechanical considerations with the exception of assembly performance. This has been done in the interests of simplicity and reading ease. Let the reader recognize that the inclusion of other yields, such as those related to thermal and stress requirements (or any others for that matter) could easily be accommodated via the same basic methodology. In other words, there would be more terms to multiply with respect to the application of Eq. (2-1). Thus, an overall rolled-throughput yield could be derived which considers all i mechanical requirements.

3.4 THE ROLE OF ELECTRICAL ENGINEERING

In the context of electrical circuit performance, let us turn our attention to the PCB illustrated in Figure 3-3. Within this particular PCB are several circuits. Let's consider just one. Suppose that circuit V was intended to output a certain electrical response – say, some level of voltage within certain specified limits. Let us also say that it was possible to artificially create a response (e.g., voltage) using a computer simulation program. If we were to input the statistical characteristics of each part into the computer simulation, it would be possible to study the effect of component variation on voltage from a short- and long-term perspective. From such study, we could ascertain the projected first-time test yield of circuit voltage.

---

[2] Short-term capability data reflects "instantaneous reproducibility" – i.e., the ability of a process to repeat itself in a short period of time. Note that short-term capability data must only reflect random variations. If so, the resultant variance describes random error. If the data reflects only random error, it is reasonable to say that it is free of perturbing, systematic influences which emanate from the network of causal variables. Such influences are reflected in the long-term capability data. The relative difference between short- and long-term indices of capability reflects the extent to which existing process, material, and component controls are effective. In short, it is a measure of how robust the response characteristic is to systematic, nonrandom variations in the underlying system of causal variables; i.e., it is an indirect measure of manufacturing control. From this vantage point, it is easy to see why such data is vital to a quantitative producibility assessment.

[3] Rational estimation is usually based on extensive engineering and manufacturing experience. For example, it is well known that many manufacturing processes operating under the auspices of SPC display a capability ratio between $1.00 < C_p < 1.33$; therefore, the pessimistic assumption would be $C_p = 1.00$ and the optimistic assumption would be $C_p = 1.33$. Such assumptions are often (not always) considered "rational" because many of the textbooks on SPC provide this particular range as a target for purposes of manufacturing. As a consequence, many novice practitioners control their respective processes to this level, simply because "the book said so." In fact, they are often rewarded for such performance, which does nothing more than reinforce the behavior, not to mention the antiquated textbook – and the cycle goes on and on. As a sideline to this discussion, the reader must recognize that many experienced practitioners no longer accept the aforementioned capability range as satisfactory. Today, some organizations require $1.5 < C_p < 2.0$, or even $C_p = > 2.0$.

[4] In specific, the probability would be ascertained from the maximum and minimum standard normal deviates (Z values) associated with the assembly specifications (i.e., the lower and upper assembly gap specifications). The Z value is found by calculating the ratio of nominal assembly gap (numerator term) and assembly gap standard deviation (denominator term). Notice that the assembly gap standard deviation is derived by the root-sum-squares (RSS) method. The reader is directed to Harry and Stewart (1988) should additional information on this topic be required.

[5] Such estimation may be by direct calculation (in the instance of our assembly gap example) or by way of computer simulations driven via mathematical algorithms. Regardless of the form of estimation, the reader must recognize that the output is only as good as the input. By using actual short- and long-term input as the basis of calculation/simulation, the outcome would be more intelligent and, as a consequence, provide a better vehicle for conducting quantitative producibility analyses.

If there was a total of m = 6 independent electrical specifications associated with the PCB, and the long-term, first-time yield (Y_{FT}) projection for each of the six parameters was 99.73 percent, the rolled-throughput test yield (Y_{RT}) for the PCB, over many manufacturing intervals, would be $Y_{RT} = Y_{FT}^m = .9973^6 = .9839$, or 98.39 percent. Again, Eq. (2-1) could be applied to make this calculation. This is to say that there would be a 98.39 percent likelihood that any PCB would pass the required electrical test. Notice that all j independent circuit response yields related to the design could be treated in the same manner. Doing so would reveal the projected rolled-throughput yield for the product with respect to the electrical performance characteristics.

3.5 THE ROLE OF MANUFACTURING AND QUALITY ENGINEERING

Now, let us say that the product is subject to k inspection characteristics. If the historical defect data is available, or can be rationally postulated for each of the k characteristics, we could estimate the rolled-throughput inspection yield of the product by virtue of the Poisson relation. For example, let us say that the historical soldering performance related to a PCB similar to that depicted in Figure 3-3 was such that dpm = .000000983.

Notice that, in this instance, an opportunity is defined as an individual solder joint. Given this, the expected first-time soldering yield per joint would be $e^{-dpm} = 2.71828^{-.000000983} = .999999016$, or 99.9999016 percent. If there was a total of, say, 2750 solder joints in the product given in Figure 3-1, the rolled-throughput soldering yield of the PCB would be $Y_{RT} = Y_{FT}^k = .999999016^{2750} = .9973$, or 99.73 percent. Here again, we could have employed Eq. (2-1) to make such a calculation. If the same rolled-throughput yield applied to each of the k = 6 inspection categories, we would readily determine that the projected long-term probability of zero defects would be $Y_{RT} = Y_{FT}^m = .9973^6 = .9839$, or 98.39 percent.

3.6 ESTIMATING LONG-TERM DESIGN PRODUCIBILITY

Up to this point in our discussion concerning the AN/PRC-112(V) radio, we have only considered several unique subsets of all possible i, j, and k parameters. Let us now hypothesize that the long-term, rolled-throughput yield for all i, j, and k product-related parameters turned out to be .7467, or 74.67 percent. We shall also say that engineering determined there was a total of m = 5000 opportunities for nonconformance associated with the product. Given these constraints, the normalized long-term, rolled-throughput yield per opportunity would be calculated using Eq. (2-12)

and given as $Y_{RT:N} = .7467^{1/5000} = .999942$. In short, there would be 99.9942 percent confidence that any given opportunity could be passed through the manufacturing process without a quality-related incident. Hence, we now have a relative measure of long-term producibility with respect to our example product scenario.

If such a long-term benchmark proved to be unsatisfactory, optimization would be required. To do so would require an improvement in manufacturing capability, a reduction in design complexity, a change in the design configuration, alteration of the component/material tolerances, or some combination thereof.

Now, if we were to calibrate the previously mentioned opportunity level yield value to cumulative area under the standard normal curve, we would discover that .999942 area is approximately equivalent to 3.85σ in the context of a unilateral tolerance.[6] Thus, the long-term producibility benchmark (per opportunity) would be 3.85σ. As may be apparent, such "sigma" performance reduces to $C_p = 3.85/3.00 = 1.28$. It may also be expressed in parts-per-million opportunities (ppmo): e.g., ppmo = $(1-.999942)$ x $10^6 = 58$. We'll say more about these metrics later in the booklet.

Now, let us turn our attention to a competing design. If the competing design revealed a long-term, rolled-throughput yield of .98 and consisted of m = 4000 opportunities for nonconformance, the normalized long-term, rolled-throughput yield per opportunity may again be calculated using Eq. (2-12). In this instance, the computation revealed $Y_{RT:N}^{1/m} = .98^{1/4000} = .999995$, or 99.9995 percent. This would be equivalent to approximately 4.42σ. In terms of a capability ratio, $C_p = 4.42/3.00 = 1.47$. Expressed in parts-per-million opportunities, ppmo = $(1 - .999995)$ x $10^6 = 5$. Obviously, the competing design is superior in terms of producibility. In terms of ppmo, there is about one order-of-magnitude difference.

3.7 ESTIMATING SHORT-TERM DESIGN PRODUCIBILITY

We shall now consider the producibility analysis of the original design under the constraint of short-term capability data (as related to the process, material, and components). Essentially, whenever a producibility study is based on this type of parameter capability data, the analytical output reflects "instantaneous producibility." In other words, it describes the capability of any given parameter free of perturbing temporal influences. Hence, if the short-term capability data is used as the basis of computer modeling, the outcome projects what would be expected when only random variations are present.

---

[6] Since cumulative probability of conformance is used as the basis of benchmarking, only one tail of the standard normal distribution need be considered – hence, the reference to an equivalent unilateral tolerance.

To illustrate, let's postulate that the product illustrated in Figure 3-1 was subjected to certain performance simulations using the short-term capability database associated with the i, j, and k performance parameters. In this context, let us further suppose that Y_{RT} for all i, j, and k parameters was such that Y_{RT} = .99954, or 99.95 percent. Again, we may find the normalized rolled-throughput yield by virtue of $.99954^{1/m}$, where m = 5000. In this instance, the short-term, rolled-throughput yield expectation would be $Y_{RT:N}$ = $.99954^{1/5000}$ = .9999999, or approximately 99.99999 percent. Calibrating this to an area under the standard normal curve would reveal that .9999999 cumulative area is given by 5.21σ ; hence, the short-term or "instantaneous" producibility benchmark is 5.21σ.

3.8   ANALYSIS OF DESIGN ROBUSTNESS

Now, if one were to consider the discrepancy between the normalized short-term and long-term producibility estimates, the degree of design "robustness" could be readily ascertained. To exemplify, let us study the original design

alternative. As you may recall, the short-term estimate of producibility was 5.21σ (per opportunity) and the long-term was 3.85σ (per opportunity). It may then be reasoned that the discrepancy was $5.21\sigma - 3.85\sigma = 1.36\sigma$. We may now say that 1.36σ represents an equivalent mean shift. This would be like offsetting an otherwise centered 5.21σ parameter by a factor of 1.36σ. In essence, the offset (e.g. $\delta\sigma$ = 1.36) represents the effects of perturbing nonrandom influences (per opportunity) over many intervals of production.

Expressed as a ratio, the design robustness may be given as (3.85σ / 5.21σ) = .739. Hence, the design is 74 percent robust to perturbing influences of a temporal nature. On the flip side, we may say that the instantaneous design producibility was degraded by (1.00 – .74)100 = 26 percent. In this context, the ratio is a quantitative statement of how hermetic the design is to systematic, nonrandom influences. The reader is directed to Figure 3-4 for a better understanding of the relationship between capability, complexity, and robustness.

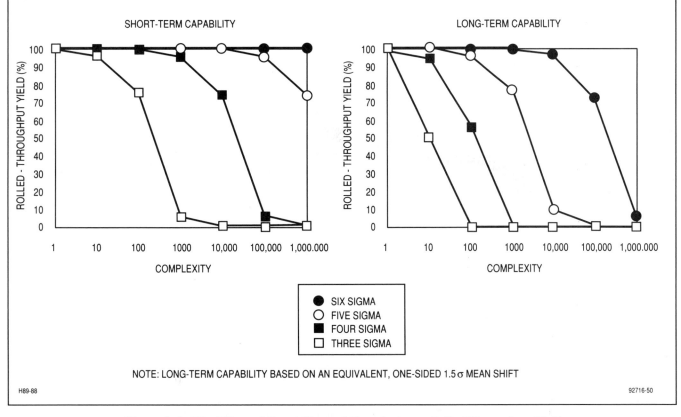

Figure 3-4. The Effect of Capability and Complexity on Rolled-Throughput Yield

3.9 PRODUCIBILITY OPTIMIZATION ALTERNATIVES

It is easy to see how m could be the number of process steps, operations, specifications, etc. In fact, m could be just about anything that relates to complexity. In essence, normalized rolled-throughput yield allows us to study producibility from many different perspectives. However, only such traditional variables as the number of opportunities, part count, and process operations should be used as the basis of normalization. Also note that m can be weighted by relative cost; however, it must be recognized that most weighting schemes introduce an additional layer of computational complexity. This is not to say that cost should not be considered in a quantitative producibility analysis, but rather to say that there are better ways of studying it.[7]

If any given design fails to reveal a satisfactory index of producibility, several alternatives are available. First, it would be necessary to hierarchically study the producibility metrics – i.e., create a Pareto breakdown of the design to isolate leverage. Once leverage is isolated, one can "what if" the baseline design via the manipulation of part count and manufacturing capability. For example, one could explore possible product and/or process design changes that would result in a reduced complexity factor; e.g., m could be minimized to obtain the desired rolled-throughput yield. Also, various aspects of the design could be optimized in terms of variation robustness via theoretical factorial experimentation, linear programming techniques, etc.

Another exploratory procedure would be to artificially minimize the process, component, and material capabilities to determine the feasibility of a manufacturing and/or procurement solution. Yet another alternative would be some combination of all three. Again, Figure 1-7 highlights many of the approaches often associated with producibility optimization.

Regardless of optimization strategy, it is quite clear that the independent and joint effects of product/process design complexity/configuration and manufacturing/component capability largely determine the functional producibility of a product design. The reader must recognize that "Postmortem" optimization efforts can be avoided via a proactive and concurrent design process. For example, the methodology presented in this section of the booklet can be worked in reverse to establish initial, baseline design goals.[8]

3.10 SYNOPSIS OF THE PRODUCIBILITY ASSESSMENT MODEL

As a consequence of the aforementioned arguments, we can now see how rolled-throughput yield and robustness can be related to all three of the circles given in Figure 1-4. However, it is also quite apparent that such a system of analysis is highly dependent upon timely and accurate capability data. But how do we go about getting such data? And what indices should the data be reduced to? In order to answer such questions, we must delve into the issue of process, component, and material characterization.

As a final point on the topic of producibility metrics, the reader is again reminded that any given quantitative assessment of producibility is only as good as the data and assumptions that underlie the final numbers. The age-old saying "garbage in, garbage out" certainly applies to the methodologies proposed in this booklet. In addition, we are all reminded of the precarious balance that must exist between the real world of practical constraints and the abstract domain of mathematical precision. Too much of the former can easily invalidate a quantitative analysis. On the other hand, too much of the latter can lead to perpetual "analysis paralysis."

---

[7] For example, it is possible to apply the quadratic loss function to illustrate the unit change in economic loss as a function of some unit change in parameter variation, complexity, or both. The reader is directed to the bibliography should additional information on this topic be required.

[8] For example, one can establish a desired rolled-throughput yield for all the "test" parameters and then back compute the maximum allowable part count, given a per-part capability figure, via an mth root transform. In the instance of process design, the inspection rolled-throughput yield target can be decomposed and subsequently allocated in the same fashion. When this is done, producibility can be structured prior to the creation of engineering drawings – i.e., before the design gets "cast in concrete."

SECTION 4
THE MODEL FOR PROCESS CHARACTERIZATION

Manufacturing industries are becoming increasingly aware that the practice of concurrent or "simultaneous" engineering can extend many benefits to the practitioners, as well as to their customers. Some of those benefits include, but are not limited to a) reduced total cost, b) enhanced product quality and reliability, c) lower manufacturing cycle time, and d) fewer design changes after release for production. As mentioned earlier in the booklet, such benefits can only be realized if the product has been designed for robustness to natural sources of unavoidable process, material, and component variations. Naturally, all of this assumes that the producer has a means for obtaining the necessary characterization data.

This portion of the booklet will discuss the general strategy, tactics, and tools for properly characterizing one or more product response characteristics. More specifically, we shall focus our discussion on what is often referred to as "process characterization." After the discussion, it should be readily apparent how the strategy and related tactics/tools can be applied to component and material characterization, as well as to many other activities such as yield enhancement, variable search, etc.

4.1 TOWARD A DEFINITION OF PROCESS CHARACTERIZATION

As with many things, a good place to start a discussion is with a clarification of key terms. In this case, we are concerned with a definition of the term "process characterization." As a first order of business, we shall decompose the term into its component parts, to gain greater resolution.

First, we shall consider the term "process." Webster's dictionary (1986) defines it as "a particular method of doing something, generally involving a number of steps or operations." Obviously, this is a fairly straightforward concept and can easily be related to manufacturing.

Given the latter understanding of a process, let us now turn our focus to the term "characterization." Again, Webster's may be employed to better structure our discussion and ensuing generalizations. In this case, "characterization" is defined as a means "to describe or portray the particular qualities, features, or traits of [something]."

If we were to integrate the previously mentioned definitions, we would discover that the term "process characterization" may be defined, in a generic sense, as "a description of the particular qualities, features, or traits of a method which involves a number of steps or operations." If we were to generalize this understanding to a manufacturing process, we would be able to say that process characterization provides us with "a description of the unique qualities, features, or traits related to the progressive steps, individually and/or collectively, used in manufacturing a product."

While the latter definition seems to be palatable, there is much to be considered. For example, what qualities, features, and/or traits related to the manufacturing steps are we talking about? Are we talking about their respective capabilities and, if so, what capabilities? Should we express the description "as is" or should we express it in terms of an optimum? After all, each of the former questions allude to the "traits" associated with the process. Because of this, we are tempted to say "yes" to all of the previous questions. But is this possible?

Well, in order to provide greater focus, we must recall two key notions. First, we must remember what Lord Kelvin (1891) had to say, as stated in Section 1: only a quantitative description can provide satisfactory knowledge. Second, we must "let the product do the talking in the form of numbers" – i.e., let the product response measurements tell us about process performance. Thus, we may now add greater resolution to our previous understanding of process characterization by saying that any given description of the qualities, features, and/or traits must be made on the basis of process output measurements; otherwise, the description would be unsatisfactory. This would be to say that any such description of the process must be given in terms of product performance, in a numerical sense – i.e., via measurement of the various product performance parameters correlated to the process. After all, the output quality does have something to say about the input/process interaction.

At this point in our discussion, we need to consider the scope of characterization. That is to say, how extensive does the process description need to be? For example, must we consider only the independent effects of the process, irrespective of input effects, or does the description include the input/process interactions? After all, an interaction is a "feature" of a manufacturing process and, in many instances, worthy of quantitative description. Should the description be based upon a cursory study of a simple collection of measurements, or should it be founded on sampling theory and inferential statistics so that generalization is possible?

This leads us to the question – to whom is the description targeted? If the target audience is primarily engineers and scientists, the description would need to be in technical form. However, if the description is to be used by senior management for decision making, it must be global, concise, and unconfounded by technical details. Obviously, such questions give rise to much debate and even more questions. So where does it all end?

So that we do not become paralyzed by such questions, let us consider Figure 4-1. As you can see, this figure provides the basic objectives of process characterization on columns, and analytic levels (in progressive order of technical sophistication) on rows. As we shall see later on, these objectives form the four progressive phases of our process characterization strategy: (a) parameter definition, (b) parameter analysis, (c) parameter optimization, and (d) parameter control.

ANALYSIS LEVEL	ANALYSIS DESCRIPTION	OBJECTIVE				
		DESCRIBE	CLASSIFY	DECIDE	REGULATE	IMPROVE
1	NO DATA - EXPERIENCE ONLY					
2	DATA COLLECTED - JUST "LOOK" AT THE NUMBERS, ETC.					
3	GROUPED DATA - CHARTS, GRAPHS, DIAGRAMS, ETC.					
4	DESCRIPTIVE STATISTICS - MEAN, STANDARD DEVIATION, ETC.					
5	CHARACTERIZATION STATISTICS - C_p, C_{pk}, GOODNESS-OF-FIT, ETC.					
6	CONTROL STATISTICS - SPC CHARTS					
7	INFERENTIAL STATISTICS - ANOVA, REGRESSION, EXPERIMENT DESIGN, ETC.					

H89-88   92716-51

Figure 4-1. The Potential Scope (Columns) and Extent (Rows) of a Process Characterization Study

As may be apparent, those cells in the upper left-hand corner of the table are perhaps the least sophisticated in terms of application and analytical output, whereas the cells in the lower right-hand corner are the most sophisticated. Since task difficulty increases across columns, and prerequisite knowledge (as well as "dedicated time") increases down rows, several conclusions may be drawn. First, we may say that breadth of process understanding increases as we move across columns. Second, we may say that generalizability and specificity increase as we move down the rows. Hence, costs increase as we move from left to right and top to bottom, for many reasons (e.g., computation time, number of tasks to be performed, amount of time per task, etc.).

We should now recognize, in any given situation, the overall balance which must be realized in terms of (a) the characterization objective, (b) related material and production costs, (c) direct/indirect labor in terms of time, and (d) organizational skills, knowledge, and ability – just to mention a few of the potential criterion. If a characterization study is to be undertaken for a "non-critical" product response parameter, it is doubtful that we would want to plan for a "full-tilt banquet in the grand ballroom." On the other hand, we may want more than a cursory "burger and fries" study. As a consequence, Figure 4-1 is not only used to define and better understand the nature of process characterization, it can also be directly employed as a planning tool, as we shall discover later.

Based on the latter discussion, we may safely say that there is no single, inclusive definition of the term "process characterization," no more than there is a single definition of the term "design producibility." Consequently, we must remain satisfied with the applied concept and its related business, engineering, and manufacturing implications. However, as we shall see, there are several key principles which are present in virtually every process characterization study and, when taken together, form the foundation of what many would call a "quasi-expert system." Through the study of this system, we shall gain greater insights into the concept of process characterization.

4.2   THE FOUR PHASES OF PROCESS CHARACTERIZATION

The characterization strategy essentially consists of four primary phases: (1) product parameter definition, (2) product parameter analysis, (3) process parameter optimization, and (4) process parameter control. As may be apparent, this strategy seeks to link the process to the product in a scientific manner. The general structure of the four-phase approach is shown in Figure 4-2. Let us now explore each of the phases in greater detail.

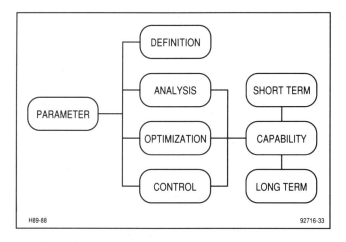

Figure 4-2. Parameter Characterization Strategy

PHASE 1

The first phase involves defining the critical product response characteristic to be studied, after a manufacturing process has been selected. Although more than one response variable may be identified and subsequently studied, we shall constrain our discussion to only one, for the sake of reading ease and simplicity of communication.

PHASE 2

The second phase of the strategy entails the collection of baseline product data. It should be pointed out that the baseline data is gathered on a short- and long-term basis. The short-term data is used to estimate the instantaneous reproducibility of the response characteristic (Y). In this manner, it is possible to establish the extent to which the process is capable of meeting the specified product quality standards – free of perturbing influences. The long-term data is used to estimate the sustained reproducibility of the dependent variable over a very large number of production intervals. Intuitively, one may reason that such data not only reflects instantaneous or random noise, but systematic nonrandom influences as well.

From these two measures, it is possible to study the extent to which Y is robust to perturbing influences stemming from the network of causal variables related to the process. From another vantage point, we may view the disparity between the short- and long-term metrics as a measure of how well the process is controlled over time.

PHASE 3

Once the product parameter capability has been established, the third phase is initiated. This is most often done by identifying the key process variables ($X_1 ... X_N$) within the network of causation that exerts an undue influence on Y. Such work is regularly accomplished through the application of statistically designed experiments and various diagnostic tools. The intent of such activity is threefold: (1) isolate leverage within the network of causation, (2) study competing

settings among the major causal variables, and (3) assess the feasibility and relative efficacy of control with respect to the key causal variables. Of course, the capability may need to be reassessed after such activity.

In some instances, it may be necessary to extend the third phase to "fine tune" the independent variables identified earlier. Naturally, the extension of Phase 3 is exercised only if the parameter capability data and manufacturing situation so warrant. At this time, it may also be necessary to focus on desensitizing the response characteristic to systematic and nonsystematic sources of variation. Therefore, the application of advanced inferential statistics, response surface methodology, and computer modeling is often required. Here again, it may be desirable to reassess capability upon completion.

PHASE 4

Finally, the fourth phase is related to monitoring the dependent variable (Y) and controlling the "vital few" process variables (Xs) within their respective operating tolerances. This is most often accomplished by way of SPC charts or automated feedback control. After a "settling in" period, the product and process parameter capabilities would be reassessed. Depending upon the outcomes of such a follow-on analysis, it may be necessary to revisit one or more of the preceding phases.

As we can now see, the process characterization strategy is a scientific and deductive method for structuring a product response problem. As may be noted, the strategy emphasizes deductive inquiry and repeatability, two of the central issues associated with scientific investigation. In this sense, the strategy constitutes "working smarter, not harder." Table 4-1 shows a highly generalized step-wise progression related to the process characterization strategy. Table 4-2 presents the analytical tools often used during the course of a characterization strategy.

4.3 FOCUSING THE OUTPUT FROM CHARACTERIZATION STUDIES

In the context of this booklet, the first step toward the quantitative assessment of producibility entails the capture of process, material, and component data. Next, the data are statistically summarized into indices of capability. Following this, the summary information is transferred to a computer data file. During the course of product design simulation, the file is periodically accessed by the product and/or process designer in order to develop the most rational combination of parts, materials, processes, etc. Naturally, if actual capability data does not exist, the designer is forced to postulate the state-of-affairs based on best engineering judgment and manufacturing experience. Once the baseline simulations and engineering studies are complete, the projected parameter yields are multiplied and subsequently normalized. In turn, the normalized yield is used to create an overall statement of producibility.

Table 4-1. General Step-Wise Progression Associated with the Process Characterization Strategy

Step	Phase	Step Description
1	Definition	Select a manufacturing process to be characterized
2		Identify the independent steps related to the selected process
3		Develop a process flow diagram based on the listed steps
4		Define the key product characteristics which the process creates
5	Analysis	Establish an appropriate measurement scale for each product characteristic
6		Select measurement apparatus to be used in the study
7		Establish capability of the selected measurement apparatus
8		Determine the existing short- and long-term capability of each product characteristic
9	Optimization	Identify the key independent variables related to each process step
10		Conduct experiments to verify the influence of the key independent variables
11		Establish optimum operating tolerances for all leverage variables
12	Control	Implement an appropriate control strategy for all leverage variables
13		Verify capabilities after an extended period of process operation
14		Monitor product characteristics over time

When this process is applied across many different products, an organization can benchmark its overall design and manufacturing capability. Through the careful analysis of such benchmarking information, the organization can discover how to best capitalize on its strengths and overcome its limitations.

4.4 PLANNING PROCESS CHARACTERIZATION STUDIES

Perhaps the best place to begin this discussion is with a recognition of the need for planning. Intuitively, we all clearly understand why planning is such a vital link in the success chain. However, we often lose sight of this fact as we move toward the threshold of a project. Some may often say, "Well, this project isn't as big as it looks . . . so we really don't need a whole lot to get it off the ground . . . the details can be worked out as we go along!" Obviously, such reasoning seemingly passes the common sense test; however, in many instances, things are not always as they seem.

4.4.1 Key Ingredients For Successful Planning

To illustrate the latter point, let us consider an amphibious military operation. As may be apparent, the objective of such an operation is to put soldiers on a ship, along with the appropriate supplies, and then transport them to a beachhead to confront a resistive force. Given this mission, it becomes crystal clear that logistics plays a major role. After all, we certainly recognize the importance of "beans, bullets, and band-aids" to a soldier.

Without the basic supplies, the mission cannot be achieved, no matter how motivated the troops are; therefore, it makes proper sense to put the high-priority items at the top of the "be-sure-to-put-on-the-ship" list, right? Well, it may seem so, however, we have forgotten to consider the other end of the mission. More specifically, our planning did not consider how the ship would be unloaded once the Commander calls back to the ship and says, "Hey, send the beans, bullets, and band-aids – we're just about out!"

Because the high-priority items were at the top of the ship's manifest, they were the first to be loaded into the ship's hull. Consequently, they were the last to come off. In the case of our example, the commander had to surrender because it took three days to unload the ship and reach the critical supplies. The moral is quite simple – reverse planning has many practical benefits.

Table 4-2. Analytical Tools Commonly Applied During the Course of Process Characterization
Broken Down by Phase and Likelihood of Use

Characterization Phase					Characterization Phase				
1	2	3	4	Analytical Tool Description	1	2	3	4	Analytical Tool Description
C	C	C	B	Positrol Logs	C	A	A	A	Probability Density Functions
A	B	C	B	Process Flow Diagrams	C	B	B	C	Median Test
B	A	C	A	Line, Bar, Pie Charts	C	A	A	B	Chi-Square Test of Independence
C	C	A	B	Fishbone Diagrams	C	A	A	B	Chi-Square Test for Goodness-of-Fit
B	B	C	C	Force Field Diagrams	C	B	A	C	Regression (Linear, Nonlinear,
B	A	C	A	Pareto Diagrams and Charts					Multivariate, Univariate)
C	A	A	B	Brainstorming Techniques	C	C	C	B	Pre-control
A	A	B	B	Cross Tabulation Tables	C	B	C	A	Tests for Randomness
C	A	B	B	Cause and Effect Matrix	C	A	A	B	t Test
C	A	A	A	Check Sheets	C	A	A	B	F Test
C	A	A	A	Data Collection Sheets	C	A	A	B	Mathematical Transformations
B	A	A	A	Indices of Location	C	A	A	B	Sample Size Equations and Tables
B	A	A	A	Indices of Variability					(Discrete, Continuous)
C	B	A	A	Confidence Intervals	C	B	A	C	Full Factorial Experiment Designs
C	A	A	A	Statistical Tables	C	C	A	B	Fractional Factorial Experiment
C	A	A	A	Random Number Generation					Designs
B	A	C	A	Statistical Process Control Charts	C	B	A	C	Group Screening Experiment
C	A	A	C	Correlation (Discrete, Continuous)					Designs
C	B	A	A	Hypotheses	C	B	A	C	Response Surface Experiment
C	A	A	C	Analysis-of-Variance					Designs
C	B	A	C	Analysis-of-Covariance	C	B	A	C	Random Strategy Experiment
B	A	A	A	Indices of Process Capability					Designs
C	A	A	A	Histograms	C	B	A	C	Mixture Experiment Designs

1 = Definition
2 = Analysis
3 = Optimization
4 = Control

A = Often Applied
B = Sometimes Applied
C = Seldom Applied

NOTE: *The Reader must recognize that not all of the analytical tools have been listed. Only those tools which are considered the "vital few" have been tabulated.*

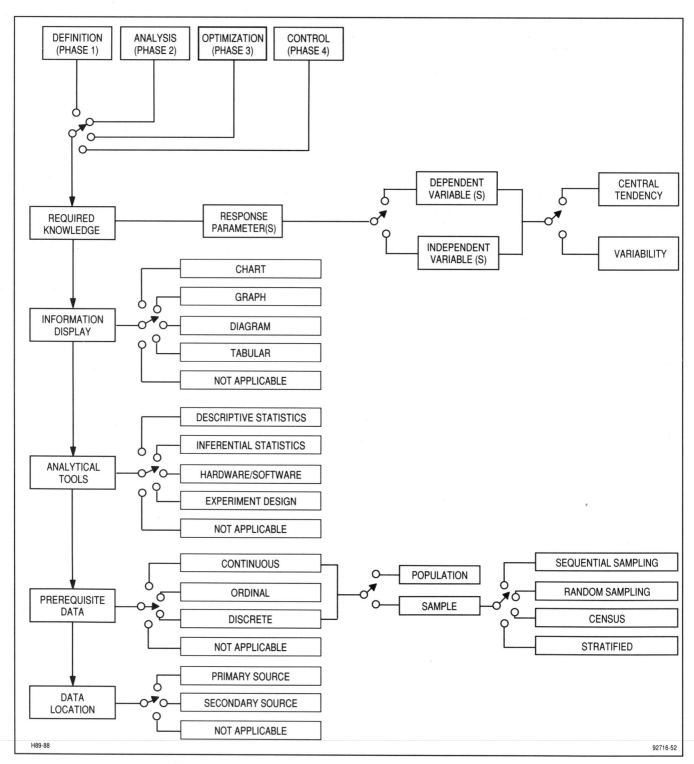

Figure 4-3. *The Basic Conceptual Structure for Translating the Critical Planning Questions into Application Terminology*

In many respects, planning a process characterization study is no different than planning a military operation, or any other undertaking, for that matter. The fundamental elements related to the planning process are much the same; i.e., certain strategies, tactics, and tools need to be identified and subsequently organized to successfully achieve a particular goal. For example, let us consider a simple capability study of a certain response characteristic. In this situation, we must "reverse load" the planning. To do this, we must answer the following questions for each phase of the process characterization strategy:

Question 1: What do we ultimately want to know?

Question 2: How do we want to see what we need to know?

Question 3: What type of analytical tool will best generate what we must see?

Question 4: What type of data is required of the selected tools?

Question 5: Where can the specified type of data be gathered?

Translating these questions into application reveals the basic conceptual structure presented in Figure 4-3 and Figure 4-4. It is essential that the experienced reader recognize the highly limited scope of these Figures. Here again, the intent is to present a simple visualization which will provide a limited set of "mental connectors" for the novice.

All too often, the reasoning process described in Figure 4-3 is turned upside down. In other words, the engineer first says, "Where can I get some data to accomplish the task?" Not so obvious is the fact that whenever a data collection point is fixed, the type of data which can be gathered at that point is also fixed. When this happens, the range of applicable analytical tools is greatly restricted because most statistical devices (i.e., methods and equations) will only work properly with certain types of data. As now may be apparent, the analytical tool which is used largely controls the type of information which will be extracted from the data. Naturally, this limits the number of ways in which the resultant information can be displayed. Now comes the downside to it all: the latter outcome dictates what the engineer ultimately will know about the response characteristic under investigation – which may or may not be related to the original objectives of the study. Again, the moral is one of reverse planning.

Much too often, the authors of this booklet have had well-intentioned engineers call for consultation on how best to analyze a particular set of data only to discover, much to their dismay, that the given data cannot be "crunched" to provide an answer to what they originally wanted to know. Usually, the call for consultation comes just before their "conclusions and recommendations" are to be submitted to management. In such instances, it is quite clear that various links in the "success chain" were very weak or even nonexistent. The reader is directed to Figure 4-5 for an overview of the elements which constitute the chain of analytical success.

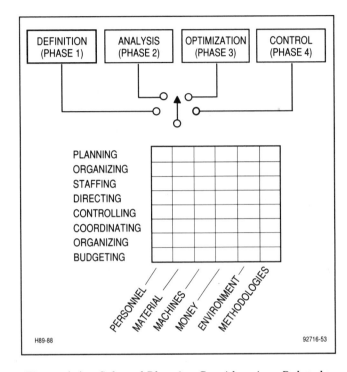

Figure 4-4. Selected Planning Considerations Related to a Process Characterization Study

Unfortunately, some engineers try to force fit their data into an improper format to comply with their respective submission date. Needless to say, such action can set up a domino chain of decisions that often leads to the loss of precious resources, not to mention the engineer's reputation. The underlying principle at hand is quite simple. Just as a given rifle is designed to accommodate a certain size bullet (or vice-versa), a selected statistic will only work with a certain type of data. Imagine being dropped off on a beachhead, only to discover that your rifle has the wrong kind of bullets! Obviously, the original strategy of a frontal assault would prove unsuccessful under such conditions.

It is far beyond the scope and intent of this booklet to present a full discussion of project planning. For more information, the reader is directed to the bibliography.

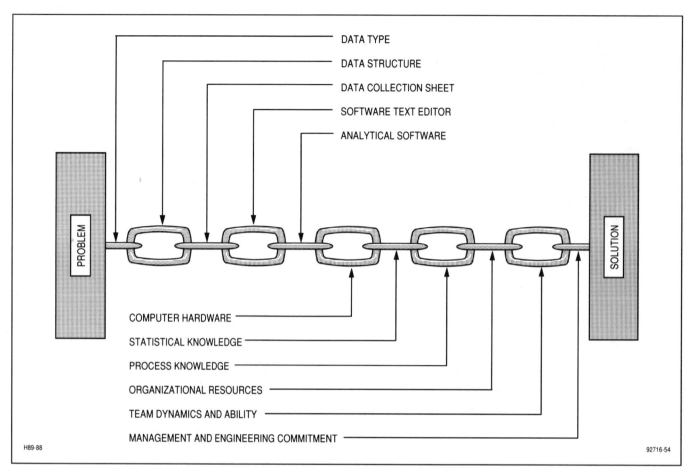

DATA TYPE
DATA STRUCTURE
DATA COLLECTION SHEET
SOFTWARE TEXT EDITOR
ANALYTICAL SOFTWARE

PROBLEM

SOLUTION

COMPUTER HARDWARE
STATISTICAL KNOWLEDGE
PROCESS KNOWLEDGE
ORGANIZATIONAL RESOURCES
TEAM DYNAMICS AND ABILITY
MANAGEMENT AND ENGINEERING COMMITMENT

H89-88
92716-54

Figure 4-5.   The Fundamental Elements Which Constitute the Chain of Analytical Success

4.4.2   *The Generic Activities*

For virtually all of the technical disciplines associated with modern industry, problem solving plays a major role. In fact, it is so entrenched within some technical disciplines, it is often taught as a separate, but interrelated topic. For some individuals, the art and science of problem solving becomes a primary career focus.

Over the course of many years, the professional problem solver encounters a wide array of analytical situations (often of a cross-functional nature), each with its own set of nuances. Such exposure over time forces the practitioner to integrate experience and knowledge. When this occurs, common principles come to light; hence, the practitioner is able to see the common elements which unfold across many situations. From such insight, a unified philosophy often emerges.

Presented herein is a highly flexible planning system which can be applied in virtually all industrial settings. At the heart of this system is a series of unstructured, generic problem-solving activities. In this sense, the activities are like a smorgasbord of general actions which often transpire in most problem-solving situations. More specifically, the activities can be organized *a priori* to establish a problem-solving road map in almost any production situation. For example, the generic activities can be selected and sequentially organized in such a combination as to define an action plan for the purpose of (a) establishing control over a manufacturing process, (b) solving a production yield problem, (c) conducting a laboratory experiment, or (d) characterizing a manufacturing process, just to mention a few. For the reader's convenience, these activities have been grouped into planning blocks and are so displayed in Table 4-3. The specific checklist associated with each of the problem-solving activities has been located in Appendix A.

Table 4-3. Generic Planning Activities for Problem Solving Presented in the Context of the Process Characterization Strategy Coded by Relative Frequency of Use

Planning Block	Block Number	Activity Description	Characterization Phase			
			1	2	3	4
Organization	1	Conduct Situation Analysis	A	C	C	B
	2	Conduct Literature Review	A	B	C	C
	3	Conduct Training Activities	B	A	A	A
	4	Synthesize and Focus	A	A	A	A
Variables	5	Define Dependent Variables	A	B	C	B
	6	Define Independent Variables	C	A	C	B
	7	Define Control Variables	C	A	A	C
Measurement	8	Establish Measurement System	B	A	C	B
	9	Identify Data Vehicle	B	A	C	B
Analytics	10	Design Parameter Capability Study	C	A	B	A
	11	Design Pareto Study	B	A	C	B
	12	Design Diagnostic Study	C	A	C	B
	13	Design Experimental Study	C	A	A	B
	14	Design Parameter Control Study	C	B	C	A
	15	Design Measurement Validation Study	C	A	C	B
Data	16	Design Data Analysis System	C	A	A	A
	17	Develop Data Tracking System	C	A	A	A
	18	Develop Data Collection System	C	A	A	A
	19	Implement Data Collection System	C	A	A	A
	20	Conduct Data Analysis	B	A	A	A
Sampling	21	Derive Sample Size	C	A	A	B
	22	Identify Sample Methodology	C	A	A	A
	23	Design Test Vehicle	C	B	B	C

1 = Definition   A = Often Applied
2 = Analysis   B = Sometimes Applied
3 = Optimization   C = Seldom Applied
4 = Control

Considering the planning device displayed in Figure 4-6 concurrently accomplishes a variety of tasks while simultaneously providing many benefits. Some of those benefits include:

- Standardizing an approach to planning statistically based studies; e.g., helping to prevent the "reinvent the wheel" syndrome each time a study is undertaken.

- Reducing the planning time, which translates to more "technical thinking time."

- Providing a common language that enhances and clarifies, therein avoiding ambiguous communication and documentation.

- Allowing the study to be decomposed into smaller elements which, in turn, translate to more realistic goals, expectations, and projection/allocation of resources.

- Providing the engineer with a quasi-expert system.

- Allowing for computer-based documentation and task management.

- Serving as the foundation for benchmarking; i.e., the novice practitioner can reference similar studies to assess the rationality of project flow, costs, etc.

These are but a few of the advantages of the planning system presented in this booklet. With careful study and judicious application, the reader will come to see many of the hidden benefits.

4.4.3 The Sequencing Methodology

At this point, we shall direct our attention to how the generic activities can be efficiently and effectively organized into a process characterization action plan.

Perhaps the best place to begin is with a close examination of Figure 4-6. As you can see, the generic problem-solving activities have been cross-tabulated by the four phases of process characterization. To use the matrix, an engineer would sequence the selected activities for each phase by placing the corresponding step number within the appropriate box. Recognize that Table 4-3 can greatly assist the novice practitioner at this point in the planning process. Naturally, the previously mentioned principles related to reverse planning should be employed. Of course, the assistance of an experienced SPC practitioner should be solicited at the onset of planning, for obvious reasons.

	PHASE 1: PARAMETER DEFINITION	PHASE 2: PARAMETER ANALYSIS	PHASE 3: PARAMETER OPTIMIZATION	PHASE 4: PARAMETER CONTROL
ORGANIZATION				
CONDUCT SITUATION ANALYSIS				
CONDUCT LITERATURE REVIEW				
CONDUCT TRAINING ACTIVITIES				
SYNTHESIZE AND FOCUS				
VARIABLES				
DEFINE DEPENDENT VARIABLES				
DEFINE INDEPENDENT VARIABLES				
DEFINE CONTROL VARIABLES				
MEASUREMENT				
ESTABLISH MEASUREMENT SYSTEM				
IDENTIFY DATA VEHICLE				
ANALYTICS				
DESIGN PARAMETER CAPABILITY STUDY				
DESIGN PARETO STUDY				
DESIGN DIAGNOSTIC STUDY				
DESIGN EXPERIMENTAL STUDY				
DESIGN PARAMETER CONTROL STUDY				
DESIGN MEASUREMENT VALIDATION STUDY				
DATA				
DESIGN DATA ANALYSIS SYSTEM				
DEVELOP DATA TRACKING SYSTEM				
DEVELOP DATA COLLECTION SYSTEM				
IMPLEMENT DATA COLLECTION SYSTEM				
CONDUCT DATA ANALYSIS				
SAMPLING				
DERIVE SAMPLE SIZE				
IDENTIFY SAMPLING METHODOLOGY				
DESIGN TEST VEHICLE				

H89-88   92716-55

Figure 4-6.   General Planning Matrix Used to Sequence the Generic Problem-Solving Activities in the Context of Process Characterization

After the activities have been selected and sequenced, the engineer would assign a start- and stop-date to each activity. For purposes of accountability, a specific person should be listed, as well as such items as projected budget, labor hours, material requirements, etc. Doing so establishes a "baseline of expectation" to which actual performance can be benchmarked during the course of execution. An example project plan related to a plasma-cleaning characterization study is shown in Figures 4-7 through 4-9. The novice practitioner is cautioned against the transfer of the example plan to some other manufacturing scenario. As a final point, recognize that many project planning software tools exist for a wide variety of computers. The use of such tools can greatly facilitate the construction and subsequent presentation of an action plan.

PROCESS CHARACTERIZATION PLANNING GUIDE	RESPONSIBLE	TASK NO.	FEBRUARY 13-17	20-24	27-3	MARCH 6-10	13-17	20-24	27-31	APRIL 3-7	10-14	17-18
1.0 PHASE: PARAMETER DEFINITION												
CONDUCT SITUATION ANALYSIS	TEAM	COMPLETE										
DEFINE DEPENDENT VARIABLE(S)	TEAM	COMPLETE										
IDENTIFY MEASUREMENT SYSTEM	TEAM	COMPLETE										
SYNTHESIZE AND FOCUS	TEAM	COMPLETE										
2.0 PHASE: PARAMETER ANALYSIS												
DESIGN PARAMETER CAPABILITY	TEAM	COMPLETE										
DESIGN DATA ANALYSIS SYSTEM	JG	COMPLETE										
DEVELOP DATA COLLECTION SYSTEM	JG	COMPLETE										
IMPLEMENT DATA COLLECTION SYSTEM	JG	COMPLETE										
CONDUCT DATA ANALYSIS	JG	1	▨									
SYNTHESIZE AND FOCUS	TEAM	2	▨									
3.0 PHASE: PARAMETER OPTIMIZATION												
SCREENING												
DEFINE INDEPENDENT VARIABLES	RF/KB	3										
DEFINE DATA VEHICLE	TEAM	COMPLETE										
DESIGN EXPERIMENTAL SYSTEM	RF/KB	4		▨								
DEVELOP DATA TRACKING SYSTEM	RF/JG	5		▨								
DESIGN DATA ANALYSIS SYSTEM	RF/JG	6		▨								
DEVELOP DATA COLLECTION SYSTEM	RF/JG	7		▨								
CONDUCT TRAINING ACTIVITIES	CJ/RF	8			▨							
IMPLEMENT DATA COLLECTION SYSTEM	CJ/RF	9				▨▨▨						
CONDUCT DATA ANALYSIS	KB	10						▨				
SYNTHESIZE AND FOCUS	TEAM	11						▨				
REFINING		12										
DEFINE INDEPENDENT VARIABLES	DK/RF	13						▨				
DESIGN EXPERIMENTAL SYSTEM	DK/RF	14						▨				
DEVELOP DATA TRACKING SYSTEM	DK/KB	15						▨				
DESIGN DATA ANALYSIS SYSTEM	DK/KB	16						▨				
DEVELOP DATA COLLECTION SYSTEM	DK/KB	17						▨				
CONDUCT TRAINING ACTIVITIES	CJ/RF	18						▨				
IMPLEMENT DATA COLLECTION SYSTEM	CJ/RF	19						▨▨				
CONDUCT DATA ANALYSIS	KB	20							▨			
SYNTHESIZE AND FOCUS	TEAM	21							▨			
OPTIMIZING												
DEFINE INDEPENDENT VARIABLES	GN/RF	22							▨			
DESIGN EXPERIMENTAL SYSTEM	GN/RF	23							▨			
DEVELOP DATA TRACKING SYSTEM	GN/DG	24							▨			
DESIGN DATA ANALYSIS SYSTEM	GN/DG	25							▨			
DEVELOP DATA COLLECTION SYSTEM	GN/DG	26							▨			
CONDUCT TRAINING ACTIVITIES	CJ/RF	27								▨		
IMPLEMENT DATA COLLECTION SYSTEM	CJ/RF	28								▨▨		
CONDUCT DATA ANALYSIS	KB	29									▨	
SYNTHESIZE AND FOCUS	TEAM	30									▨	
4.0 PHASE: PARAMETER CONTROL												
DEFINE CONTROL VARIABLES	RF/JG	31									▨	
DESIGN PARAMETER CONTROL SYSTEM	RF/JG	32									▨	
DEVELOP DATA TRACKING SYSTEM	RF/JG	33									▨	
DESIGN DATA ANALYSIS SYSTEM	RF/JG	34									▨	
DEVELOP DATA COLLECTION SYSTEM	RF/JG	35									▨	
CONDUCT TRAINING ACTIVITIES	CJ/RF	36									▨	
IMPLEMENT DATA COLLECTION SYSTEM	CJ	37										▨
CONDUCT DATA ANALYSIS	RF	38										

H89-88

92716-56

Figure 4-7. Action Plan and Time Line Related to the Characterization of a Plasma-Cleaning Process.

PROCESS CHARACTERIZATION PLANNING GUIDE	RESPONSIBLE	TASK HOURS			TOTAL HOURS	LABOR/ TASK	TASK LIKELI-HOOD (0-100%)	WEIGHTED LABOR/ TASK	MATERIALS/ MACHINES
		412	413	417					
1.0 PHASE: PARAMETER DEFINITION									
CONDUCT SITUATION ANALYSIS	TEAM								
DEFINE DEPENDENT VARIABLE(S)	TEAM								
IDENTIFY MEASUREMENT SYSTEM	TEAM								
SYNTHESIZE AND FOCUS	TEAM								
2.0 PHASE: PARAMETER ANALYSIS									
DESIGN PARAMETER CAPABILITY	TEAM								
DESIGN DATA ANALYSIS SYSTEM	JG								
DEVELOP DATA COLLECTION SYSTEM	JG								
IMPLEMENT DATA COLLECTION SYSTEM	JG								
CONDUCT DATA ANALYSIS	JG	8			8	143.68	100	143.68	a
SYNTHESIZE AND FOCUS	TEAM	7	1		8	138.73	100	138.73	
3.0 PHASE: PARAMETER OPTIMIZATION									
SCREENING									
DEFINE INDEPENDENT VARIABLES	RF/KB								
DEFINE DATA VEHICLE	TEAM								
DESIGN EXPERIMENTAL SYSTEM	RF/KB	6			6	107.76	100	107.76	
DEVELOP DATA TRACKING SYSTEM	RF/JG	2			2	35.92	100	35.92	
DESIGN DATA ANALYSIS SYSTEM	RF/JG	2			2	35.92	100	35.92	
DEVELOP DATA COLLECTION SYSTEM	RF/JG	2			2	35.92	100	35.92	a
CONDUCT TRAINING ACTIVITIES	CJ/RF	2	2	2	6	81.14	100	81.14	ijkl / bcdefg
IMPLEMENT DATA COLLECTION SYSTEM	CJ/RF	8	8	32	48	307.2	100	307.2	
CONDUCT DATA ANALYSIS	KB	4			4	71.84	100	71.84	a
SYNTHESIZE AND FOCUS	TEAM	7	1		5	138.73	100	138.73	
REFINING									
DEFINE INDEPENDENT VARIABLES	DK/RF	1			1	17.96	50	8.98	
DESIGN EXPERIMENTAL SYSTEM	DK/RF	4			4	71.84	50	35.92	
DEVELOP DATA TRACKING SYSTEM	DK/KB	2			2	35.92	50	17.96	
DESIGN DATA ANALYSIS SYSTEM	DK/KB	2			2	35.92	50	17.96	
DEVELOP DATA COLLECTION SYSTEM	DK/KB	2			2	35.92	50	17.96	a
CONDUCT TRAINING ACTIVITIES	CJ/RF	2	2	2	6	81.14	50	40.57	b
IMPLEMENT DATA COLLECTION SYSTEM	CJ/RF	4	4	16	24	153.6	50	69.37	ijkl / bcdefg
CONDUCT DATA ANALYSIS	KB	4			4	71.84	50	35.92	a
SYNTHESIZE AND FOCUS	TEAM	7	1		5	138.73	50	69.37	
OPTIMIZING									
DEFINE INDEPENDENT VARIABLES	GH/RF	1			1	17.96	100	17.96	
DESIGN EXPERIMENTAL SYSTEM	GH/RF	4			4	71.84	100	71.84	
DEVELOP DATA TRACKING SYSTEM	GH/DG	2			2	35.92	100	35.92	
DESIGN DATA ANALYSIS SYSTEM	GH/DG	2			2	35.92	100	35.92	
DEVELOP DATA COLLECTION SYSTEM	GH/DG	2			2	35.92	100	35.92	a
CONDUCT TRAINING ACTIVITIES	CJ/RF	2	2	2	6	81.14	100	81.14	b
IMPLEMENT DATA COLLECTION SYSTEM	CJ/RF	2	2	8	12	138.74	100	138.74	ijkl / bcdefg
CONDUCT DATA ANALYSIS	KB	4			4	71.84	100	71.84	a
SYNTHESIZE AND FOCUS	TEAM	7	1		5	138.73	100	138.73	
4.0 PHASE: PARAMETER CONTROL									
DEFINE CONTROL VARIABLES	RF/JG	1			1	17.96	100	17.96	
DESIGN PARAMETER CONTROL SYSTEM	RF/JG	2			2	35.92	100	35.92	
DEVELOP DATA TRACKING SYSTEM	RF/JG	2			2	35.92	100	35.92	
DESIGN DATA ANALYSIS SYSTEM	RF/JG	2			2	35.92	100	35.92	a
DEVELOP DATA COLLECTION SYSTEM	RF/JG	2			2	35.92	100	35.92	b
CONDUCT TRAINING ACTIVITIES	CJ/RF	2	2	2	6	81.14	100	81.14	ijkl / bcdefg
IMPLEMENT DATA COLLECTION SYSTEM	CJ	2	2	2		81.14			a
CONDUCT DATA ANALYSIS	RF	CONTINUOUS							
TOTALS		66	19	36		2691.6		2281.64	

MACHINE CODES			MATERIAL CODES	
a = IBM PC	c = ALUMINUM EVAPORATOR	e = K&S SAW	i = LITHIUM NIOBATE WAFER	k = PHOTOLITHOGRAPHY MATERIALS
b = MARCH PLASMA ETCHER	d = PHOTOLITHOGRAPHIC EQUIPMENT	f = K&S WIRE BONDER	j = ALUMINUM METAL	l = 1 MIL ALUMINUM WIRE
		g = WIRE PULL TESTER		

H89-88

92716-58

Figure 4-8.   Resource Allocation Plan Related to the Characterization of a Plasma-Cleaning Process

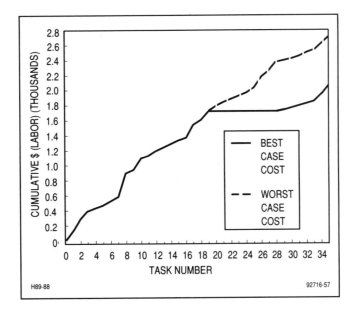

*Figure 4-9.   Resource Tracking Profile Related to the
Characterization of a Plasma-Cleaning Process*

SECTION 5
THE STATISTICAL BASIS FOR CHARACTERIZATION METRICS

Perhaps the best way to present the statistical principles underlying parameter characterization is by product example. Although using a specific product as a vehicle for demonstration certainly enhances understanding of the major points, the real issues often are easily confounded with the physical nuances surrounding the product. When this happens, the application principles often are muddled, to say the least.

5.1 THE EXAMPLE PRODUCT FOR ILLUSTRATION

In order to minimize the likelihood of confounding nuances, we will hypothesize a simple, yet plausible product – say, a widget. Figure 5-1 illustrates the basic configuration of such a product. Using the widget as a basis for discussion, we will generalize to more complex products. For instance, it's easy to see how the widget configuration can be related to a frame or rack that has been designed to support a series of printed wiring boards. As you can see from Figure 5-1, our widget consists of five components: the housing, or "envelope" as it is often called, and the internal parts. Therefore, we will designate the envelope with an e and the parts with p.

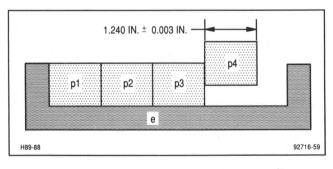

Figure 5-1.   Illustration of the Widget Product

5.2 MEASURES OF CENTRAL TENDENCY

Now that we have become somewhat familiar with our example product, let's continue by supposing that we have a lot of 10,000 parts (P_1 ... $P_{10,000}$) – say, lot #1 – and we do not know what the actual physical dimensions of the parts are. How can we find out? Well, we could measure each and every part or we could randomly select a sample of say, 100, and then carefully record the values from that sample. Obviously, this would save us a lot of time and money. If the sample truly was random, then any statistical estimates thereof should be reasonably representative of the total, or "population". But what estimates would we be making? From a statistical point of view, we could summarize the 100-part measurements into two basic indices: the mean and standard deviation.

5.2.1   The Arithmetic Mean of a Population

At this point, we may elect to compute the arithmetic average, or "mean". In a sense, the mean can be thought of as the balance point of the measurements. With this in mind, the population mean may be defined as

$$\mu = \sum_{i=1}^{N} X_i/N \qquad \text{Eq. (5-1)}$$

where Σ symbolizes "the sum of," X_i represents the ith part measurement, and N is the total number of parts in the population.

5.2.2   The Arithmetic Mean of a Sample

Because we are not dealing with the entire population of parts in our example, but rather a randomly selected sample, we must substitute the terms in Eq. (5-1) to reflect the difference. This may be expressed as

$$\overline{X} = \sum_{i=1}^{n} X_i/n \ . \qquad \text{Eq. (5-2)}$$

Notice that the sample mean is now designated by $\overline{X}$. Also note that the number of measurements in the sample has now been defined as n. In general, the Greek symbols are most often associated with the population, whereas Roman letters are reserved for the sample. For the sake of discussion, suppose that we made the necessary calculation using Eq. (5-2) as a guide, and noted the sample average ($\overline{X}$) to be 1.240 inches (in.).

5.2.3   Properties of the Arithmetic Mean

Let us now consider several statistical properties of the mean. First, the mean is very responsive to every value in the data set from which it was computed. When we say that it is "responsive," we are saying that its numerical value is sensitive to the values of the other numbers. That is, if any of the other numbers were to change in magnitude, then the mean would also be affected to some degree. The larger the change, the more the mean will change.

Along these same lines is the second property of the mean – its sensitivity to extreme values. For instance, if we had two small numbers (say, 2 and 4), it is readily apparent that the mean would be 3. Now, let us add a third number (say, 6). Given this, the new average would be 4. This would represent a location change of 1 unit in the mean (from 3 to 4). However, if that third number had been 21, the mean would now be 9. As you can see, this would represent a location change of 6 units. In the first set of three numbers (2, 4, and 6) there was only a 1.33-fold change in the average; however, in the second set of three numbers (2, 4, and 21), there was a 3-fold change in the location. This would tend to tell us that the arithmetic mean is very sensitive to any unbalanced change in the data, as well as extreme values.

In the instance of our widget example, if more were to be produced, say three more, it is possible than the mean (μ) would change in value. Should this happen, we could say the mean shifted to some higher or lower level. In other words, if the cause system ($X_1...X_N$) underlying Y were to change, we would see some degree of change in the population or "universe" average (μ). In short, if the cause system were to be suddenly altered, μ would "shift" its location.

Yet another property of the mean would be its ability to resist the influence of sampling fluctuations. This particular property is extremely important whenever random sampling is performed and the assumption of normality is reasonable. For example, let us suppose that we were randomly to draw 100 samples of size 5 from a normally distributed population. If we were to determine the mean, median, and mode for each of the 100 samples and then compare how much each measure of central tendency changed from sample to sample, we would find that the arithmetic average (mean) would be the most resilient to fluctuation.

In general, this holds true for most of the different types of distributions that are commonly used in statistical work. Given these, as well as other properties, the mean is perhaps the most useful measure of central tendency – hence its wide application, reputation, and use in the 6σ quality philosophy.

5.2.4 Other Measures of Central Tendency

Although the median (that point which divides a data set in half, based on a rank ordering of the data) and mode (the most frequently occurring value in a set of data) are also measures of central tendency, we shall only consider the mean. The reason for this is that the median and mode are seldom used in parametric statistics and play a very small role in the case at hand. They may be mentioned from time to time during the discussion but will not be given consideration other than by definition or reference. For more information on these indices, the reader is directed to Juran (1979) or Ott (1977).

5.3 MEASURES OF VARIABILITY

Perhaps one of the most perplexing of all the statistical indices is the standard deviation. It seems to escape intuitive understanding. That is to say, many newcomers to the game of statistical analysis find the standard deviation without plausible definition other than by mathematics. In many situations, the standard deviation is used, but the exact nature of its true meaning is something else – it is just accepted on faith. Well, so that we don't just have to accept this creature blindly, let's try to develop a feel for what it is all about.

5.3.1 Purposes of the Standard Deviation

If we accept the fact that variation exists, then we must also recognize that variation in data is nothing more than some form of dispersion or scatter. Expressed differently, continuous data often disperses or spreads out relative to a particular location on some scale of measure or, as one might say, "it is scattered about the average." What this means is that the individual observations (measurements) tend to be "sprinkled" around the balance point of the data.

To illustrate, let us suppose that we were holding a funnel full of sand directly over a large piece of white paper. If we were to project a line from the center of the funnel to the paper, the point at which the line intersects the paper can be thought of as point of contact or a center point. Let us further suppose that we were to allow the sand to pour out of the funnel onto the paper while holding the funnel perfectly steady. What would happen?

As we might expect, the grains of sand would be scattered all over the piece of paper; however, the grains would tend to be most concentrated at the center point. If enough sand were to be released from the funnel, we would expect to see a pile start to form about the center point. In addition, we would also expect to see fewer grains of sand as we move farther away from the peak of the pile – assuming that the person holding the funnel did not shift it to a new center point on the paper. In this analogy, the center of the sand pile would be the arithmetic average, or balance point. But how can we describe the dispersion of the individual grains of sand? How can we express the scatter we see?

One way of expressing the degree of scatter we see would be to measure the distance between the two outermost grains of sand. This is most often called the range. One problem with using the range to express dispersion is that it does not use the additional information that all of the other individual grains of sand could give us, nor does it give us information that is relative to the center point of the pile.

In order to make the individual grains of sand relative to the total width and center point of the pile, we would need to devise an index which takes advantage of the information related to each grain of sand. As previously indicated, one such index is called the standard deviation. This particular index is a summary number that conveys to us the relative distance any particular observation is from the arithmetic balance point of its distribution.

5.3.2 Calculating the Standard Deviation via the Deviation Method

Again, we will use our 100 measurements to estimate the population standard deviation (σ). The method which we will first consider is founded on squared deviations from the mean and, as a consequence, is called the "deviation method." Using this method, we may say that the standard deviation for the population can be defined as

$$\sigma = \sqrt{\sum_{i=1}^{N} (X_i - \mu)^2/N} \qquad \text{Eq. (5-3)}$$

whereas the sample standard deviation is described by

$$S = \sqrt{\sum_{i=1}^{n} (X_i - \overline{X})^2/(n-1)} \ . \qquad \text{Eq. (5-4)}$$

Recognize that the squared standard deviation (σ^2, S^2) is called the "variance." More will be said about the variance later in the booklet.

It is interesting to note that Eq. (5-4) uses $n-1$ in lieu of N. This is done so as not to derive a "biased" estimate of σ. As a general rule, whenever $n \geq 30$, it makes little difference if N or $n-1$ is used.[1]

As may be apparent from Eq. (5-3) and Eq. (5-4), the standard deviation is a statistical unit of measure that relates to the dispersion of the measurements around their balance point. In this sense, σ would be the measuring device with which we can describe the amount of scatter present in the data. Again, suppose that we estimated the population standard deviation by virtue of Eq. (5-4) and found S to be .001 in.

In the interest of simplifying our discussion and subsequent use of statistical notation, let's suppose that, in all cases, we have unique knowledge in knowing that our sample is perfectly representative of the population such that $S = \sigma$ and $\overline{X} = \mu$. Thus, we may now use the population symbols μ and σ to denote the mean and standard deviation, respectively.[2]

Now, if we increased the value of μ by, say, 3σ, what value would we have? If we multiplied the number 3 times the standard deviation ($3\sigma = 3 \times .001$ in. = .003 in.) and then added the resultant number to the mean ($\mu + 3\sigma = 1.240$ in. + .003), we would have the correct answer: 1.243 in. If we considered the same problem, but decreased μ by 3σ instead of increasing it, we would have calculated the value to be 1.237 in. Thus, the $\pm 3\sigma$ limits would have a spread or "range" of 1.243 in. $- 1.237 = .006$ in.

5.3.3 Calculating the Standard Deviation via the Range Method

Because this particular method of computing the sample standard deviation is based on the sample ranges, it is sometimes referred to as the "range method." In general, the range method should be used when rational subgrouping serves as the basis of the sampling scheme. In general, the deviation method should be employed when it is not possible to define rational subgroups. The notion of a "rational subgroup" will be presented in great detail later in the discussion. For the moment, we need only recognize that it is related to a sampling technique designed to limit systematic variations within the sample.

Computing the sample standard deviation via the range method is a relatively easy task. First, the range (R) of each subgroup (G_1, ..., G_6) must be determined. This may be done by subtracting the minimum value (X_{min}) in a particular subgroup – say, G_j – from the maximum value (X_{max}) contained within G_j. This may be expressed as

$$R_j = X_{max} - X_{min} \ . \qquad \text{Eq. (5-5)}$$

---

[1] The use of n–1 is a mathematical device employed for the purposes of deriving an unbiased estimator of the population standard deviation. In the given context, n–1 is referred to as "degrees of freedom." When the total sums-of-squared deviations is given and the pair-wise deviation contrasts are made for n observations, the last contrast is fixed; hence, there are n–1 degrees of freedom from which to accumulate the total. More specifically, degrees of freedom may be defined as $(n-1)$ independent contrasts out of n observations. For example, in a sample with n = 5, measurements X_1, X_2, X_3, X_4, and X_5, are made. The independent contrasts are $X_1 - X_2$, $X_2 - X_3$, $X_3 - X_4$, and $X_4 - X_5$. The additional contrast, $X_1 - X_5$, is not independent since its value is known from

$$(X_1 - X_2) + (X_2 - X_3) + (X_3 - X_4) + (X_4 - X_5) = X_1 - X_5$$

Therefore, for a sample of n = 5, there are four $(n-1)$ independent contrasts or "degrees of freedom." In this instance, all but one of the contrasts are free to vary in magnitude, given that the total is fixed. Thus, when n is large, the degree of bias is small; therefore, there is little need for such a corrective device.

[2] The informed reader should know that the authors have deviated from statistical convention by omitting the estimator symbol "^" in those instances where a population parameter estimate has been made without data. For example, if an engineer hypothesizes a population parameter value (say μ), the convention for statistical notation would dictate the use of $\hat{\mu}$. Although such notation is statistically proper, it has been circumvented for the sake of reading ease on the behalf of the uninformed reader. In all instances in this booklet, the population parameters related to hypothesized universes are known; thus, $\hat{\mu} = \mu$ and $\hat{\sigma} = \sigma$.

Next, we need to find the average range ($\overline{R}$). In the context of Eq. (5-5), the average range may be given by

$$\overline{R} = \sum_{j=1}^{N} R_j/N \qquad \text{Eq. (5-6)}$$

where R_j is the range of the jth subgroup (G_j) and N is the total number of subgroups.[3] Once the average range ($\overline{R}$) has been computed, the sample standard deviation may be calculated by dividing the average range ($\overline{R}$) by the appropriate constant (d_2*) listed in Table 5-1. This operation may be expressed as

$$S = \overline{R}/d_2* \qquad \text{Eq. (5-7)}$$

where $d_2* = 2.353$ for the case when there are N = 6 subgroups, under the special condition n = 5. Obviously, if there were more or less subgroups, the value of d_2* would be different.[4]

Table 5-1. Tabulated Values of d_2*
for a Selected Number of Subgroups (N)
of Size n = 5

N	d_2*	N	d_2*
1	2.474	8	2.346
2	2.405	10	2.342
3	2.379	11	2.339
5	2.358	20	2.334
6	2.353	∞	2.326

5.3.4 Properties of the Standard Deviation

Yet another way to describe the nature of the standard deviation is by its unique properties. First, much like the mean, it is very sensitive or responsive to the position of every value in a distribution. If a single value out of a reasonably large distribution of values is shifted to an extreme position, the standard deviation will change noticeably. Expressed differently, the standard deviation is not robust against extreme values. As a result of this property, the standard deviation may not be the best choice among measures of

variability when the distribution is markedly skewed or extreme values are present. Of course, mathematical transformations can sometimes be employed to rectify the undesirable situations.[5]

When the deviations are calculated from the arithmetic average, the sum of squares (SS) is smaller than if another measure of central tendency had been used (e.g., mode, median, etc.). Given this, we have yet another way to describe the arithmetic average (mean): that point which minimizes the sum of squares. Another property of the standard deviation would be its resistance to sampling fluctuations. That is to say, the standard deviation does not change a whole lot, as compared to other measures of variability, given normal fluctuations in repeated random samples.

Still another characteristic would be its similarity to the mean in that it is "kind of like" the average of all of the squared deviations. In this respect, it is highly sensitive to extreme values and location. Like the mean, it is used in many descriptive and inferential statistics. In addition, it is probably the most used measure of variability (indicator of dispersion or "scatter").

For additional information on this topic, see Dixon and Massey (1969) and Burr (1953).

5.4 GRAPHICAL DISPLAY OF VARIATION

At this point, we should be on some common conceptual ground with respect to μ and σ. We will continue by introducing the notion of a histogram. A histogram is very much like a simple bar chart. It shows how the values tend to group themselves together across the range of values (upper-left illustration of Figure 5-2). Notice that the width of each bar is the same. It also is interesting that the height of any given bar represents the number of part measurements associated with that bar's width. Juran, Gryna, and Bingham (1979) present many of the details associated with the construction of histograms.

If we drew a smooth curve through the top of each bar, we would form a shape that looks like a bell. For this reason, the curve is often called the "bell curve." Statisticians call it a "normal distribution." Although there are other shapes, this is the one used most often. A thorough discussion of the normal distribution is given by Bowker and Lieberman (1972).

As you may have noticed, most of the measurements tend to cluster around the center of the bell – the location on the measurement scale directly below the hump in the curve. If you said that this point is the average (μ), you would be

---

[3] It should be noted that the use of N may also be used to reference the total number of observations in a population. Recognize that the usage is dependent upon context.

[4] Strictly speaking, the standard d_2 factor (commonly associated with SPC charts) assumes that the ranges have been averaged for a fair number of subgroups – say, 20 or more. Where only a few subgroups are available, a more precise estimate of the universe standard deviation is obtained by using d_2*. For additional values of d_2*, the reader is directed to Appendix B.

[5] Perhaps the most commonly applied transformations are x^2, $1/x$, $\sqrt{x}$, e^x, e^{-x}, and $\log x$.

right. It is the balance point of the distribution. Furthermore, it is interesting that the "tails" of the distribution never touch the baseline (horizontal axis of the measurement scale). They get closer to the baseline the farther out to the right and left they go, but they never touch it.[6] This would mean that out of an infinite number of parts, there would always be some likelihood that an extreme valued part could be encountered. Regardless of how low the probability may be, the possibility always exists. Okay, so what? Why do we need to know all of this stuff? The answer is quite simple: CUSTOMER SATIS-FACTION.

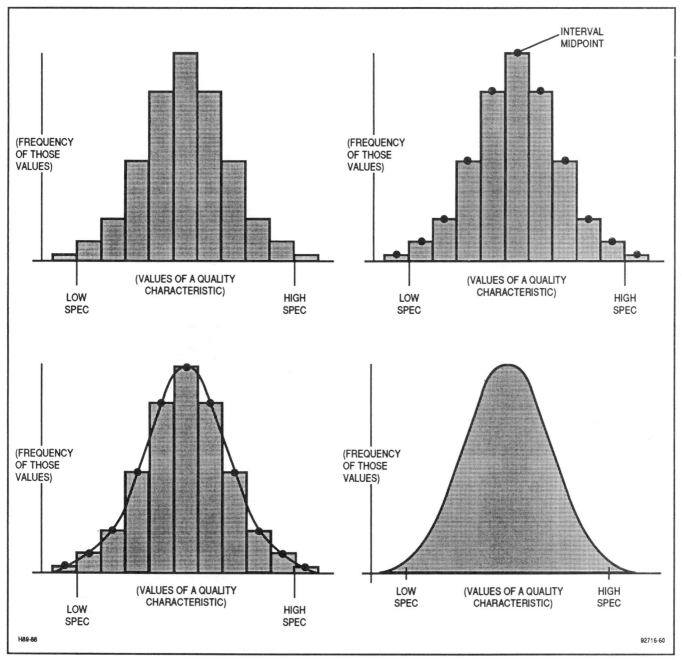

Figure 5-2. Progressive Development of the Normal Distribution

---

[6] In the strict mathematical sense, it would be said that each tail of the related distribution asymptotically approaches zero.

5.5 PROBABILITY AND THE NORMAL CURVE

To illustrate how the normal distribution is used and what implications it holds for our customers, let's return to our widget example and ask, "How many parts in lot #1 should we expect to find between the ±1σ limits of the distribution?" Again, unless we actually measure all of them, what other way is there to know? With the assistance of the normal distribution, we could make a pretty good estimate.

5.5.1 Using the Normal Curve as a Probability Model

You see, statisticians already have determined how much area there is under the normal curve at various points on a scale that uses the standard deviation (σ) as a basis of measurement. For example, statisticians have determined that 68.26 percent of the area under the curve lies within ±1σ of μ. In terms of our example, this would tell us that 68.26 percent of the parts are between 1.239 in. and 1.241 in. Figure 5-3 displays a normal curve with some other σ values and their respective areas.

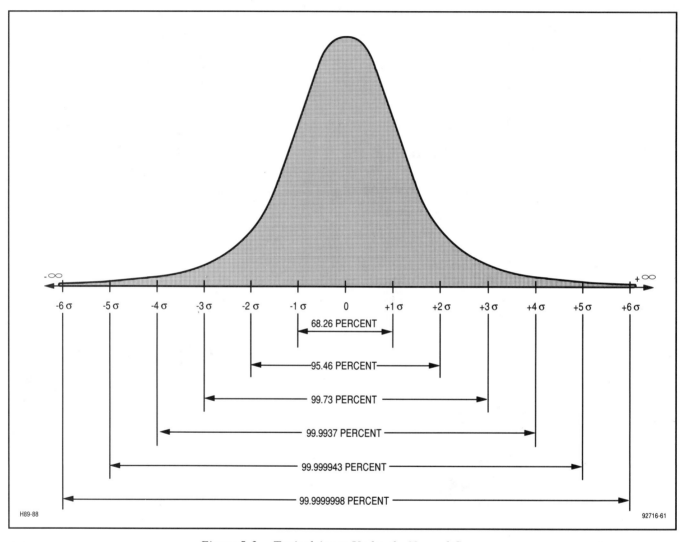

Figure 5-3. Typical Areas Under the Normal Curve

Yet another way of thinking about this would be to say that there is a 68.26 percent probability of reaching into the lot and pulling out a part whose length is somewhere between 1.239 in. and 1.241 in. If a product's engineering specification calls for 1.240 in. ±.003 in., then only those parts between 1.237 in. and 1.243 in. would be fit for use. As you can see from Figure 5-3, we could expect 99.73 percent of the parts to fall within the engineering specification range because the upper and lower specification limits (USL and LSL, respectively) are ±3σ from the center or "nominal" value of the specification. Expressed differently, 0.27 percent would be considered defective (or nonconforming) since 100 percent − 99.73 percent = 0.27 percent. This would equate to

2700 nonconforming parts per 1,000,000 parts. Simply stated, this would be 2700 parts per million (ppm) nonconforming. Historically, this was considered acceptable from a process control point of view; however, times have changed.[7] The customer now demands higher levels of quality at lower cost. Do you suppose 2700 ppm is really good enough? Well, let's extend our example and see.

5.5.2 *Impact of Distribution Parameters on Probability of Nonconformance*

Suppose that another lot of parts – lot #2 – had the same mean (μ = 1.240 in.), but a smaller standard deviation (say, σ = .0005 in.). Under this condition, 99.9999998 percent of the area under the curve would be within the engineering specification (1.237 in. to 1.243 in.). This means that the likelihood of any given part length falling between the specification limits would be extremely high. Thus, we would have an exceptionally high level of confidence that any given measurement would be somewhere within the specification window. Inversely stated, the probability of encountering a part measurement less than 1.237 in. or greater than 1.243 in. would be extremely low – or almost nonexistent – for all practical purposes, that is. Here again, this may be reasoned from Figure 5-3. The area under the curve that is beyond the USL and LSL would translate to .002 ppm nonconforming.

As may be apparent, such a level of quality represents "Six Sigma" performance, Motorola's foundation for customer satisfaction. Figure 5-4 graphically defines the concept of "Six Sigma" performance. Notice that the distribution is centered on the nominal specification value. In this state, it is a model of instantaneous reproducibility or "short-term" manufacturing capability. However, as we all realize, such a model does not always hold true over time – the mean often varies from the target value due to perturbing nonrandom influences. As we shall see later in the discussion, the impact of shifts and drifts in the mean can have a profound effect on the probability of nonconformance. Because of this, the long-term model for "Six Sigma" manufacturing capability reflects the effects of "typical" shifts and drifts in the mean. In other words, the short-term model (Figure 5-4) describes "instantaneous reproducibility" while the long-term model (Figure 5-5) describes the typical effect of perturbing influences over many manufacturing cycles.

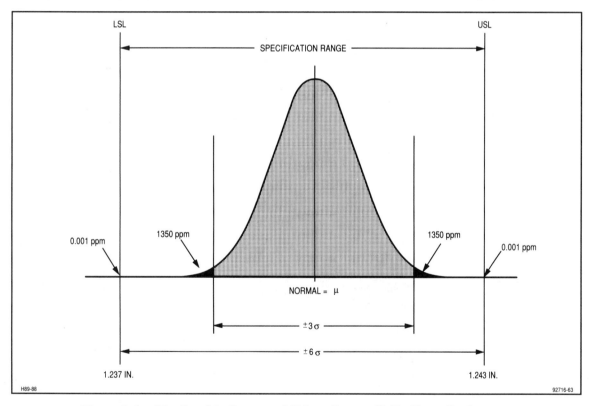

Figure 5-4. The Graphic Concept of "Mean Centered" Six Sigma Performance

---

[7] A more comprehensive discussion on the historical conventions and practices related to such issues is given by Grant and Leavenworth (1974).

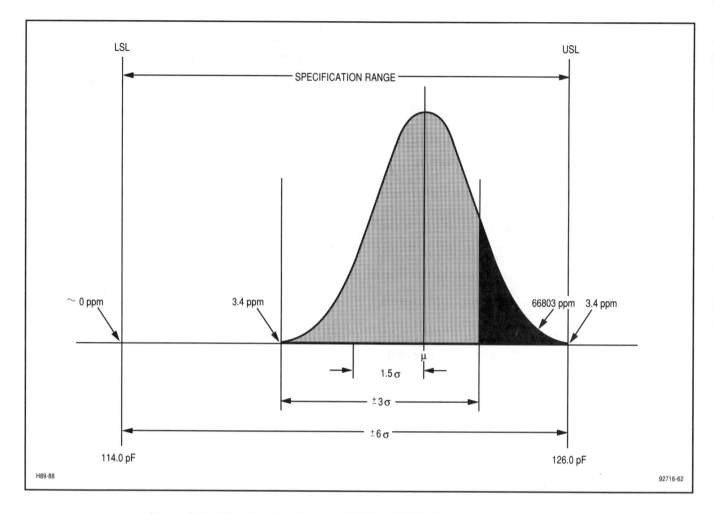

Figure 5-5.   The Graphic Concept of "Mean Shifted" Six Sigma Performance

5.5.3   *The Theoretical Basis for Calculating Probability of Nonconformance*

In order to estimate the statistical probability of exceeding any given specification limit, we must first postulate a probability distribution. Next, we may decide to make the assumption that the specification is tied to a normal random variable.[8] Given this, the manufacturing distribution function may be defined by

$$f(x) = \frac{1}{\sigma\sqrt{2\pi}}e^{-(1/2)[(x-\mu)/\sigma]^2}, \qquad \text{Eq. (5-8)}$$
$$-\infty < x < \infty$$

where x is a random variable, f(x) is the probability density

function of x, and μ and σ are constant parameters – i.e., the mean and standard deviation, respectively. Recognize that NID (μ, σ) may be used to denote the normal probability density function.[9] Furthermore, the probability (p) that x is greater than some criterion value (a) may be found by integrating the normal density function from a to ∞. This may be mathematically expressed as

$$p(x > a) = \int_{a}^{\infty} \frac{1}{\sigma\sqrt{2\pi}}e^{-(1/2)[(x-\mu)/\sigma]^2}dx \; . \qquad \text{Eq. (5-9)}$$

---

[8] In some instances, other types of assumptions are made: uniform, triangular, log-normal, etc. The most commonly applied model, however, is the normal distribution. Because of this, and for the sake of uniformity and simplicity, the normal distribution is used in this booklet. See the Bibliography for a more detailed consideration of other distribution assumptions.

[9] The notation NID (μ, σ) means "normal independent distribution with a mean μ and standard deviation σ."

As you might surmise, the use of Eq. (5-9) as a practical tool for deriving probabilities is questionable at best. Although a simple form is not readily available for evaluating the integral, probabilities may be quickly ascertained via application of the Z transformation, which will be discussed in greater detail later. With a given Z value, the corresponding tail area probability may be located in a table of area under the normal curve (Appendix C). The reader is directed to Brownlee (1965) for additional information on the normal density function.

5.5.4 Relating the Normal Distribution to the Poisson Distribution

The reader is enthusiastically encouraged to recognize that the normal limiting distribution, as previously discussed, can tell us the number of events to expect when the distribution parameters are known or estimated. For example, we could determine how many occurrences of x to expect within any interval from x = a to x = b. Extending this line of reasoning, Taylor (1982) stated that

In practice, the observed number [within the interval x = a to x = b] is seldom exactly the expected number. Instead it fluctuates in accordance with the Poisson distribution. In many situations it is reasonable to expect numbers to be distributed approximately according to the Poisson distribution. The approximation is called the Gaussian approximations to the Poisson. It is analogous to the corresponding approximation for the binomial distribution and is useful under the same conditions, namely, when the parameters involved are large. In fact, it can be proved that as $\mu \rightarrow \infty$, the Poisson distribution becomes steadily more symmetrical and approaches the Gauss [normal] distribution with the same mean and standard deviation.

To illustrate the practical implications of this relation, let us postulate that a given, normally distributed response characteristic (say p_1, as related to our widget example) has a capability such that the specification limits are $\pm 3\sigma$. Such a capability would translate to a first-time yield of .9973, or 99.73 percent as evidenced by Figure 5-4. It is now possible to calculate the equivalent defects-per-unit (dpu) metric. In this instance, dpu = .0027. Given this, we may employ Eq. (2-8) and subsequently compute $e^{-.0027}$ = .9973, or 99.73 percent yield. More will be said about this transformation later. Until then, let us simply accept that it is related to the Poisson model.

Hence, we may directly compare discrete defect data to continuous capability data so long as the corresponding distributional assumptions are reasonably adhered to. In this case, we may say that a defects per unit (dpu) of .0027 is directly equivalent, for all practical purposes, to a normal distribution, which is $\pm 3\sigma$ in relation to the bilateral specification limits. As a consequence, it is possible to align the various metrics founded on discrete data to those metrics which are designed for continuous data, and vice-versa.

Such "metric interconnectivity" will take on immense value and applied meaning in subsequent discussions; however, for now, let us simply recognize the existence of interconnectivity between the Poisson and normal distribution, as well as the binomial model.

5.6 THE STANDARD TRANSFORM

In many instances, we need to be able to compute the probability of exceeding a given design constraint without the aid of an illustration like the one displayed in Figure 5-3, or the complexity of mathematical integration. In such instances, we need only employ what is known as the "standard Z transform." Notice that it is also referred to as the "standard normal deviate." The reader should be aware that both usages will be employed in subsequent discussions and illustrations.

Essentially, the standard transform, or "Z" scale of measure, transforms a set of data such that the mean is always equal to zero ($\mu = 0$) and the standard deviation is always equal to one ($\sigma = 1.0$). Of course, the use of such a transformation assumes that the underlying distribution is normal. Statistically speaking, this would be to say $Z \sim NID (0, 1)$. Figure 5-6 contrasts the "raw" scale (as related to our widget part example) to its equivalent Z scale. In addition, the raw units of measure (e.g., inches as related to our widget example) are eliminated, or lost, by virtue of the transformation process. That is to say, the Z measurement scale is without units.

To illustrate how the standard transform is used, let's suppose we wanted to know how many σs are equivalent to 1.242 inches. To get the answer, we must transform the measurement of interest into a Z value by applying the following equation:

$$Z = \frac{(X - \mu)}{\sigma} \, . \qquad \text{Eq. (5-10)}$$

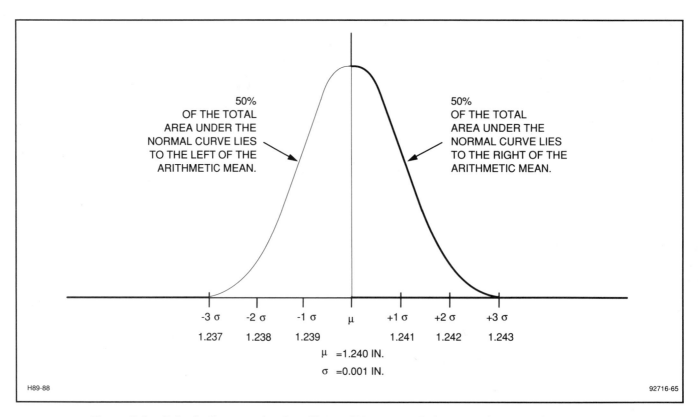

50%
OF THE TOTAL
AREA UNDER THE
NORMAL CURVE LIES
TO THE LEFT OF THE
ARITHMETIC MEAN.

50%
OF THE TOTAL
AREA UNDER THE
NORMAL CURVE LIES
TO THE RIGHT OF THE
ARITHMETIC MEAN.

-3 σ	-2 σ	-1 σ	μ	+1 σ	+2 σ	+3 σ
1.237	1.238	1.239		1.241	1.242	1.243

μ = 1.240 IN.
σ = 0.001 IN.

H89-88   92716-65

Figure 5-6.   Z Scale Contrasted to Raw Units of Measure in Relation to the Normal Distribution

This particular equation is for population values. If a sample is used, then substitute $\overline{X}$ for μ and s for σ. Substituting the values of our known population parameters into the equation, we would have:

$$Z = \frac{1.242 - 1.240}{.001} \ . \qquad \text{Eq. (5-11)}$$

Making the necessary calculations reveals Z = 2.000. This tells us that the length measurement of 1.242 lies 2σ to the right of μ. It would be to the right because the Z equivalent of 1.242 in. is positive. If Z were a negative number, say –2.000, then the corresponding product measurement value would lie to the left of μ. This may be directly verified by studying Figure 5-6. See Dixon and Massey (1969) for additional information. We shall see later why the standard transform is so important, but for now, let's just recognize that it's an invaluable tool.

5.7   APPLICATION OF THE Z TRANSFORM

The Z transform is most useful when we want to know how much of a distribution lies beyond a certain point – say, above and/or below a given design specification. In manufacturing and quality work, the previous statement would translate into. "How many nonconformities or defects could we expect?" To answer such a question, we would need to turn to the Z scale and normal distribution for help.

For example, let's suppose that we want to know how much of the area under the normal curve there is beyond the upper specification limit (USL) of our example widget part, given a new population mean such that μ = 1.242 in. To work this problem we would want to modify Eq. (5-10) to include the USL term. Doing this would give us

$$Z = \frac{\text{USL} - μ}{σ} \ . \qquad \text{Eq. (5-12)}$$

Thus, we would compute Z = 1.000. The USL lies to the the right of μ by 1σ. In other words, we would have to move 1σ from μ to reach the USL. The question now becomes, "How much of the area under the normal curve lies beyond 1σ?" We must consult a table of area under the normal curve for the answer – such as the table in Appendix C. This particular table already has the areas calculated for the corresponding Z values, so you can save a lot of time by using it for most problems dealing with area under the normal curve. Also note that this particular table only contains the areas for the right one-half of the distribution. Because the distribution is the same on both sides of μ, only one half of the total possible area is needed.[10] Using the table in Appendix A as a guide, we can see that 100 (1.587E-01) = 15.87 percent of the part measurements lie to the right of the USL.

Of course, this entire discussion assumes that the underlying distribution is normal. We must always remain cognizant of the fact that whenever a table of normal area is used to establish a rate of nonconformance, and the actual distribution is markedly skewed (i.e., non-normal), the likelihood of grossly distorted estimates is quite high. To avoid such distortion, it is often possible to mathematically transform the raw data, as discussed earlier in this section of the booklet. If the transformation is done correctly, the data are artificially forced to a state of normality. Only then can reliable estimates of nonconformance be rendered. Even then, one must always check to be sure that the transformed data retains correlation to the raw data. If not, resultant estimates could be highly misleading.

It should now be apparent that raw data should always be plotted and/or statistically tested for compliance to the assumed distribution.[11] In addition, we may also say that, whenever mathematical transformations are used, one must always correlate the data. Following these two simple rules of thumb can avoid costly and often embarrassing decision errors. In particular, Gunter (1989) discusses the use of mathematical transformations and their impact on estimates of nonconformance. The reader is also directed to Juran (1979) for a more detailed discussion on some of the commonly used transformations. Ford Motor Company (1984) presents several other interesting applications of the Z transform.

5.8 MEASURES OF CAPABILITY FOR CONTINUOUS DATA

Rather than characterizing the quality of our parts in terms of σ, μ, yield or defects, we could define it in terms of a capability ratio. Such a ratio or "performance index" would contrast the distribution width to the engineering specification width, thereby providing us with a number for comparative purposes. The advantage of such a number is that it is unitless: i.e., free of measurement scale units. This gives us the ability to directly compare the inherent quality of one product characteristic to another, even though the characteristics may be "apples and oranges." We also may compare the capability ratio to some criterion value so that we can determine how close we are to meeting a given performance objective.

5.8.1 The Short-Term Capability Ratio

By statistical convention, the short-term capability index is used to establish the ratio of the specification width to that of the process, regardless of centering.[12] It is most frequently defined as

$$C_p = \frac{USL - LSL}{6\sigma} \qquad \text{Eq. (5-13)}$$

where the upper and lower engineering specification limits are described by USL and LSL, respectively. Be aware that Eq. (5-13) is restricted to the bilateral case: i.e., when both upper and lower limits are prescribed. It should be apparent that Eq. (5-13) is applicable to each of the components related to our widget example.

---

[10] With the assistance of an electronic spreadsheet, the process of converting a standard normal deviate (Z) to tail area probability (P) can be greatly simplified via the following relation:

P = (((((((1 + 0.049867347*B3) + 0.0211410061*B3^2) + 0.0032776263*B3^3) + 0.0000380036*B3^4) + 0.0000488906*B3^5) + 0.000005383*B3^6)^ – 16/2)

where B3 is the cell reference for the given Z value. Recognize that B3 is an arbitrary reference used solely for the purpose of illustration. Should it be necessary to convert in the opposite direction (i.e., P to Z), the following relation can be used:

Z = (SQRT(LN(1/B2^2))) – (2.515517 + 0.802853*(SQRT(LN(1/B2^2))) + 0.010328*(SQRT(LN(1/B2^2)))^2)/(1 + 1.432788* (SQRT(LN(1/B2^2))) + 0.189269*(SQRT(LN(1/B2^2)))^2 + 0.001308*(SQRT(LN(1/B2^2)))^3)

where B2 is the cell location of P. Be aware that the given relations should provide more than enough precision for virtually any application of a practical nature (e.g., process capability studies, etc).

[11] Testing for normality may be accomplished by way of log paper, a chi-square goodness-of-fit test, etc.

[12] Over the course of many years, it has become a statistical convention to treat the $\pm 3\sigma$ limits of the normal density function as the constraints for describing unity. This convention is most often invoked in the interest of practical application.

In the event a unilateral specification is affixed to some characteristic, the capability index may be defined as

$$C_p = \frac{USL - \mu}{3\sigma} \qquad \text{Eq. (5-14)}$$

or

$$C_p = \frac{\mu - LSL}{3\sigma} . \qquad \text{Eq. (5-15)}$$

Of course, Eq. (5-14) and Eq. (5-15) assume that a nominal or "target" value has not been given; e.g., the equations assume $T = \mu$. Should a target value be specified in the instance of a unilateral tolerance, then T should be substituted for μ, with respect to Eq. (5-14) and Eq. (5-15).

By virtue of Eq. (5-10), we may simplify and express the capability ratio as

$$C_p = \frac{Z_{SL}}{3} \qquad \text{Eq. (5-16)}$$

where SL is a limiting specification.

Thus, lot #2 (as related to the widget example) may be characterized by $C_p = 2.0$. A capability of 2.0 would tell us that the specification width is twice as wide as the distribution. Another way of looking at this would be to say that the $\pm 3\sigma$ range of the distribution only consumes 50 percent of the specification width: e.g., $100\,(1/C_p) = 100\,(1/2) = 50$ percent.

At this point in the discussion, the reader should notice that Eq. (5-13) through Eq. (5-16) do not consider the location of μ. Initially, this may seem insufficient for describing manufacturing capability; however, as we shall see later, such a figure of merit takes on great meaning. For example, it is possible that a given response characteristic may be capable in the short-term, in relation to the specification limit(s), but not capable over many manufacturing intervals. In this situation, we would say that the "instant reproducibility," or short-term capability, as described by Eq. (5-16), is acceptable, but the perturbing effects of long-term nonrandom variations in μ degrades this estimate to such an extent that the estimate of long-term capability is undesirable. Hence, Eq. (5-16) is a measure of the relative potential for reproducibility: i.e., the extent to which the process is capable of "cloning" the response characteristic independent of perturbing nonrandom influences of a temporal nature.

5.8.1   The Mid-Term Capability Ratio

Yet another capability index would be C_{pk}. First, the number associated with C_{pk} tells us how far μ is from the nominal condition of the specification in light of the

distribution width. Again, by statistical convention, we may describe the relationship of μ to the nominal specification value (T) by

$$C_{pk} = C_p\,(1 - k) \qquad \text{Eq. (5-17)}$$

where

$$k = \frac{|\,T - \mu\,|}{(USL - LSL)/2} . \qquad \text{Eq. (5-18)}$$

In the case of a unilateral specification,

$$C_{pk} = \frac{T - LSL}{3\sigma} \left\{ 1 - \frac{|\,T - \mu\,|}{T - LSL} \right\} \qquad \text{Eq. (5-19)}$$

or

$$C_{pk} = \frac{USL - T}{3\sigma} \left\{ 1 - \frac{|\,T - \mu\,|}{USL - T} \right\} . \qquad \text{Eq. (5-20)}$$

As before, we may make direct substitution and calculate the capability ratio as

$$C_{pk} = \frac{Z_{SL;\,min}}{3} \qquad \text{Eq. (5-21)}$$

where $Z_{SL;min}$ is the minimum number of standard normal deviates required to encounter a specification limit. Also notice that whenever μ is the same value as the nominal specification, or T, then $C_p = C_{pk}$. As μ departs from the nominal specification, or the target value (left or right), C_{pk} gets smaller in value, assuming σ remains constant. Figure 5-7 illustrates the concepts underlying C_p and C_{pk}.

Interestingly, Gunter (1989) has indicated that the use of C_{pk} can be a very misleading indicator of process stability. This particular conclusion was based on extensive experience, empirical data, and also via computer modeling. Specifically, Gunter stated

> *... there is one more fact of life to be recognized: the variability in the data just due to the luck of the draw – sampling variability. That is, if the data could be collected again under the same process conditions that existed the first-time around, we'd get somewhat different data, and thus different means and standard deviations, and C_{pk}'s. In other words, the C_{pk} we have collected is only one of the many that might be obtained by sampling the same number of items under the same condition. This uncertainty is unavoidable and any reasonable*

approach to using capability indexes must deal with it. All in all, this ... shows that unless a large amount of good data is taken from a stable process, C_{pk} doesn't reveal a lot about what's going on, even when it's used only as a rough indicator and not as a hard measure of percentage within specification.

Obviously, the implications are clear – the calculation requires a substantial amount of data from a fairly stable (and presumably mature) manufacturing process prior to using the index as a decision-making tool. Thus, we may say that C_{pk} is an intermediate or "mid-term" index which may not necessarily report on the "true" state of affairs over many manufacturing intervals. However, in subsequent discussions, we shall discover a methodology which overcomes many of the aforementioned limitations.

Be aware that the metric associated with this particular methodology reflects long-term capability and is designated as C_p^*, where * denotes the inclusion of perturbing nonrandom influences over a great many manufacturing cycles. The reader should also be aware that Gunter provides many other illustrative examples and caveats concerning the use of C_{pk}. A more thorough discussion on the topic of capability indices, from a mathematical perspective, is found in an article authored by Kane (1986).

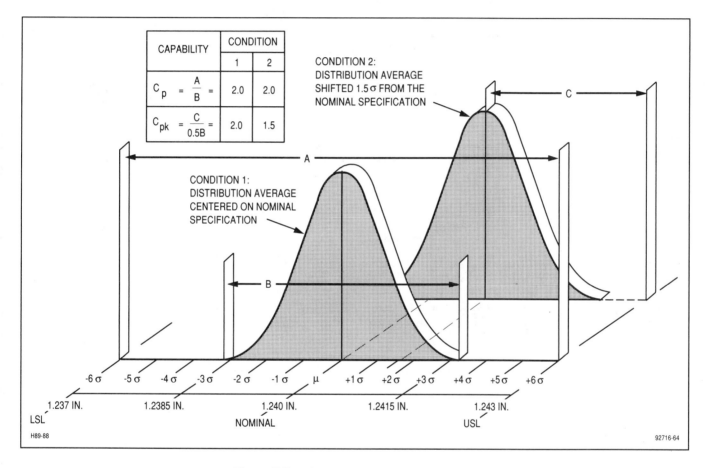

CAPABILITY		CONDITION	
		1	2
C_p	$= \dfrac{A}{B} =$	2.0	2.0
C_{pk}	$= \dfrac{C}{0.5B} =$	2.0	1.5

CONDITION 2: DISTRIBUTION AVERAGE SHIFTED 1.5 σ FROM THE NOMINAL SPECIFICATION

CONDITION 1: DISTRIBUTION AVERAGE CENTERED ON NOMINAL SPECIFICATION

-6σ -5σ -4σ -3σ -2σ -1σ μ +1σ +2σ +3σ +4σ +5σ +6σ

1.237 IN. 1.2385 IN. 1.240 IN. 1.2415 IN. 1.243 IN.
LSL NOMINAL USL

H89-88 92716-64

Figure 5-7.   Concepts Underlying C_p and C_{pk}

5.9   MEASURES OF CAPABILITY FOR DISCRETE DATA

When a product or process is characterized by the number of defects detected under a specific set of sampling conditions, one often seeks to formulate an index of capability from this discrete data. As stated earlier, the number of defects can often be modeled by the tail area of a normal distribution, given that certain conditions can be reasonably complied with or assumed.

The probability for a normally distributed parameter value to be within a given interval can be obtained by computing the ratio of the area of the interval under the normal curve to the entire area under the curve. As mentioned earlier, the standard Z transform is normally distributed with a mean of 0 and a standard deviation of 1. The total area under the curve of the Z transform is one, is unitless, and represents the entire population. Given this, we may say that a portion of the area under the curve would represent the portion of the population that fits into that interval. A table of the areas of intervals under the curve of the Z distribution (Appendix C) directly gives the percentage of the total population that would be included in the interval. In order to use this property of the normal distribution in the instance of discrete data, one has to relate numbers of defects to areas under the normal curve.

If several production units are inspected and a number of defects are found, one can readily compute defects per unit (dpu) to ultimately determine the defects per opportunity (dpm). One can think of this quantity, dpm, as a proportion of the total population of opportunities that are defective. Hence, this fraction defective is directly equivalent to the area under the tail of the normal curve. An equivalent limiting standard normal deviate (Z_{EQ}) can then be associated with this value of dpm. Once Z_{EQ} has been estimated, the capability ratio can be computed as

$$C_p = \frac{Z_{EQ}}{3} . \qquad \text{Eq. (5-22)}$$

Thus far, we've made no mention of the temporal nature of the data: i.e., whether or not it reflects perturbing nonrandom influences. Also, it should be evident that at least one defect must be observed in order to make the calculations, for reasons which will be discussed later on. Because of this, the choice of a rational subgroup for sampling is different for discrete data than that for continuous data.

When the probability for a defect is low, as is the case in many of today's improving processes, the sample size must be quite large to satisfy the need for observing defects. Consequently, for a capability value to be assigned, it is necessary that the sampling be continued until at least one defect is detected. When it is feasible, the sampling should be continued until more defects are detected. Since this is not always practical, the confidence in results can be improved by using the "best" estimate rather than the "point" estimate for obtaining the value of dpm. The distinction between these two estimates will be described in a later section.

The reader must also recognize that the temporal nature of the capability index must be determined by the sample size. If the sample size is large – spanning a period of time which would adequately allow for the influence of perturbing nonrandom effects to be captured within the data – the capability index should be considered as long-term. Given this, the resultant of Eq. (5-22) would then represent C_{pk} or C_p*. Short-term capability would then be approximated, provided a value for k can be determined. Since the data is discrete, k cannot be calculated in a conventional manner, as per Eq. (5-18). Instead, it must be estimated from experience or determined by comparison of short-term and long-term data, as will be demonstrated later. When the latter is not practical, it will be shown later that typical values of k lie in the range, .286 < k < .375, and that a recommended value for k in the absence of confirming data is 0.333.

If the time interval required to observe one or more defects is short, such that the perturbing influences of a temporal nature are not present, the capability index (C_p) would be considered short-term. A mid- or long-term capability index, C_{pk} or C_p*, would then be calculated. Here the arguments concerning the choice of k would still hold. However, since the time needed to observe defects is short in this case, it would seem logical that one could extend the measurements over a longer time frame, find a comparison between C_p and C_{pk}, and thereby generate an empirical value for k. Again, the discussion concerning such calculations will be presented in greater detail later in the booklet.

SECTION 6
THE THEORETICAL BASIS FOR CHARACTERIZATION METRICS

The process characterization metrics referenced herein represent a substantive effort to quantify and characterize short-, mid-, and long-term producibility. This particular section offers a dynamic and, in some instances, highly innovative methodology for the statistical analysis of continuous, as well as discrete data in the context of parameter characterization and process standardization. As may be apparent, our intent is to provide a valid and reliable basis for benchmarking key product, process, material, and component characteristics. As we've said, "You cannot hope to understand what cannot be expressed in numbers." Hence, the need for characterization metrics.

6.1 THE CONCEPT OF INSTANTANEOUS REPRODUCIBILITY

The concept of short-term process capability is largely based on classical Shewhart control chart theory and statistics.[1] In essence, this theory subscribes to the basic notion that the true capability or "reproducibility" of a characteristic can be determined only when the measurements display random variations. In fact, some authors have referred to such estimates of short-term capability as a measure of "instantaneous reproducibility."[2] This means that the sample will only reflect "white noise." Under this condition, the cause system of variables is deliberately constrained in such a manner as to exclude nonrandom perturbing influences. This is most often accomplished by way of blocking.[3] If such extraneous variations exist at the time of data capture, resultant estimates of short-term capability will be biased. Hence, we need to establish how well the process can replicate a given characteristic under relatively ideal conditions.

6.1.1 The Importance of Short-Term Capability

Perhaps the best way to discuss the need for estimating short-term capability is by example. To do this, we shall use our widget product. More specifically, we will estimate the short-term capability of p_1. For the sake of discussion, let us suppose that a sampling plan was adequately devised. In this instance, we shall say that the plan called for the sequential selection of N = 6 subgroups, each consisting of n = 5 consecutive measurements. Notice that such a sampling strategy (e.g., rational subgrouping coupled with sequential sampling) has the effect of limiting the number of variables within the "normal" cause system to some smaller subset. In this manner, each of the subgroups would reflect only random variations, therein providing the data necessary to make a reasonably precise estimate of instantaneous reproducibility, free of perturbing nonrandom variations which occur over time.

Based on the resulting measurements, the average range was determined, using Eq. (5-6), to be .002326 inches. Next, the short-term limiting standard normal deviate (Z_{ST}) was calculated via

$$Z_{ST} = \frac{|T - SL|}{\overline{R}/d_2} \qquad \text{Eq. (6-1)}$$

where T is the target specification value (nominal condition), SL is a specification limit (USL or LSL), and the sample standard deviation is given by the denominator term.

Since N = 6 and n = 5, it was determined that $d_2* = 2.353$ by way of Appendix B. Given the value for $\overline{R}$ and d_2*, the sample standard deviation was subsequently computed and reported as S = .001 in. In this instance, the short-term limiting standard normal deviate was calculated and determined to be Z_{ST} = .003 in. / .001 in. = 3.0. Hence, the short-term manufacturing capability was expressed as "3σ." This represents the instantaneous reproducibility of the process free of perturbing systematic influences of a temporal nature. Yet another way of expressing this would be to say that Z_{ST} is a measure of background noise.

The short-term capability ratio was computed and subsequently reported as C_p = 1.0 by way of Eq. (5-6). Assuming NID (μ,σ), the yield was determined to be 99.73 percent using a table of area under the normal curve (see Appendix C).

---

[1] For additional information, see Shewhart (1931) as well as Grant and Leavenworth (1980).

[2] The reader is directed to Juran (1979) for additional information.

[3] In the given context, the use of blocking variables has much the same effect as the use of control variables. From an experimental frame of reference, it can be said that an experimental block allows the response to be evaluated free of any effects which may be attributable to the blocking variable. The use of such variables provides an avenue for constructing rational subgroups. As may be apparent, the most frequently used blocking variable is time. Thus, if blocking is adequately performed, there will exist maximum opportunity for the measurements to be alike within a subgroup, and maximum likelihood that each of the subgroups will be different across many sampling intervals. In other words, the purpose of blocking is to minimize within-group variance and maximize sensitivity to mean differences between and across subgroups. In this sense, rational subgrouping maximizes the likelihood of homogeneity of variance across subgroups.

Finally, the parts per million was computed and given as ppm = $(1 - .9973)10^6 = 2700$.

Now, let us suppose that we let the process run under normal operating conditions over a great many manufacturing intervals. Doing so would reveal the long-term performance of p_1. Notice that such performance reflects random variations and virtually all sources of systematic nonrandom influence. In this case, we shall say that the long-term capability was determined to be $Z_{LT} = 2.0$. In this context, the short-term capability study served as the baseline or "benchmark" for gauging the relative efficacy of manufacturing control over an extended period of production.

As may be surmised, the disparity between the short- and long-term estimates reflects how well the process is controlled over time. This will be discussed in greater detail later. The key at this point is to recognize the benchmarking role of short-term capability.

6.1.2   The Issue of Manufacturing Error

As we all know, there are many manufacturing, component, material, and environmental variables which can, if uncontrolled, significantly distort numerical estimates of the true short-term process capability, thereby introducing unnecessary error into the situation. Of course, we do not mean the kind of error typically associated with the term "mistake." On this topic, Taylor (1982) stated

> *In science the word "error" does not carry the usual connotations of "mistake" or "blunder." "Error" in a scientific measurement means the inevitable uncertainty that attends all measurements. As such, errors are not mistakes; you cannot avoid them by being very careful. The best you can hope to do is ensure that errors are as small as reasonably possible.*

Based on this understanding, we may say that the intent of a short-term manufacturing capability study is to quantify the potential repeatability of a manufacturing process. As previously indicated, this translates to how well the process performs, independent of systematic perturbing influences of

a temporal nature. When such an operating condition has been properly established, error is at or near some minimum which, in turn, assures minimum uncertainty about the process's ultimate technological potential. As you can surmise, this provides a solid foundation for decision making.[4]

6.1.3   The Issue of Compounding Error

To better understand the formulation of uncertainty, we must turn to a quantitative definition. Strictly speaking, we may say that the total uncertainty in any manufacturing situation results from the sum of all contributing uncertainties. Expressing this in terms of error variance, we may state

$$\sigma^2_{TOT} = \sigma^2_1 + \sigma^2_2 + ... + \sigma^2_N \qquad \text{Eq. (6-2)}$$

where, σ^2_{TOT} is the total observed variance of the response characteristic Y, and σ^2_1, σ^2_2, ... , σ^2_N are the independent variances associated with those variables which comprise the underlying cause system.[5] In the instance of p_1, the independent sources of error might include measurement apparatus, operator differences, materials, machines, and environment, just to mention a few. From this vantage point, it is easy to see why σ^2_{TOT} may be viewed as a measure of precision.[6] Hence, the relative precision of a manufacturing process is a function of all the contributing variations.

Of course, we fully recognize that Eq. (6-2) assumes the N sources of error are independent. If, for example, σ^2_1 and σ^2_2 are interrelated, the correlation would have to be taken into account, therein altering the linear combination of variances to another form.[7] In this instance

$$\sigma^2_{TOT} = \sigma^2_1 + \sigma^2_2 + 2\,\rho_{12}\,\sigma_1\,\sigma_2 \qquad \text{Eq. (6-3)}$$

where ρ is the correlation coefficient. For most types of work in industry, the assumption of independence (i.e., $\rho = 0$) is considered to be reasonable, thereby allowing the linear combination of variances to serve as a plausible first-order model.

---

[4] At this point in our discussion, the reader should remember that the variance of a response parameter represents a relative measure of error; thus, it is a direct measure of uncertainty and manufacturing risk.

[5] From a statistical perspective, we must recognize that it is possible to show $V(X_1 + X_2) = V(X_1) + V(X_2) + 2\,COV\,(X_1, X_2)$ and $V(X_1 - X_2) = V(X_1) + V(X_2) - 2\,COV\,(X_1, X_2)$ where V is the variance and $COV\,(X_1, X_2) = E[X_1 - \mu_1)\,(X_2 - \mu_2)]$ is the covariance. Thus, if X_1 and X_2 are independent, $V(X_1 \pm X_2) = V(X_1) + V(X_2) = \sigma_1^2 + \sigma_2^2$ where $\pm 2\,COV\,(X_1, X_2) = 0$. Hence, the linear sum of component variances may be used to describe the total error – e.g., $\sigma^2\,TOT = \sigma_1^2 + \sigma_2^2 + ... + \sigma_N^2$, assuming independence – otherwise, the pairwise covariances must be considered. Of course, independence may not be inferred directly by virtue of $COV\,(X_1, X_2) = 0$. Related theorems and proof pertaining to the variances of linear combinations is given by Mendenhall and Schaffer (1973) as well as Pearson (1983).

[6] The reader must distinguish between precision and accuracy. Precision is most often associated with the scatter inherent to a set of data while accuracy describes the central tendency of the data set in relation to a target value. In this sense, precision is given by the variance, whereas accuracy is denoted by the relative difference between the arithmetic mean and nominal specification value.

[7] See Juran (1979) as well as Grant and Leavenworth (1980).

6.1.4 The Issue of Leverage

We should now recognize that some of the error components do not have a significant impact on σ^2_{TOT} relative to some established interval or volume of production. Given this, it should be apparent that σ^2_{TOT} will, in general, decrease as the interval of production is shortened. Of course, this assumes a fairly stable rate of production. Obviously, the inverse of this relation would also hold, as a general rule. As a consequence, one would anticipate a point of diminishing return relative to the minimum and maximum size of σ^2_{TOT} and the number of terms on the right-hand side of Eq. (6-2).

If all sources of error were to be rank ordered and then entered into the equation on the basis of greatest or least influence, we could expect σ^2_{TOT} to quickly taper off in size as the terms are introduced. This phenomenon is most often called the Pareto Principle. Figure 6-1 illustrates the Pareto Principle in the context of cumulative manufacturing error. In essence, this principle advocates the notion of diminishing return. That is, a point were the output does not appreciably change as a function of the number of inputs. In short, the principle would suggest that 80 percent of the total error in most any situation can be accounted for by 20 percent of the variables.

To better understand the practical impact of Pareto's Principle, let us assume that some performance characteristic (Y_i related to a certain product) currently exhibits some amount of error as given by σ^2_{TOT}. Of course, σ_{TOT} is given by finding the square root of the right-hand side of Eq. (6-2). Furthermore, let us assume that there are only six sources of error ($X_1...X_6$). Table 6-1 displays the contributing error inherent to each one of the variables within the cause system.

In this case, the application of Eq. (6-2) would reveal

that $\sigma_{TOT} = 12.33$. Given these facts, any number of strategies could be implemented to improve the overall situation. To limit the exploration of all possible strategies, only three will be considered. The first strategy entails reducing the contributing error of each variable by one unit. The second strategy involves completely eliminating the error inherent to each variable except X_2. In this instance, X_2 will not be considered as an "improvement candidate;" therefore, it will be left at 11 units. The third strategy will consider reducing the error inherent to X_2 by 3 units, with the remaining variables left at their existing levels. Table 6-2 presents the outcomes associated with each of the three strategies.

It is very apparent that the third strategy is superior to the first and second strategies, as evidenced by the last column in Table 6-2. As may be apparent, X_2 exerts an undue influence in the total cause system; therefore, it is leverage in nature. In Pareto terms, it is the "vital few" (20 percent), whereas the other sources of error are among the "trivial many" (80 percent). Working smarter, not harder, means searching a situation for leverage before taking action.

Table 6-1.   Components of Error Related to the Given Product Example

Variable (X)	Units of Contributing Error
1	4
2	11
3	3
4	2
5	1
6	1

Table 6-2.   Display of the Outcomes Related to the Three Error Reduction Strategies

Option Number	Strategy Description	Amount Error						Summation of Error Reduction	Net Effect (σ_{TOT})	Change Over Baseline (%)
		σ_1^2	σ_2^2	σ_3^2	σ_4^2	σ_5^2	σ_6^2			
NA	Baseline Condition	4	11	3	2	1	1	0	12.33	NA
1	Reduce each source of error by one unit	3	10	2	1	0	0	6	10.67	13.5
2	Reduce all sources of error to 0 except X_2	0	11	0	0	0	0	11	11.00	10.8
3	Reduce the contributing error of X_2 by 3 units	4	8	3	2	1	1	3	9.74	21.0

Given the Pareto Principle, we may say that σ^2_{TOT} can be decomposed into the "vital few" and the "trivial many" components of error. In other words, a few key sources of error account for the overwhelming majority of uncertainty across many intervals of manufacturing. As such, the vital few sources represent leverage.

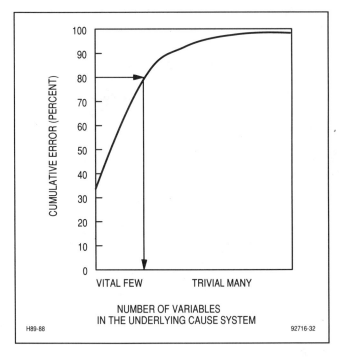

Figure 6-1. Graphic Depiction of the Pareto Principle

In the context of Figure 6-1, we must conclude that the "vital few" sources of nonrandom error should be discerned and subsequently neutralized to make a reliable estimate of instantaneous capability. To do this, it would be necessary to block or otherwise control the "vital few" effects. If the variable called "sampling interval" or "time" was used for this purpose, it should be apparent that as time approaches zero, the number of terms remaining on the right-hand side of Eq. (6-2) approaches zero. In the context of a short-term capability study, our objective would be to discover the sampling interval size which reduces σ^2_{TOT} to white noise. Hence, we must be able to classify the underlying cause system such that it would be possible to calculate

$$\sigma^2_{TOT} = \sigma^2_{SYS} + \sigma^2_{RND} \qquad \text{Eq. (6-4)}$$

where σ^2_{SYS} is the composite effect of peturbing nonrandom errors which are leverage in nature and σ^2_{RND} is the random or "residual" error component.[8] Of course, it is assumed that such error sources can be identified in some practical and economical manner.

Hence, the major task associated with the conduct of any short-term capability study is one of separating σ^2_{TOT} into its major component parts. Once separated, $\sigma^2_{TOT} - \sigma^2_{SYS} = \sigma^2_{RND}$ is used as the measure of instantaneous reproducibility. With such a measure, the boundaries of potential manufacturing precision can be quantitatively established in a practical and economical manner with a known degree of probabilistic certainty. Of course, this is often easier said than done. In many situations, this becomes a very difficult task, as evidenced by the thoughts of E. F. Schumaker:

> *When the Lord created the world and people to live in it – an enterprise which, according to modern science, took a very long time – I could well imagine that he reasoned with himself as follows: If I make everything predictable, these human beings, whom I have endowed with pretty good brains, will undoubtedly learn to predict everything, and they will thereupon have no motive to do anything at all because they will recognize that the future is totally determined and cannot be influenced by any human action. On the other hand, if I make everything unpredictable, they will gradually discover that there is no rational basis for any decision whatsoever and, as in the first case, they will thereupon have no motive to do anything at all. Neither scheme would make sense. I must therefore create a mixture of the two. Let some things be predictable and let others be unpredictable. They will then, amongst many other things, have the very important task of finding out which is which.*

6.1.5   The Basis for Characterization Metrics

As the reader might have already surmised, the long-term variance of a characteristic (σ^2_{LT}) may be used in lieu of the total variance (σ^2_{TOT}). As already indicated, the short-term variance (σ^2_{ST}) may be given by the random error component (σ^2_{RND}). When we substitute such terms, it is apparent that

---

[8] Strictly speaking, the residual variations may not necessarily be purely random in a mathematical or physical sense; i.e., they cannot be practically discerned. As a consequence, they are referenced as random influences, or "white noise" as some would say.

$$\sigma_{LT}^2 = \sigma_{SYS}^2 + \sigma_{ST}^2 \qquad \text{Eq. (6-5)}$$

Hence, the effect of perturbing sources of systematic nonrandom error may be expressed as

$$\sigma_{SYS}^2 = \sigma_{LT}^2 - \sigma_{ST}^2 \quad . \qquad \text{Eq. (6-6)}$$

Given Eq. (6-6), it becomes apparent that the ultimate manufacturing goal is to control the process over time so that $\sigma^2_{SYS} = 0$. Under this condition, the process will remain consistently predictable, in terms of precision, over a great many intervals of manufacturing.[9] In turn, this tends to stabilize many key indicators of factory performance. Along these lines, Juran (1979) stated that

> . . . there is great value in standardizing on a formula for process capability based on a state of statistical control (i.e., free of assignable causes of variation). Under this state, the product variations are the resultant of numerous small variables (rather than being the effect of a single large variable) and hence have the character of random variation. The practitioner cannot reduce this "natural" or inherent instantaneous reproducibility, which thereby becomes "unavoidable" so long as this process is used; i.e., the variability of the process can be reduced to the size of the process capability, but no further. It is most helpful for planners to have such limits in quantified form.

In addition, he states:

> Some practitioners advocate a standard formula which does take into account the "extraneous" variables such as drift and sudden changes. However, use of such a formula would remove the commonality possessed by all processed, i.e., inherent instantaneous variability. Instead, the standard formula would include the "extraneous" variables, which differ widely from one process to another.

Simply stated, this means that any estimate of the true capability of a manufacturing process should be made free of assignable causes if one is to have a valid and reliable predictor of process capability. In other words, the sample variance should not reflect systematic sources of variation; otherwise, one could not (a) make comparisons across processes or factories, (b) have valid benchmarks from which to gauge improvement efforts, or (c) understand the degree to which a process can perform if it is relatively well controlled. Along the same line of reasoning, Kane (1986) stated that

> . . . the number of sources of variation increases as the time interval between samples within a subgroup increases. Spreading out the samples within a subgroup over time will increase $\overline{R}$, widening the control limits, and thus makes achieving statistical control more likely. However, increasing $\overline{R}$ will increase the estimate of σ and thus decrease process capability. Conversely, it is possible to increase process capability by using consecutive piece sampling (i.e., obtaining a small $\overline{R}$) to obtain a minimum estimate of σ and maximum capability.

Based on the latter arguments, it becomes all too obvious that, if σ^2_{SYS} is to be minimized, a rational sampling strategy must be invoked to effectively block the influence of certain key variables within the cause system. If an adequate sampling plan is not contrived, the potential for unacceptable producer risk is high. Of course, the derivation of a sampling plan requires that the sample size be established *a priori*. As we shall see, the sample size interacts with the method of data collection.

6.1.6 The Issue of Sample Size

In most instances it is not practical or economical to make all possible measurements relative to a universe: hence, the need for sampling. If the sample is too small, the margin of predictive error will be large. In turn, a large margin of error confounds, or even prevents, subsequent decision making. On the other hand, if the sample is too large, much of the economy associated with sampling is diminished, or even lost. In turn, this implies a balance point between "statistical purity" and utilitarian need. Both are of concern. To better understand the practical impact of sample size on decision making, we must consider the basic notions that underlie statistical confidence intervals.

In essence, a statistical confidence interval is merely a probabilitic range in which the "true" universe parameter of interest resides. The confidence limits are the upper and lower boundaries of the interval. For the arithmetic mean, such an interval may be given by

$$\overline{X} - t_{(1-\alpha/2);\, v}\frac{S}{\sqrt{n}} \leqslant \mu \leqslant \overline{X} + t_{(1-\alpha/2);\, v}\frac{S}{\sqrt{n}}$$
$$\text{Eq. (6-7)}$$

where t is the distribution coefficient with $n-1$ degrees of freedom, α is the probability of Type I decision error, S is the sample standard deviation, and n is the sample size. A table of

---

[9] Notice that when the systematic error term is zero, the response parameter is 100 percent hermetic to perturbing sources of systematic nonrandom manufacturing error. Inversely, as the systematic error term asymptotically approaches infinity, the measure of hermeticity to nonrandom variations approaches 0 percent: hence, the quantitative basis for describing parameter robustness.

t values has been provided in Appendix E. The confidence interval associated with the standard deviation may be expressed as

$$S \sqrt{(n-1)/\chi^2_{(1-\alpha/2);\,\nu}} \leqslant \sigma \leqslant$$

$$S \sqrt{(n-1)/\chi^2_{1\,\alpha/2);\,\nu}} \qquad \text{Eq. (6-8)}$$

where χ^2 is the chi-square distribution coefficient and ν is the related degrees of freedom. A table of χ^2 values has been provided in Appendix F. Figures 6-2 and 6-3 display the 95 percent confidence interval for μ and σ relative to a selected range of n and for the case NID (0,1).

Given Figure 6-2, the reader should notice the apparent point of diminishing return at n = 5. To highlight the significance of this particular case, let us discuss it further. Since the confidence interval of the mean is approximately $-1.24 \leq \mu \leq +1.24$ for the case n = 5, it may be concluded, with 95 percent confidence, the true value of μ will be included within this range. The same line of reasoning would be applied to Figure 6-3 for the case of n = 5.

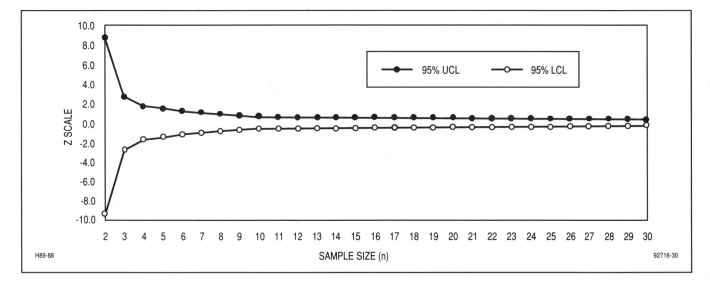

Figure 6-2. The 95 Percent Confidence Interval of μ for a Selected Range of Sample Size (n)

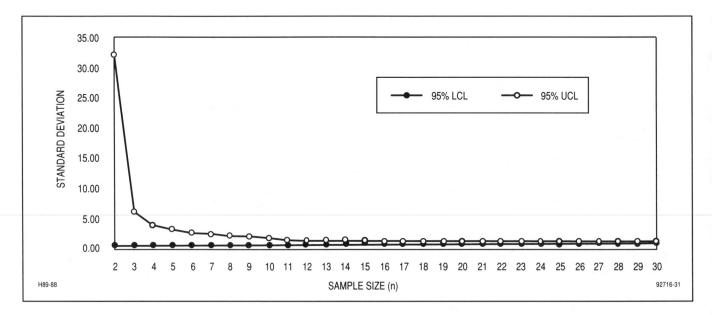

Figure 6-3. The 95 Percent Confidence Interval of σ for a Selected Range of Sample Size (n)

Assuming a relatively high volume of production, it is apparent that the point of compromise between manufacturing economy and statistical precision can be realized (in many instances) when a rational subgroup consisting of n = 5 measurements has been established. If the n = 5 measurements are made on the basis of production order, the cause system is often sufficiently constrained so that only random variations will prevail. Again, this generally assumes a fairly high production volume that is reasonably stable over time.

Further investigation will reveal that the next point of diminishing return, with respect to Eq. (6-7) and Eq. (6-8), is at about n = 30. If the number of subgroups is set at N = 6 while retaining n = 5 for each subgroup, we may say that the total sample size is N x n = 6 x 5 = 30. In this context, statistical precision can be enhanced significantly while simultaneously fulfilling the basic mission of a short-term capability study. Given this line of reasoning, it should now be apparent that instantaneous reproducibility of a manufacturing process can be estimated free of perturbing nonrandom influences, while concurrently maintaining a relatively high degree of statistical confidence and precision.

Remember that all of this is quite general in nature and, as a consequence, should not be taken out of this context. In most manufacturing situations, there are many mitigating circumstances which must be considered in the selection of N and n: e.g., production volume, process stability, product configuration, etc. More direct guidance will be presented later. The intent at this point in our discussion is merely one of recognition and rationale.

It is imperative that the reader understand the statistical reasoning which must underlie the selection of N and n for purposes of estimating short-term capability; otherwise, the likelihood of inappropriate application is high. This in turn, drives faulty manufacturing and business decisions.[10] This point cannot be overly emphasized.

6.2 THE CONCEPT OF DYNAMIC MEAN VARIATION

To help explain dynamic mean variation, we will again use our widget as a basis for discussion and illustration. To begin with, let's suppose that widget component p_1 is to be made on a numerically controlled production milling machine which has a historical standard deviation of $\sigma = .001$ in. Furthermore, we will say that the normal distribution holds true for this particular characteristic. As previously

demonstrated, a centered $\pm 3\sigma$ process capability leads us to a level of producibility such that $Y_{FT} = .9973$, or 99.73 percent. However, such an estimate of producibility or, in manufacturing lingo, "capability," assumes that the process mean of the milling machine is centered within the specification such that $\mu = T$.

As those who have had experience in such matters will testify, the recognition of such factors as tool wear often forces the operator to deliberately under-adjust the process mean in relation to the target specification value (T). This would most certainly happen upon replacement of the cutting tool. As the tool begins to wear, and other independent variables[11] come into play, μ begins to drift toward the nominal value, and subsequently away from it, thus violating the original assumption of a centered process. In general, the tail area probabilities change as the mean moves across the specification window. Figure 6-4 illustrates this phenomenon.

Thus, the overall effect across many such manufacturing cycles is a tail area probability which is greater than any artificially centered "slice in time" estimate. In short, a dynamic process mean tends to mask the instantaneous capability of the process. Also notice that the assumption of equal variances must prevail.[12]

6.2.1 The Mean-Biased Standard Deviation

Thus, we may now say that dynamic mean behavior assumes the population mean will move about within the tolerance zone, but will eventually display a very strong bias toward the target value over a great many production intervals. Naturally, this assumes a reasonable degree of control over the manufacturing technology. Another way of expressing this concept would be to say the combined effect of random and nonrandom error over a very long period of production will impact the response mean rather uniformly on both sides of the nominal specification such that the mean will eventually tend toward the condition; i.e., μ approaches T over a great many intervals of production.

The impact of such behavior is quite profound: *it ultimately translates to an inflated standard deviation which, in turn, degrades manufacturing capability.* This particular statement is based on the progressive rationale surrounding Eq. (6-4). Intuitively, it is quite easy to understand how the inflationary effects of dynamic mean behavior translate to yield loss over a great many intervals of production. Figure 6-5 graphically illustrates this point.

---

[10] Remember that the integrity of the data will ultimately determine the credibility of a characterization study. If the data are not properly gathered under appropriate conditions using realistic safeguards, it is highly likely that the "cornerstone of credibility" will crumble under the questions of a knowledgeable reviewer. When this happens, the "conclusions and recommendations for action" are most often discarded with the rubble.

[11] Such variables include, but are not limited to (a) machine-related temperatures, (b) uniformity of material hardness, (c) thermal expansion coefficients, and (d) operator nuances such as tweaking, just to mention a few.

[12] Referred to as homogeneity of variance; i.e., $\sigma_1^2 = \sigma_2^2 = \sigma_3^2 = \ldots = \sigma_N^2$

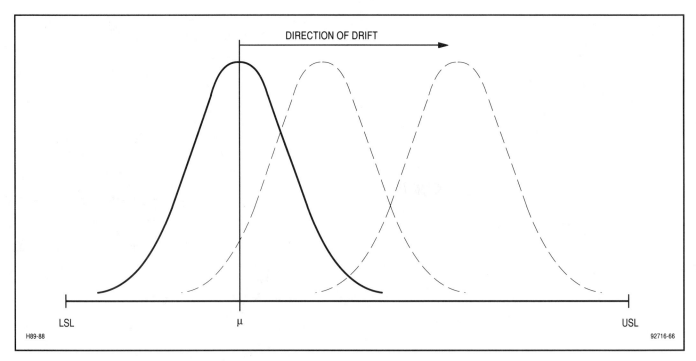

Figure 6-4. The Effect of Drift as a Function of Tool Wear Over Time

Without going into great mathematical detail at this point, suffice it to say that this position has been supported by such noted researchers as Bender (1975), Gilson (1951), and Evans (1975). In particular, Evans pointed out that

> *. . . shifts and drifts in the mean of the distribution of a component value occur for a number of reasons as do changes in the other parameters of a distribution: for example, tool wear is one source of a gradual drift, differences in raw material or change of suppliers can cause shifts in the distribution. Except in special cases it is almost impossible to predict quantitatively the changes in the distribution of a component value which will occur, but the knowledge that they will occur enables us to cope with the difficulty. A solution proposed by Bender ... allows for shifts and drifts. Bender suggests that one should use*

$$V = 1.5 \sqrt{VAR\ (X)}$$

> *as the standard deviation of the response to calculate the percentage out-of-tolerance responses and, thus, to relate the component tolerances and the response tolerance.*

Although using a slightly different approach, Gilson also expressed the same basic conclusion.[13]

If we were to synthesize their many years of experience and research, we would discover that the magnitude of inflation (c), as applied to the standard deviation, may roughly be given by the range $1.4 < c < 1.6$, with respect to "typical" manufacturing conditions and circumstances. Hence, the dynamic or "long-term" standard deviation may be described by

$$\sigma_{LT} = \sigma_{ST}c \ . \qquad \text{Eq. (6-9)}$$

Also recognize that $c = 1.5$ is perhaps the most commonly applied value and, as a consequence, the recommended value when ambiguous manufacturing circumstances prevail. As we shall see later in the discussion, the use of c allows us to derive first-order estimates of long-term producibility. Coupling these estimates with relatively precise short-term estimates of manufacturing capability, we can assess how robust the parameter of interest is to random and systematic influences, of a dynamic nature, which stem from the underlying network of independent variables.

6.2.2   The Equivalent Mean Shift

In light of the previously mentioned research concerning c, we may now discuss the concept of an equivalent mean shift and its general utility in the context of producibility analysis and process characterization work.

---

[13] This phenomenon has also been investigated by the authors via extensive emperical modeling and computer simulation. An example simulation has been located in Appendix G of this booklet.

First, let us recognize that an equivalent mean shift is nothing more than a compensatory static offset in the mean which directly corresponds to dynamic inflation of the standard deviation such that the *probability of nonconformance* *is the same in both cases*. This provides us with comparable tail area when considering both types of occurrences. Figure 6-6 and Figure 6-7 provide a visual definition of this relationship for the unilateral and bilateral cases, respectively.

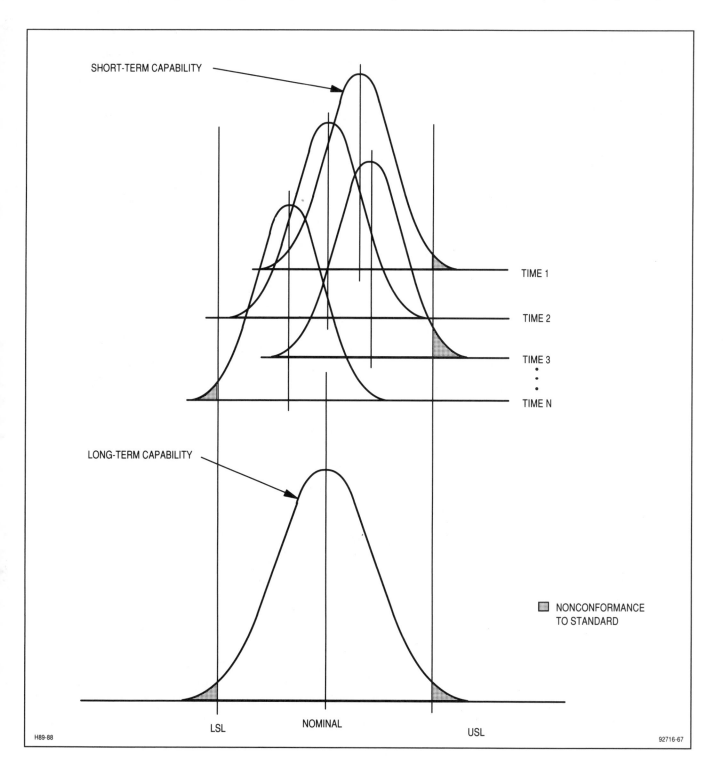

Figure 6-5. The Effect of Dynamic Mean Variation on Production Yield

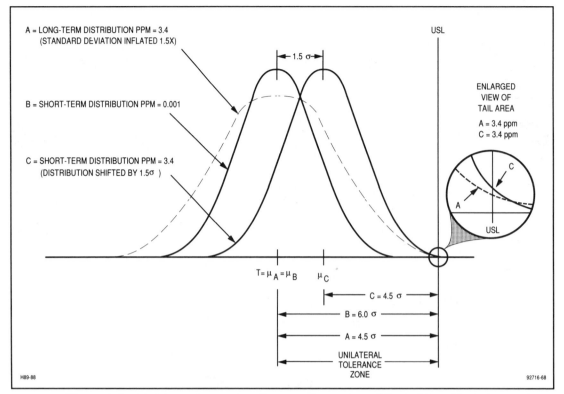

Figure 6-6. *Tail Area Comparison Between Dynamic and Static Mean Variation Under the Constraint of a Unilateral Tolerance*

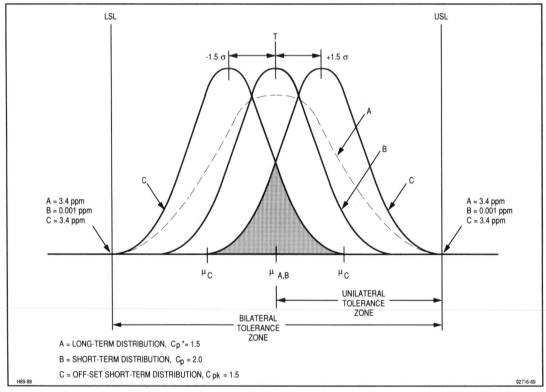

Figure 6-7. *Tail Area Comparison Between Dynamic and Static Mean Variation Under the Constraint of a Symmetrical Bilateral Tolerance*

Based upon the notion of equivalent tail area, it would be reasonable to postulate equivalent capability. In terms of the capability ratio, such equivalency could be defined as

$$C_{pk} = C_p*$$ Eq. (6-10)

where C_{pk} is the equivalent mid-term capability ratio given by Eq. (5-13) through Eq. (5-16) and C_p* is the corresponding dynamic long-term capability ratio. In this instance, the dynamic long-term capability ratio may be expressed as

$$C_p* = |T - SL|/(3\sigma_{ST}c)$$ Eq. (6-11)

where c is the inflation factor applied to the short-term standard deviation to reflect long-term perturbing influences. In partially expanded form, such equivalency takes the form

$$[\, |T - SL|/(3\sigma_{ST})\,](1 - k) = |T - SL|/(3\sigma_{ST}c)\ .$$ Eq. (6-12)

Recognize that Eq. (6-12) is expressed in unilateral form; however, it may also be applied to the bilateral case by virtue of symmetry. Also notice that the left side of this relation considers a linear mean shift (by virtue of k), while the right side considers an expanded standard deviation (by virtue of c). When simplified, we discover that Eq. (6-12) reduces to

$$Z_{ST}(1 - k) = Z_{ST}/c\ .$$ Eq. (6-13)

Therefore, Eq. (6-13) is an expression of long-term capability given as a standard normal deviate (Z_{LT}).

Further reduction of Eq. (6-13) reveals that

$$k = 1 - \frac{1}{c}\ .$$ Eq. (6-14)

With respect to Eq. (6-14), we may expand the left side to reflect

$$\frac{|T - \mu|}{|T - SL|} = 1 - \frac{1}{c}$$ Eq. (6-15)

and subsequently solve for the extent of linear mean shift via

$$|T - \mu| = |T - SL|\left(1 - \frac{1}{c}\right).$$ Eq. (6-16)

We may again normalize to the special case of NID (0,1) to reflect

$$|\delta\sigma_{EQ}| = |Z_{ST}|\left(1 - \frac{1}{c}\right).$$ Eq. (6-17)

Thus, we may translate c to an "equivalent" sustained mean shift ($\delta\sigma_{EQ}$), expressed in Z units of measure. Now, by substitution, it is possible to demonstrate that

$$k = \frac{|\delta\sigma_{EQ}|}{|Z_{ST}|}\ .$$ Eq. (6-18)

For the reader's convenience, the relationship between $\delta\sigma_{EQ}$ and c (for selected short-term limiting standard normal deviates) is displayed in Figure 6-8.

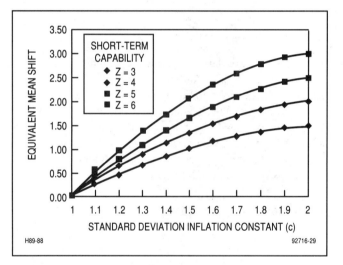

Figure 6-8. *The Relationship Between $\delta\sigma_{EQ}$ and c for Selected Values of Short-Term Unilateral Capability*

To illustrate the equivalency of the previous equations, let us consider an example of a unilateral specification with a nominal value of T and a short-term capability of $C_p = 1.0$. Of course, this would translate to 3σ performance, without regard to centering. Now, we shall say that historical manufacturing data revealed $c = 1.5$.

Based on Eq. (6-17), it is apparent the equivalent static-state mean offset or "shift" would be $\delta\sigma_{EQ} = 3[1-(1/c)] = 3[1-1/1.5] = 1$. Substituting $\delta\sigma_{EQ} = 1$ into Eq. (6-18) reveals that K = .333. From the left side of Eq. (6-13) it follows that $Z_{LT} = Z_{ST}(1 - K) = 3(1 - .333) = 2$. From the right side of Eq. (6-13) it is apparent that $Z_{LT} = Z_{ST}/c = 3/1.5 = 2$. Hence, we may conclude that a linear mean shift ($\delta\sigma_{EQ}$) may be expressed as an inflationary constant (c) applied to the standard deviation (σ). In addition, we may now say $\delta\sigma_{EQ} = Z_{ST}K = Z_{ST} - Z_{LT}$. Given such calculations involving Z, it follows that the unilateral tail area probability is equivalent.[14]

Since k = .3333 by virtue of Eq. (6-14) or Eq. (6-18), we may conclude that approximately 33 percent of the tolerance zone would be consumed by dynamic mean behavior over a great many manufacturing intervals. Hence, parameter robustness (C_R) may be given by

$$C_R = \frac{Z_{LT}}{Z_{ST}} = \frac{Z_{ST} - |\delta\sigma_{EQ}|}{Z_{ST}} = \frac{Z_{ST}(1-k)}{Z_{ST}} = 1 - k = \frac{1}{c} \ .$$
Eq. (6-19)

6.2.3 The Metrics for Describing Long-Term Dynamic Capability

As previously demonstrated, the limiting long-term standard normal deviate of any given dynamic parameter may be expressed as

$$Z_{LT} = Z_{ST}(1 - k) \qquad \text{Eq. (6-20)}$$

regardless of how large or small the actual tolerance zone may be in raw units of measure. By virtue of the previously specified range for c and Eq. (6-14), the equivalent range of k may now be given as $.286 < k < .375$; however, the use of k = .333 is recommended for most ambiguous manufacturing situations. In short, we now have a metric for expressing the inflationary effects of dynamic mean behavior in terms of the limiting standard normal deviate.

Based on Eq. (5-16) and Eq. (6-20), we may now calculate the long-term dynamic process capability ratio (C_p^*) as

$$C_p^* = \frac{Z_{ST}(1 - k)}{3} \ . \qquad \text{Eq. (6-21)}$$

At this point in the discussion, the reader should note that the overall process may be reversed. This is to say that the short-term capability may be estimated or hypothesized when the long-term capability is known, or has been estimated. Under such circumstances, we may rearrange Eq. (6-20) to calculate Z_{ST}. This would take the form of

$$Z_{ST} = \frac{Z_{LT}}{1 - k} \ . \qquad \text{Eq. (6-22)}$$

In terms of the short-term capability ratio, it can be demonstrated that

$$C_p = \frac{Z_{LT}}{3(1 - k)} \qquad \text{Eq. (6-23)}$$

assuming that k is known, empirically estimated, or can be rationally postulated on the basis of manufacturing experience or best engineering judgement. Naturally, the prevailing circumstances will dictate whether Eq. (6-20) or Eq. (6-22) is used.

To better illustrate practical utility, we shall return to our widget product. Let us suppose that the short-term capability of p_1 was calculated using Eq. (6-22) and determined to be Z_{ST} = 4.0. We shall also say manufacturing experience indicates that μ is dynamic by nature such that $\delta\sigma_{EQ} = \pm1.5$. Given this, we would estimate k via Eq. (6-18) to be 1.5/4 = .375. Thus, the long-term process capability ratio would be estimated by Eq. (6-21) and given as C_p^* = .833. We may also say that the parameter is $C_R = (1 - k) = (1 - .375) = .625$, or 62.5 percent robust to perturbing influences of a temporal nature.

Conversely, let us suppose that the long-term capability of some other part (say, p_2) is known to be Z_{LT} = 3.0 and manufacturing data reveals that k = .333, in a dynamic sense. In this instance, we would calculate the short-term process capability ratio. Doing so would reveal C_p = 1.5. Notice that this may also be expressed as $\pm4.5\sigma$ performance. Hence, the characteristic would be $C_R = (3.0/4.5) = .67$, or 67 percent robust to perturbing nonrandom influences of a temporal nature. More discussion will be given to this topic later on; however, for now, let us just recognize such transformation and estimation is essential to process characterization work.

---

[14] The reader is encouraged to recognize that, in the instance of a unilateral specification, equivalent tail area results only when the mean shift occurs in the direction of the specification limit. Obviously, a mean shift in the opposite direction would not produce a corresponding probability of nonconformance. Based on this discussion, we may conclude that C_{pk} can be compared to C_p^* only when the researcher is willing to acknowledge that a mid-term estimate of capability; e.g., C_{pk}, will prove to be a dynamic index over additional periods of sampling. With respect to the latter point, we must remember that k is most often computed after a fairly limited number of samples has been taken; e.g., often after 50 or fewer rational subgroups have been gathered. Because of this, there is an intuitively high likelihood that, in a great many manufacturing situations, the observed mean shift has the potential to occur in the opposite direction if the sampling procedure was replicated at a different point in time. Thus, it is reasonable, if not preferable, to postulate symmetrical mean behavior (e.g., $\mu\pm\delta\sigma$, vice $\mu+\delta\sigma$ or $\mu-\delta\sigma$, as the empirical case may be): hence, the basis for arguing the equivalency of C_{pk} and C_p^* in the instance of a unilateral tolerance, or even the bilateral case, for that matter. The reader must also remember that C_{pk} has been previously defined as a mid-term estimate of capability and C_p^* as a long-term metric; hence, use of the word "equivalent." This will take on applied meaning in subsequent discussions.

6.2.4 The Long-Term Dynamic-State Six Sigma Capability Model

Again, let us return to our widget product example as a basis for discussion, using p_1 as the platform. In order to define the nature of a dynamic $\pm 6\sigma$ manufacturing model,[15] we must take into account naturally occurring, long-term sources of variation, such as the effect of tool wear, differences in lots of material, etc. As the reader may recall, the nominal value of p_1 was given as 1.240 in., and the short-term process standard deviation was determined to be $\sigma_{ST} = .0005$ in. Now, if we assume a level of inflation such that $c = 1.333$, it can be readily demonstrated via Eq. (6-17) that the equivalent sustained mean shift would be $\delta\sigma_{EQ} = 6[1-(1 / 1.333)] = \pm 1.5$. Thus, the equivalent k would be calculated using Eq. (6-18) and given as $k = 1.5/6 = .25$. The long-term limiting standard normal deviate would be given by Eq. (6-20) and subsequently calculated as $6 (1 - .25) = 4.5$. Next, the long-term dynamic capability ratio would be computed via Eq. (6-21). Such computation would reveal $C_p^* = 1.5$, with C_p remaining the same at 2.0. From the adjusted estimate, we would say that the "long-term dynamic first-time yield expectation" is 99.99966 percent for the unilateral case, and 99.99932 percent for a bilateral tolerance.

The long-term, first-time yield estimate takes into account the dynamic change in μ. Expressed differently, we would say that the change in yield reflects the recognition of dynamic mean variation over time. Figure 6-9 displays the condition where μ behaves in a dynamic manner such that $\delta\sigma_{EQ} = 1.5$, accounting for natural sources of manufacturing variation. If we compare the distribution presented in Figure 6-9 to that displayed in Figure 6-10, we can gain substantial insight into the effects of dynamic mean variation on product yield.

6.3 THE CONCEPT OF STATIC MEAN VARIATION

On the other end of the spectrum is the notion of static, mean behavior. Essentially, this relates to a sustained condition in mean location relative to the target value of a specification and/or the tolerance limits. It may be given as the actual, derived, or postulated number of standard normal deviates from the nominal value (T) of a specification: e.g., the extent of mean offset ($\delta\sigma$). To illustrate, let us return to part p_1 of our widget.

6.3.1 Accounting for Static Mean Behavior

Let us now postulate that p_1 is plated with some type of metal after the machining operation. Given this, we are forced to recognize that the process will, in all likelihood, be intentionally run slightly off-center in order to reap certain manufacturing efficiencies. One such efficiency is related to the avoidance of scrap; i.e., it is less costly to add metal via replating than it is to overplate and create scrap. As a consequence, the process is deliberately set up so that the mean will always be less than the nominal specification; i.e., $\mu = T - \delta$, where δ is the extent of intentional offset. Thus, μ will be in a sustained static shift condition with respect to T.

Assuming that the short-term capability is known, estimated, or can be rationally postulated, such that Z_{ST} can be given, we may express the long-term static capability, in Z units of measure, as

$$Z_{LT} = Z_{ST} - |\delta\sigma| \, . \qquad \text{Eq. (6-24)}$$

Of course, if we know the long-term Z, we may calculate the short-term capability via

$$Z_{ST} = Z_{LT} + |\delta\sigma| \, . \qquad \text{Eq. (6-25)}$$

Now, by virtue of the previous definitions, we may say that the long-term, static-state capability ratio may be calculated by

$$C_p^* = \frac{Z_{ST} - |\delta\sigma|}{3} \, . \qquad \text{Eq. (6-26)}$$

---

[15] As an informed reader, you should recognize that the 6σ model entertains the assumption that the mean and variance are independent; i.e., the mean can be relocated relative to a given scale of measure without altering the variance. The reverse of this also would hold true: the variance can be altered without impacting the mean. Although the Motorola 6σ model distribution appears to be a 6σ distribution shifted by a factor of $\pm 1.5\sigma$ relative to a set of engineering specifications, the shift is merely a compensatory measure for the cumulative effects of variation in μ over an infinite number of consecutive lots composed of n articles. Of course, this implies the commonly held assumption of homogeneity of variance. Another way of looking at this would be to say that μ varies randomly (and systematically in many instances) within a specification range; however, μ eventually will display a bias toward the nominal specification over a great many intervals of production. Interestingly, this particular assumption also is embedded within the DRSS design tolerancing methodology discussed by Harry and Stewart (1988).

If the long-term limiting standard normal deviate (Z_{LT}) is known, estimated, or can be rationally postulated, it should be evident that the short-term capability ratio may be given by

$$C_p = \frac{Z_{LT} + |\delta\sigma|}{3} \ . \qquad \text{Eq. (6-27)}$$

Since $\delta\sigma$ can also be expressed as $Z_{ST}K$, it should be apparent that Eq. (6-21) and Eq. (6-26) are interchangeable with respect to outcome. The same can be said for Eq. (6-23) and Eq. (6-27).

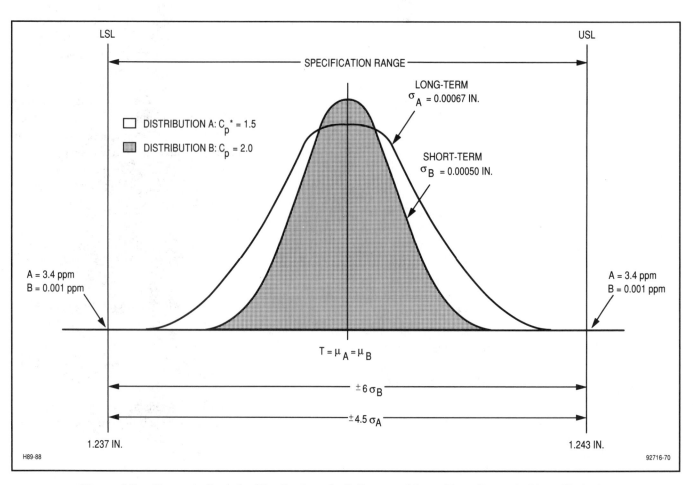

Figure 6-9.   Dynamic-State 6σ Distribution: the Influence of Long-Term Dynamic Mean Variation (parameters: $C_p = 2.0$, $c = 1.333$, and $C_p* = 1.5$)

6.3.2   The Long-Term Static-State Six Sigma Capability Model

As previously indicated, we must take into account naturally occurring sources of manufacturing variation in order to define the nature of a $\pm 6\sigma$ characteristic; however, when the mean variation assumes the form of a sustained static shift (such as a molo or die with fixed bias) we must handle the variation in a slightly different manner.

For example, let's now suppose that $\mu = 1.2415$ in. and $\sigma_{ST} = .0005$ in. as related to p_1 of our example widget product.

Thus, C_{pk} would be 1.5, with C_p remaining the same at 2.0. From the adjusted estimate, we would say that the "long-term yield expectation" is not 99.9999998 percent, but rather, 99.99966 percent. The adjusted yield estimate (99.99966 percent) takes into account the sustained shift in μ. Figure 6-10 displays the condition where μ is shifted toward the specification limit such that $|T-\mu| = \delta\sigma = 1.5$. Here again, if we compare the distribution presented in Figure 6-10 to that displayed in Figure 6-9, we can gain a much better understanding of the philosophy which underlies Motorola's Six Sigma initiative.

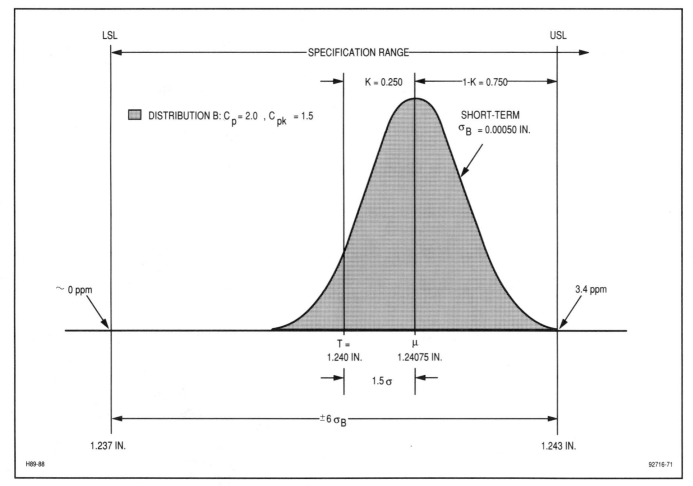

Figure 6-10. Static-State 6σ Distribution: the Influence of a Long-Term, Sustained Mean Offset (parameters: $C_p = 2.0$, $k = .250$, $\delta\sigma = 1.5$, and $C_{pk} = 1.5$)

6.4 THE SIMULTANEOUS OCCURRENCE OF DYNAMIC AND STATIC MEAN BEHAVIOR

At this point in the discussion, the reader may have noted the possibility that, in some situations, both forms of mean behavior may be present. For example, it is entirely possible that some parameter mean could be deliberately offset from the nominal specification to reap certain manufacturing efficiencies, therein forcing the recognition of a sustained mean shift; however, it may also be known that the parameter is dynamic by nature. In such instances, it would be necessary to simultaneously account for both forms of mean variation.

For example, a plating process might be deliberately run off-center so as to gain certain manufacturing efficiencies; however, the operating conditions of the process might cause the mean to behave in a dynamic manner. Hence, both forms of mean behavior would come into play. In such a situation, the long-term estimate of capability should consider the deliberate mean offset as well as the dynamic influences that result over time. Since the mean offset is most often fixed in

advance of production, we may say that the portion of mean variation due to dynamic variations (k*) may be given by

$$k^* = 1 - [(Z_{LT} + \delta\sigma^*)/Z_{ST}] \quad \text{Eq. (6-28)}$$

where $\delta\sigma^*$ represents the given extent of intentional static offset in the mean.

To illustrate the practical utility of Eq. (6-28), let us consider an example. Suppose that a certain manufacturing capability study revealed $Z_{ST} = 6.0$ and $Z_{LT} = 4.5$. Thus, k may be given by $1-(Z_{LT}/Z_{ST}) = .25$. We shall also suppose that the process was deliberately run off-center by a factor of 1.0σ. In this instance, we would say that $\delta\sigma^* = 1.0$. Application of Eq. (6-28) would reveal that $k^* = .0833$. In this instance, we would say that 8.33 percent of the semi-tolerance zone would be consumed by dynamic mean behavior, and that $(.250-.0833)\,100 = 16.67$ percent of the same zone would be consumed by the deliberate mean offset.

In some other situation, in order to establish a manufacturing convention, it may be necessary to determine how much offset is being deliberately induced. In this instance, we would rearrange Eq. (6-28) to solve for $\delta\sigma^*$. Doing so would reveal

$$\delta\sigma^* = [Z_{ST}(1 - k^*)] - Z_{LT} \quad \text{Eq. (6-29)}$$

The utility of the latter equations should be apparent to the experienced practitioner; however, further discussion is beyond the scope and intent of this booklet. With careful study, the reader should be able to advance the application of Eq. (6-28) to many other manufacturing situations.

6.5 EXAMPLE APPLICATION TO DESIGN ANALYSIS

To better understand the need for the various equations called out in this section of the booklet, we shall overview an example application. In this instance, we will use a mechanical design tolerance optimization model originally presented by Harry and Stewart (1988).

6.5.1 The Basis For Tolerance Analysis

As previously indicated, we must "design for manufacturability" if we are to sustain "best-in-class" quality. In terms of mechanical design tolerancing, we must be able to establish the nominal values and tolerances in such a fashion that the overall design is "robust" to naturally occurring sources of manufacturing and material variation. In other words, when the design is put into production, it is relatively impervious to expected shifts and drifts in the process mean. Thus, the assembly yield will not be driven significantly below the minimum expected value. This is not to say that the tail area probability associated with the assembly gap will not change over time, because it does. It is to say, however, that the change is anticipated *a priori* and dealt with accordingly during the design phase – not during the manufacturing phase. Consequently, manufacturing yields are higher and simultaneously more consistent. In a nutshell, we must learn how to design quality into the product – not inspect it in. In other words, proactive design circumvents reactive manufacturing.

As we all know, organizations with a highly consistent assembly yield are much more manageable than those organizations with erratic, less-predictable assembly yield. Such stability and consistency also means less firefighting on the shop floor. Remember, existing manufacturing technology and procedures are often modified, upgraded, and in some instances, even replaced at a very high cost – simply because designs are not robust to natural sources of variation. At the risk of redundancy, it is far easier and less costly to create designs in recognition of variation (e.g., shifts and drifts in μ)

than it is to believe that the organization's manufacturing people need to do a better job of controlling their processes. Well, all of this sounds good, but the bottom line still remains – how do we go about creating robust designs?

6.5.2 The Basic Tolerance Analysis Model

The answer to the latter question is quite simple: we must adjust the known or estimated process standard deviation associated with each nominal design value to account for natural shifts and drifts in the process mean. Essentially, such an adjustment has the effect of inflating the standard deviation, thereby decreasing the Z value related to any given assembly gap constraint or limitation which, in turn, decreases the probability of assembly.

Historically, the probability of assembly was computed using the root-sum-of-squares (RSS) as a basis for deriving the assembly gap standard deviation. In this form, the gap standard deviation (σ_G) may be computed as

$$\sigma_G = \sqrt{\sigma_1^2 + \sigma_2^2 + ... + \sigma_m^2} \quad \text{Eq. (6-30)}$$

where $\sigma_1^2 ... \sigma_m^2$ are the variances related to the assembly parts and m is the total number of parts that influences the assembly gap. Recognize that the variances reflect process error or "capability."

In most analytical situations, using Eq. (6-30) would prove to be of value; however, it is seldom the case that $\sigma_1^2 ... \sigma_m^2$ has been adequately estimated on the basis of emperical data. Hence, the mechanical designer is often forced to approximate by calculating

$$\sigma_G = \sqrt{(T_1/3)^2 + (T_2/3)^2 + ... + (T_m/3)^2}$$
$$\text{Eq. (6-31)}$$

where T is the semi-tolerance zone of a specification. Obviously, this approach is quite subjective. However, if the process capabilities were adequately estimated via empirical characterization, Eq. (6-31) could be adjusted via

$$\sigma_G = \sqrt{(T_1/3C_{pk_1})^2 + (T_2/3C_{pk_2})^2 + ... + (T_m/3C_{pk_m})^2}$$
$$\text{Eq. (6-32)}$$

where C_{pk} is the process capability ratio. The reader should also recognize that

$$\sigma_{LT_i}^2 = (T_i/3C_{pk_i})^2 \quad \text{Eq. (6-33)}$$

when k > 0; otherwise, $\sigma_{LT\,i}^2$ becomes $\sigma_{ST\,i}^2$.

From this perspective, the short- or long-term limiting standard normal deviate associated with the point of assembly interference (Z_Q) could be readily calculated as

$$Z_Q = \frac{Q - \sum_{i=1}^{m} N_i V_i B_i}{\sqrt{\sum_{i=1}^{m} (T_i B_i / 3 C_{pk_i})^2}} \ . \qquad \text{Eq. (6-34)}$$

where Q is the point of assembly interference (e.g., Q = 0), m is the number of dimensions in the design circuit, B_i is a circuit correction factor (used for fixed and floating fasteners, etc.), and V_i is the dimensions's vector within the circuit; i.e., +1 or –1, depending on the nature of the design circuit.

Given these particular adjustment mechanisms, the resultant critical Z value will decrease as the mean of each component departs from its respective nominal design value. As a statistical consequence, the tail area that exceeds any given gap constraint or limitation will increase. This in turn, decreases manufacturing confidence. In short, whenever 1–k at the component level decreases, the likelihood of assembly deteriorates.

From Eq. (6-33) it is evident that k is used to adjust the instantaneous capability to account for the effects of perturbing nonrandom influences of a dynamic nature. Hence, the design analysis is more realistic in terms of Z_Q. It should now be apparent why σ_{ST}, σ_{LT}, $\delta\sigma_{EQ}$, and k must be discovered during the course of process characterization. Such metrics serve as the basis for *a priori* tolerance analysis and the subsequent study of design robustness.

6.5.3 The Basic Tolerance Optimization Method

Optimization of a baseline design involves several steps. First, Eq. (6-34) must be applied to obtain an understanding of the baseline performance with respect to Z_Q. Naturally, the baseline design and process parameter values would be used for such a calculation.

If the resultant of Eq. (6-34) reveals a less-than-satisfactory value for Z_Q, optimization would ensue. To do this, it would be necessary to rearrange Eq. (6-34) into a more convenient form. Since the designer has little, if any, control over manufacturing capability, and given that Z_Q is the term to be optimized, it stands to reason that the numerator is the only term free for subsequent optimization. Thus the rearrangement of Eq. (6-34) would take the form of

$$Q - \sum_{i=1}^{m} N_i V_i B_i = Z_Q \sqrt{\sum_{i=1}^{m} (T_i B_i / 3 C_{pk_i})^2}$$
$$\text{Eq. (6-35)}$$

In the instance of Motorola's Six Sigma initiative, the criterion value for Z_Q would be set at 4.5.

Hence, the application of Eq. (6-35) would reveal a new nominal gap. This value would be subtracted from the baseline nominal gap value as originally used when applying Eq. (6-34). The residual is called the "nominal pool" and would be allocated back to the part nominals on the basis of a rational weighting scheme. The end result would be a mechanical design that would exhibit "4.5σ" long-term performance in terms of assembly probability. This would mean that no more than 3.4 assembly problems per million assemblies would be expected, given the existing long-term capability of the manufacturing processes required to produce the assembly parts.

The analysis could also be performed under the assumption of "worst-case" mean shifts via the application of

$$Z_Q = \frac{Q - \sum_{i=1}^{m} (N_i + W_i k_i T_i) V_i B_i}{\sqrt{\sum_{i=1}^{m} (T_i B_i / 3 C_{pi})^2}} \qquad \text{Eq. (6-36)}$$

where W_i is the "shift vector" for the ith nominal dimension. As you can now see, the mean shifts, if any, would be located in the numerator term in the form of a sustained static mean offset. In the interest of computational simplicity, it should be noted that the worst-case mean shift vector (W_i) may be established by virtue of $0 - V_i$. Recognize that the design could be optimized in the manner previously described.

Such a transitioning of "mean effects" from the denominator term of Eq. (6-34) to the numerator term of Eq. (6-36) must be expressed in raw units of measure, such as a proportion of the tolerance width: hence, the reason for using k as a correction factor in Eq. (6-33). Also notice that the merits of Eq. (6-28) and Eq. (6-29) can be incorporated into the design analysis. Using k, therefore, provides us with a plausible and flexible mechanism for both dynamic and static analysis, while simultaneously ensuring independence between the process mean and variance.

6.5.4 Synopsis of the Mechanical Design Application

At this point in our discussion, the reader should better understand the intrinsic need for such mechanisms as σ_{ST}, σ_{LT}, $\delta\sigma_{EQ}$, C_p^*, C_R and so on. When such metrics reside in a database, the designer is better positioned to configure in such a manner as to allow for the use of standard processes, components, and material. Concurrently, the designer is also able to achieve "6σ" product performance.

It is imperative that the reader see the connection between the use of certain process data and prescribed design analysis methodologies. If the data do not "fit" the tools, the previously mentioned aims related to producibility cannot be achieved. The authors fully recognize the unconventional stature surrounding several of the process characterization metrics; however, their validity has been fully demonstrated. Again, the departure from "classical" metrics has been necessary to create the "right size bullets for the guns we use." In short, the metrics and methods work together as an inseparable synergistic entity.

6.6 THE BASIS FOR ESTABLISHING k

At this point in our discussion, it is necessary to discuss the basic means by which k can be established. Perhaps some of the alternatives are already known by the reader; however, it is possible that the respective benefits and limitations are not. For this reason, we shall overview each of the methods and discuss certain features that relate to the conduct of capability studies.

6.6.1 The Control Chart Method

This method involves gathering empirical data over many periods of production. It should be recognized as the method of preference in terms of analytical precision; however, it is perhaps the most costly and time consuming. As one may readily surmise, this method relies heavily on the use of statistical process control (SPC) charts for continuous data.[16] The principal aim is to establish a reliable estimate of σ_{LT}. Once σ_{LT} has been sufficiently estimated, $\delta\sigma$ may be computed, assuming σ_{ST} has already been estimated. At this point, k may be calculated. The reader should be aware that certain SPC charts can provide an estimate of σ_{ST} and σ_{LT} in a single study. This is to say that σ_{ST} and σ_{LT} can be estimated using the same chart.

It must also be recognized that a detailed presentation of this particular method is far beyond the scope and intent of this booklet. There are simply too many charting alternatives to consider. Because some of the alternatives are fairly sophisticated in terms of their underlying statistical theory, the novice researcher should seek the advice of an experienced practitioner prior to chart selection and application. Should additional information on SPC charts be desired, the reader is directed to the bibliography.

6.6.2 The Yield Method

The yield method is predicated upon knowledge of first-time yield.[17] Again, notice that first-time-yield is designated as Y_{FT}. To use this method, one must calibrate Y_{FT} to equivalent area under the normal curve. The resultant Z value represents an equivalent limiting standard normal deviate.

For example, let us suppose that a certain characteristic displayed a first-time yield such that $Y_{FT} = .9973$ over many intervals of production. We shall also suppose that the specification is bilateral by nature. In addition, we shall assume a uniform rate of nonconformance with respect to each specification limit. Given this scenario, it should be readily apparent that each tail of the distribution would be positioned so that $(1 - .9973)/2 = .00135$ area under the normal curve would extend beyond each of the respective specification limits.

Now, if we were to reference a table of area under the normal curve, such as the one displayed in Appendix C, we would discover that .00135 area corresponds to $Z = 3.00$. If the specification had been unilateral, the corresponding Z value would have been $Z = 2.78$. Thus, first-time yield may be equated to the Z scale of measure. Notice also that such transformation can be made even when the original data is discrete by nature. Of course, such a transformation assumes $NID(\mu, \sigma)$.

Given this transformation, the disparity between Z_{ST} and Z_{LT} represents the effects of perturbing influences over time, regardless of the nature of such influences. If the short-term limiting standard normal deviate had been estimated to be $Z_{ST} = 4.00$, it may be said that the disparity is $Z_{ST} - Z_{LT} = 4.00 - 3.00 = 1.00$. In turn, the disparity may be readily converted to an equivalent $\delta\sigma_{EQ}$, k, or c, as need be.

The major point gleaned is of monumental importance: the yield method provides an avenue for merging continuous and discrete data. In many instances, the researcher may estimate short-term capability using continuous data and then switch to discrete data for the purpose of assessing long-term capability. As may be apparent, such a strategy can result in significant cost savings.

For example, most electronic production test equipment directly measures the response characteristic on a continuous scale of measure, and subsequently converts the measurement to a discrete value using a threshold measurement as the performance criterion. This is most often done to improve manufacturing efficiency. However, when only a few measurements are needed (as in the instance of estimating short-term capability) the interruption of production and/or difficulties associated with gathering the measurements can be justified. This certainly would not be the case when estimating long-term capability. Therefore, it would be far more desirable to make the long-term estimate of capability using the artificially dichotomized data.

---

[16] See Grant and Leavenworth (1974), as well as Juran (1979), for a description of the control charts which may be used with continuous data.

[17] The reader should be aware that such data can be gleaned from many of the standard manufacturing reports used in most of today's factories. Often, these reports take the form of p, np, c, and u charts. In many situations, the reports are characterized by tabular summary data. In general, such reports reflect factory performance in relative numbers which, in turn, can often be reduced to yield data and subsequently converted to equivalent Z values. Remember, the Poisson and binomial relations can be used to convert discrete data to yield information to establish an equivalent Z value.

6.6.3 The Best Estimate Method

The best estimate method relies primarily on the Poisson and chi-square distributions for estimating long-term capability under the constraint of (a) low-volume production, (b) high first-time yields, (c) high testing/inspection costs, or (d) some combination of the latter three. Once the ppm has been estimated, it is converted to an equivalent limiting standard normal deviate using a table of area under the normal curve. Recognize that this particular method assumes $NID(\mu, \sigma)$. As a result, the best estimate method is quite similar to the yield method.

Note that the effective use of this method is "situation sensitive." In general, if the likelihood of a defect is less than 10 percent and production volume is low, the method may be judiciously applied – recognizing the degree of potential error when r is small. Of course, if the production volume is high, it is the method of preference; however, it is strongly recommended that sampling continue beyond the case r = 1. When this particular technique is employed, estimation error declines as r increases, as a general rule.

If the likelihood of a defect is moderately greater than 10 percent and production volume is low, the method may still be employed; however, should "response pooling" be the terminal objective, other alternatives must be considered: e.g., binomial-based statistics. Naturally, if the probability of a defect is greater than 10 percent and production volume is high, the point estimate should be used. Again, estimation error declines as r increases.

Recognize that this method renders a "probability-based" approximation and, as a consequence, is highly dependent upon rational assumptions. Let it be known that there is no substitute for "large numbers" in the instance of discrete data.

While we recognize that a scientifically based approximation is often far superior to "experiential integration," we must also recognize that the potential decision risks associated with faulty assumptions can often negate the projected benefits resulting from such approximations. In fact, there are some situations in which an approximation should not be rendered at all. Because of these caveats, as well as others, it is highly recommended that the advice of an experienced practitioner be weighed prior to using this method.

6.6.4 Best Judgment Method

The best judgment method relies on manufacturing and engineering experience. In essence, the number of standard normal deviates from the mean to the target value ($\delta\sigma_{EQ}$) is postulated on the basis of best judgment in lieu of empirical evidence. Such judgment must be based on extensive experience and familiarity with the manufacturing process in question. Obviously, this method should only be considered when the collection of data is not feasible.

Under such circumstances, a k value equivalent to a 1.333-fold increase in σ should be used. Under no circumstances should the judgment exceed $.286 < k < .375$ without the recommendation of an experienced practitioner. The suggested constraint is based on extensive industrial experience, research, and probability theory.

6.7 BASIC METRICS FOR DISCRETE DATA

The metric that is used to describe a discrete parameter, such as number of defects, is given in Eq. (2-5). That parameter is labeled as dpm. One can extend the conceptualization of the term by considering the number of defects per million opportunities or, as it is called, parts per million (ppm). This is obtained by multiplying dpm by one million. Eq. (2-5) can be modified to give ppm as

$$ppm = \left(\frac{d}{um}\right)10^6 . \qquad \text{Eq. (6-37)}$$

Either term, dpm or ppm, represents the point estimate of the fraction of opportunities that are defective. It should be emphasized that this term is an *estimate* of the population fraction defective.

6.7.1 Theoretical Basis for a Best Estimate of ppm

As with all estimates in statistics, one can consider confidence limits. These confidence limits designate an interval of values in which the value of dpm or ppm for subsequent groups of samples would be found at least some percentage of the time. This percentage is labeled the percent confidence. Typically, one calculates confidence limits for percentages greater than or equal to 90 percent. As the percent confidence increases, the spread between the confidence limits increases. Consequently, if capability statistics were based on confidence limits, either an optimistic or a pessimistic description of the process would be obtained, depending on whether the upper or lower confidence limits were used.

Sample size affects the spread of the confidence limits. A larger number of samples improves the confidence and, therefore, reduces the interval between confidence limits. In the case of discrete data, the number of detected events also affects the confidence interval. In this case, the event is the detection of a defect. An increase in the number of defects detected will improve confidence in the estimate; that is, the width of the confidence interval will be reduced.

Let us show the mathematical representation of the confidence limits for the Poisson distribution. The estimate of the mean, x, of the Poisson distribution is bounded by confidence limits and given as

$$\frac{1}{2}\chi^2\left(\frac{\alpha}{2}, 2r\right) < x < \frac{1}{2}\chi^2\left(\frac{1-\alpha}{2}, 2(r+1)\right) \quad \text{Eq. (6-38)}$$

where $\chi^2(\alpha/2, 2r)$ is the value of the chi-square distribution evaluated for the number pair $(\alpha/2, 2r)$. The term $2r$ is the number of degrees of freedom of the chi-square parameter for the lower confidence limit in Eq. (6-38). For the upper limit, the term $2(r+1)$ is the number of degrees of freedom for the chi-square parameter; the "r" is the number of defects detected. The term α (alpha) refers to the risk associated with making an error in the statistical decision process. The α is split between the upper and lower confidence limits.

The derivation of the confidence limits for the Poisson model can be found in a variety of references: for example, in texts by Brownlee (1965) and by Hald (1952). Confidence levels are derived for the binomial distribution first. The derivation is extended to the Poisson distribution by considering the limit as m gets large and the probability, p, of finding a defect goes to x/m. In the case of the binomial model, the confidence limits are a function of the F-distribution. Brownlee (1965) shows how the F-distribution changes to the chi-square, χ^2, as the degrees of freedom related to F change with m and p. The results are shown in the inequalities represented in Eq. (6-38).

As the risk level α is increased, the right and left terms in Eq. (6-38) converge. For $\alpha/2 = 50$ percent, the convergence is complete. This point is called the best estimate and is at the point represented by χ^2 (50 percent, 2r). Appendix D lists the values of the best estimate of ppm for various combinations of trials and defects detected, up to a total of ten defects. This best estimate of parts per million (ppm*) may be calculated using the relation

$$\text{ppm*} = \frac{\chi^2_{(.50,\, 2r)}\, 10^6}{2N} \quad \text{Eq. (6-39)}$$

where N is the number of trials or units tested.

6.7.2   *Example Application of the Best Estimate Method*

As an example of the way to use Appendix D, suppose 80 units are tested and 5 defects are found. One would look for the intersection of the row representing 80 units and the column representing 5 defects. The value of the ppm at that intersection would be 58,425 ppm. Therefore, the best estimate of the fraction defective for the process tested is 58,425 parts per million. Of course, the resultant estimate can then be calibrated to Z_{ST} or Z_{LT}, as the case may be.

For defect counts above ten, the point estimate is a satisfactory representation of the fraction defective. The point estimate can be calculated using the relation

$$\text{ppm} = \left(\frac{r}{N}\right)10^6 \quad \text{Eq. (6-40)}$$

The point estimate gives a larger value of ppm than does the best estimate. This difference gets smaller as the value of r increases. Since the precision in the estimates of the Z-deviates is no more than three significant figures, this difference is considered small enough to allow a change to the use of the point estimate for defect counts above ten. In summary, if the number of defects is less than or equal to ten, the best estimate should be used for the determination of ppm. For defect counts greater than ten, calculate the point estimate using Eq. (6-40).

6.7.3   *Extending the Best Estimate Method*

If one prefers to use the best estimates for $r > 10$, one can calculate ppm from Eq. (6-39) with the appropriate value of χ^2 as obtained from a table of χ^2 which can be found in several references. In some cases, these tables do not give values of χ^2 for $\alpha/2 = 50$ percent; however χ^2 can be calculated from an approximation given by the following equation for χ^2 (50 percent, 2r):

$$\chi^2_{(.50,\, 2r)} = (2r)\left[1 - \left(\frac{2}{18r}\right)\right]^3. \quad \text{Eq. (6-41)}$$

Eq. (6-41) is derived from an equation obtained from several texts – in particular, the text by Hald (1952). A third term inside the brackets has been omitted, since that term is zero for the choice of $\alpha/2 = 50$ percent.

Eq. 6-41 was used in the generation of Appendix D. The full equation is derived as an approximation for χ^2, when the degrees of freedom are greater than 30. Since Appendix D is calculated for ten or less defects and the degrees of freedom are given by 2r, one sees that the restriction on the approximation, Eq. (6-41), is not met. However, a comparison was made between χ^2 (50 percent, 2r), calculated from Eq. (6-41), and values obtained from a three-place χ^2 table[18] for low numbers of degrees of freedom. Note that at 2 degrees of freedom, which is that used for 1 defect, the calculated value was about 2 percent higher than the tabulated value. At 10 degrees of freedom, which is used for 5 defects, the difference proved to be 0.08 percent. Here again, the precision of the resulting metrics does not suffer due to the use of Eq. (6-41). Figure 6-11 directly corresponds to the values given in Appendix D.

---

[18] The reader is directed to Hillier and Lieberman (1980) for additional information.

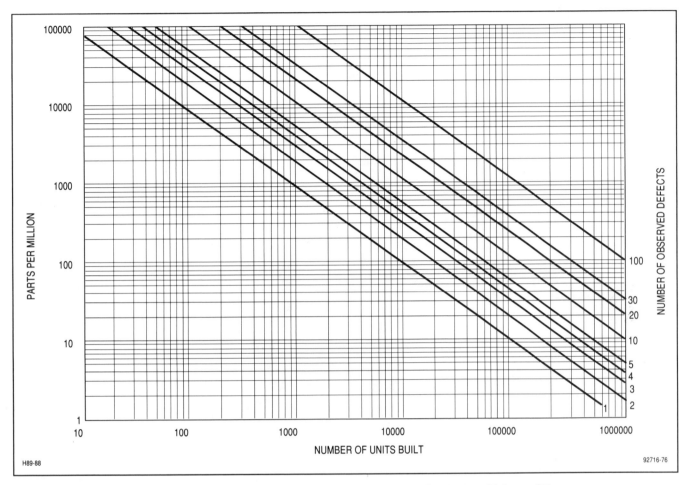

Figure 6-11. Best Estimate of the Population ppm for Various Values of N

SECTION 7
APPLICATION OF THE
CHARACTERIZATION METHODOLOGY

The purpose of this section of the booklet is to demonstrate how the process characterization metrics are applied in the context of a hypothetical manufacturing situation. To accomplish this aim, the discussion has been organized into two separate, related parts.

Part A addresses the preliminary activities generically, step by step. The reader is highly encouraged to bear in mind the importance of the steps associated with Part A. Unless careful attention is given to the inherent features of these steps, the likelihood of a successful characterization study is greatly minimized.

Part B addresses the computational aspects related to the process characterization metrics. It should be pointed out that this has been done in analytical harmony with Part A. Also recognize that the hypothetical data used in the related steps has been selected to reinforce the use of certain equations and analytical approaches.

7.1 PART A: PREPARING FOR A CAPABILITY STUDY

Step 1: Define the Response Parameter of Interest

The response parameter of interest (Y) is the dependent variable. This is the product characteristic of interest. Note that any given characterization study may consider more than one Y simultaneously, as will be the case in Part B of the discussion.

It is important to ensure that the method of measurement related to each of the selected parameters is valid and that the related measurement apparatus are reliable. This is to say that a measurement scale is valid if it reports what it purports to measure. Scale reliability is connected with the notions of repeatability – i.e., the degree to which the apparatus displays error which significantly inhibits repeatability. If in doubt, the measurement scale should be studied and the measurement apparatus should be calibrated and subjected to a separate capability analysis.[1] This is particularly true in the instance of sensory scales of measure, which should be avoided if at all possible.[2]

Furthermore, it is highly desirable to prepare a step-by-step instructional plan to assist those individuals tasked with implementing the measurement scheme. This point cannot be overstated, for obvious reasons.

Step 2: Identify the Measurement Vehicle

To gather data, one must have a source of measurements. The source is often called the "measurement vehicle." In some instances, the vehicle may be the actual product; yet in others, it may be a contrived substitute.[3] When destructive testing is involved and/or the costs associated with sample preparation are high, the use of a contrived vehicle should be considered. As a general rule, it is always better to use the actual product simply because the inferences resulting from statistical analysis are much more likely to be valid.

If a contrived vehicle is used, great care must be exercised to ensure its representativeness in terms of the target population to which it is applied. In turn, this implies a sound understanding and definition of the population. In many situations, this requires empirical testing and evaluation of a statistical nature (e.g., statistically designed experiments). In all cases, the use of a contrived vehicle should be well documented and should undergo substantive technical review by experienced practitioners prior to implementation.

Step 3: Determine the Basis of Subgrouping

As indicated earlier in the booklet, a rational subgroup is a sample in which all items are produced under conditions that only allow random effects to influence the

---

[1] See Juran (1979).

[2] Should the use of a sensory measurement scale be necessary, there are several things which can be done to minimize measurement error. First, it may be possible to alter the discrete performance criteria (e.g., pass/fail) to a crude gradient scale. For example, a solder short is most often considered a discrete characteristic; i.e., it is an electrical short or it is not a short. However, it is possible to create a 5-point scale which measures the propensity to short. In this case, the 5 points would be (1) missing solder, (2) insufficient solder, (3) acceptable solder, (4) excessive solder, and (5) bridged solder. Notice the progression from worst-case minimum to worst-case maximum. Recognize that for most soldering processes, the model case often tends toward the center of the pseudo-continuous scale (e.g., best-case condition). In previous research, the authors have discovered that the validity and reliability of such measurement scales can be significantly enhanced via consensus rating (i.e., concurrent rating by two inspectors with well-established, inspection-related credentials). Of course, there is no substitute for continuous measurements; however, when this is not possible, pseudo-continuous sensory scales can be readily developed and benchmarked for subsequent use during a process characterization exercise.

[3] This is also referred to as a product model, engineering model, data vehicle, or data platform.

measurements.[4] When this is done, the special, or as some would say, "assignable," nonrandom causes of extraneous variability (such as differing raw materials, personnel, test conditions, etc.) will then occur between subgroups rather than within them. The intent is to ensure minimum within-group variation of a random nature.

In general, subgrouping is considered "rational" if the resultant subsets of data exhibit only random variations and are also homogeneous with respect to the conditions under which the data were gathered; e.g., the same design, process, and material conditions are present at the time of data capture. When such rationality exists, an unbiased estimate of the standard deviation can be made. Remember that time is a most useful, but not unique, classification parameter for the development of rational subgroups. Other classes of variables include, but are not limited to (a) design, (b) process, (c) personnel, (d) environment, and (e) material.

In many cases, the bias resulting from an inadequate sampling strategy may be large enough to preclude the researcher from recognizing the "true" capability of the process. This point can not be overstated. The novice researcher is well advised to seek the opinion of an experienced practitioner when establishing the basis for rational subgroups; however, common principles often do exist. In this context, a discussion of these general principles would be quite relative. Also remember that in some instances, it may be necessary to test the basis of subgrouping to ensure an optimum level of compliance to the latter guidelines.[5]

Step 4:   Establish the Sampling Methodology

Before immersing ourselves in the details of this step, let us recognize its relative nature. As we all know, a sampling strategy applicable to one situation may not be generalizable to some other situation, for obvious reasons. However, the reader must remain sensitive to the fact that the intent of this portion of the discussion is to provide basic direction for the novice researcher by pointing out some of the more common concerns, issues, and practices. In other words, the ensuing discussions must not be mentally packaged as "hard rules."

Essentially, the sampling methodology is the procedure by which the measurements are gathered. Basically, there are two types of sampling methods: sequential and random. To a large extent, the type of sampling method used depends upon, but is not limited to (a) the objectives of data collection, (b) the basis by which rational subgroups are formed, (c) the basic nature of the manufacturing process, (d) production volume, (e) the time interval between observations, and (f) the type of data being gathered, just to mention a few.

Sequential sampling is often considered the preferred method simply because it has the greatest potential for realizing the intent of "rationality" where the formation of subgroups is concerned. If sequential sampling is used, it is generally recommended that the subgroup size (n) be targeted at $n = 5$ where appropriate. On this topic, Grant and Leavenworth (1980) stated that

The choice of subgroup size [i.e., sample size] should be influenced, in part, by the desirability of permitting a minimum chance for variation with a subgroup. In most cases, more useful information will be obtained from, say, five subgroups of 5 than from one subgroup of 25. In large subgroups, such as 25, there is likely to be too much opportunity for a process change within a subgroup.

Again, we can see that the basic intent is to minimize systematic, nonrandom error in light of Eq. (6-4) and Eq. (6-6). Therefore, sampling methodology plays a critical role when estimating capability. It is also generally recommended that, when making an estimate of short-term capability, the total number of subgroups (N) be $N = 6$ for reasons of statistical precision.[7] While some would say the ideal number of subgroups is $25 < N < 50$, it must be stressed that such a recommendation is usually made in the context of statistical process control (SPC) charting activities.[6]

Since the first steps in a process characterization study involve the analysis of short-term capability, the level of estimate precision afforded by such a large number of subgroups is not necessarily required – hence the lower recommended number. If, during the course of sampling, any of the

---

[4] See Nelson (1988) as well as Grant and Leavenworth (1980).

[5] Testing the rationality of a subgroup often involves analyzing (1) patterns of variation, (2) the degree to which the subgroups are homogeneous in terms of their variances and, (3) various features of mean behavior. Such testing may be accomplished with a variety of statistical process control (SPC) charts, analysis of variance procedures, regression techniques, etc.

[7] As a convenience to the uninformed reader, it should be pointed out that estimate precision relates to the standard error of the mean and standard deviation. Given $N = 25$ and $n = 5$, the 95 percent confidence interval of the mean would be approximately .18 standard errors wide (based on the normal distribution); however, given a 4-fold change in the total number of observations (e.g., $N = 6$, $n = 5$), the confidence interval of the mean would be approximately .36 standard errors wide. Thus a 4-fold decrease in the total number of observations represents only a 2-fold change in estimate precision. Essentially, when $N = 6$ and $n = 5$, the point of "practical" diminishing return is encountered with respect to the 95 percent confidence interval of the mean and standard deviation.

[6] See Juran (1979) as well as Grant and Leavenworth (1980).

subgroups should prove to be biased,[8] then all such subgroups should be discarded from the final data analysis. In the event that a subgroup is discarded, a replacement subgroup of the same size should be gathered under the same subgrouping and sampling scheme.

As a general rule, random sampling should be used if it is not possible to retain the order of production. In this case, the sample would represent all the production over a period of time, batch, lot, etc; hence, bias may be present. Again, the rule of minimizing within subgroup variation applies when attempting to estimate instantaneous reproducibility.

If multiple random samples are used, the subgroup size (n) should be $n = 5$ and the total number of subgroups (N) should be $N = 6$. If a single, random sample must be used because of practical considerations associated with taking the measurements, the subgroup size should be, in general, $n = 30$ and the number of subgroups should be $N = 1$.

Other combinations of N and n may be considered should the manufacturing or sampling circumstances so require; however, all such sampling schemes should be constructed such that the total number of samples (N x n) is in the neighborhood of 30, for statistical precision. Again, the reader is reminded of the relative nature of this discussion. As a consequence, it must not be taken out of its illustrative context and used as a basis for "statistical debate."

It should also be pointed out that no general rule or guidance can be given relative to the frequency of subgroups. Each case must be decided on its own unique merits.[9] While it is recognized that production and cost constraints significantly affect decisions regarding sampling frequency, the guidelines listed in Step 3 must also be considered. In essence, this represents the trade-off between data integrity, statistical precision, and cost.

Justifiable deviations from these guidelines are numerous and should be allowed if the manufacturing or data analysis circumstances so require; however, such deviations should be subject to documentation and undergo a substantive technical review by an experienced practitioner prior to implementation.

Step 5: Gather Data Related to the Response Parameter

In the vast majority of situations, a data collection sheet should be employed for recording data.[10] The data collection sheet should capture the following information.

- Date(s) of data capture
- Product characteristic being investigated
- Units of measure related to the product characteristic
- Type of measurement apparatus
- Date of last calibration
- Method of sampling
- Production sequence (if applicable)
- Sampling interval
- Time of data capture
- Perturbing circumstances during data capture
- Subgroup size (n)
- Total number of subgroups (N)
- Name of person responsible for data capture
- Engineering or product specification (if applicable)

In addition, the data collection sheet should reflect all other information necessary to ensure the repeatability of the study. Furthermore, it is highly desirable to prepare a step-by-step instructional plan to assist those tasked with collecting data. In all cases, those individuals should be given appropriate training in the proper use of the applied measurement apparatus, sampling methodology, and data recording procedures.

7.2 PART B: PROGRESSION FOR ESTIMATING CAPABILITY

7.2.1 Overview of the Situation

To set the stage for this part, we shall postulate a fairly typical set of manufacturing circumstances. In this instance, we will say that a certain engineer was tasked to study a particular manufacturing process, say ABC. More specifically, the objective was to characterize the various product response outputs from process ABC. In this instance, the response parameters of concern were $Y_1 \ldots Y_4$. The unique characteristics associated with $Y_1 \ldots Y_4$ are defined in Table 7-1.

---

[8] This could happen as a result of statistical testing for homogeneity of variance, randomness, run length, etc.

[9] For further discussion on this particular topic, see Grant and Leavenworth (1980).

[10] Since most data analyses are performed on computers, data collection sheets should be laid out to facilitate data entry and formatting requirements with respect to the selected computer hardware and software. The amount of time spent developing a compatible data collection sheet format is small when compared to the data entry and analysis gyrations required to overcome incompatibility.

Table 7-1.   Background Information Related to the ABC Process Example

Response Parameter (Y)	Expected Nature of Sampling Variations Related to the Mean		Nature of Measurement Scale		Specification Limits		
	Static (S)	Dynamic (D)	Continuous (CS)	Discrete (DS)	Lower (LSL)	Target (T)	Upper (USL)
Y_1	Yes	No	Yes	No	60.0	90.0	120.0
Y_2	No	Yes	Yes	No	NA	NA	11.8
Y_3	No	Yes	No	Yes	NA	NA	*
Y_4	Yes	No	No	Yes	NA	NA	NA

The response was measured with a discrete "Hi/Lo" device; consequently, it was treated as a quasi-bilateral specification.

Based on the nature of the response variables, as well as other manufacturing and engineering issues, an action plan was developed using the process characterization strategy and planning activities discussed earlier on in this booklet. At the designated time, the prescribed sampling methodology was invoked for each of the response parameters. Of course, the required measurement apparatus were checked for accuracy and were properly calibrated.

After collecting the appropriate data, the engineer derived estimates of the short- and long-term capability of each response parameter. The step-wise mechanics associated with the calculations are discussed herein.

7.3   MECHANICS RELATED TO RESPONSE PARAMETER Y_1 – CONTINUOUS DATA

7.3.1   Estimation of Short-Term Capability

Step 1:   Organize Data

The short-term data were gathered via a sequential sampling strategy under the constraint $n = 5$, $N = 6$. The individual measurements (X) were recorded in an appropriate manner. Table 7-2 displays the raw data and related summary statistics. From this table, the mean of Y_1 has been declared as a "static" parameter. Since the sampling conditions present in the given situation would tend to reveal a static mean offset versus dynamic mean behavior. In other words, it is unlikely that $\overline{\overline{X}}$ would approach T after sampling a highly limited number of subgroups. Because of this, the expected mid-term nature of mean performance was given as "static," even though the long-term expectation would be dynamic.

Table 7-2.   Raw Data and Summary Statistics for Parameter Y_1

Observation (X_i)	Subgroup					
	G_1	G_2	G_3	G_4	G_5	G_6
X_1	103	94	86	101	89	92
X_2	90	89	78	94	77	84
X_3	95	82	71	85	72	81
X_4	81	73	65	80	69	72
X_5	75	68	61	79	68	69
R	28	26	25	22	21	23
Σ	444	406	361	439	375	398
$\overline{X}$	88.8	81.2	72.2	87.8	75.0	79.6

Notice that the range (R) was computed for each subgroup using Eq. (5-5). For example, the range for subgroup (G_1) was given as

$$R_1 = X_{max} - X_{min} = 103 - 75 = 28 \ . \qquad \text{Eq. (7-1)}$$

Step 2:   Compute Average Range

Next, the average range was computed using Eq. (5-6). The result was given as

$$\overline{R} = \sum_{j=1}^{6} R_j/N = 145/6 = 24.17 . \quad \text{Eq. (7-2)}$$

Step 3: Establish Constants

Following this, the appropriate d_2^* value was located in Appendix B. Since, in this instance, $n = 5$ and $N = 6$, it was determined that $d_2^* = 2.353$.

Step 4: Compute Standard Deviation

The sample standard deviation was computed by dividing the average range by the given d_2^* value using the relation defined in Eq. (5-7). In this case, the standard deviation was given as

$$S = \overline{R}/d_2^* = 24.17/2.353 = 10.27 \; . \qquad \text{Eq. (7-3)}$$

Step 5: Compute Z

Since the sampling objective associated with Y_1 was to estimate "instantaneous reproducibility," it was determined that the next activity should be the calculation of the short-term limiting standard normal deviate (Z_{ST}). This was accomplished via Eq. (6-1). Notice that, in this instance, the data were first plotted in the form of a histogram. Subsequent analysis of the histogram gave reason to believe that NID (μ, σ) was a reasonable assumption. Hence, the analytical process was continued by calculating Z_{ST}. The result of that calculation was given as

$$Z_{ST} = \frac{|SL - T|}{S} = \frac{|120 - 90|}{10.27} = 2.92 \; . \qquad \text{Eq. (7-4)}$$

It is interesting to note that the sample standard deviation (S) was substituted for the population standard deviation (σ).

Step 6: Establish Yield

Once Z_{ST} had been estimated, the short-term parts per million (ppm_{ST}) was established with the aid of Appendix C. By entering the table in the left-most column, the row Z value of 2.9 was located. Next, the .02 column was located. The Z value of 2.92 proved to be the intersect of the given row and column. Application of Eq. (6-37) revealed that ppm = 1750; however, this was only for one side of the given symmetrical bilateral specification. In the instance of Y_1, the total ppm_{ST} was determined to be 1750 x 2 = 3500. Thus, the equivalent short-term, first-time yield was calculated as $Y_{FT;ST} = 1 - (3500/10^6) = .9965$.

Step 7: Compute Capability Ratio

Continuing with the sequence of activity, the short-term capability ratio for parameter Y_1 was calculated using Eq. (5-16) as a guide. The result was given as

$$C_p = \frac{Z_{ST}}{3} = \frac{2.92}{3} = .973 \; . \qquad \text{Eq. (7-5)}$$

As may be apparent from the estimate of short-term parameter capability, Y_1 exhibited a very marginal level of performance. If the mean of this parameter was to vary over time, the estimates of capability would deteriorate appreciably. As a consequence, Y_1 proved to be a likely candidate for short-term variance optimization.

7.3.2 Estimation of Mid-Term Capability (Y_1)

Step 1: Compute Grand Mean

In order to estimate the mid-term capability of Y_1, a longitudinal control chart study was undertaken. In this instance, an $\overline{X}$ and R chart was selected such that $N = 100$ and $n = 5$. Recognize that, in this instance, the sampling frequency was such that the information contained within the $N = 100$ subgroups was classified as mid-term. From this study, the population mean for Y_1 was estimated. This was done via the generalization of Eq. (5-2). Thus, the grand mean for all $N = 100$ subgroups was given as

$$\overline{\overline{X}} = \sum_{j=1}^{100} \overline{X}_j/N = 99.2 \qquad \text{Eq. (7-6)}$$

where $\overline{\overline{X}}$ is the grand average of the subgroup means and N is the total number of subgroups used in the study. Notice that each of the subgroup means was computed using Eq. (5-2).

Step 2: Compute k

Next, the actual degree of mean offset (k) was computed using Eq. (5-18); however, the grand sampling average ($\overline{\overline{X}}$) was substituted for μ as follows:

$$k = \frac{|T - \overline{\overline{X}}|}{|SL - T|} = \frac{|90.0 - 99.2|}{|120 - 90|} = .307 \; . \qquad \text{Eq. (7-7)}$$

Thus, it was determined that approximately 31 percent of the semi-tolerance zone was consumed by the observed mean-offset, or "shift."

Step 3: Compute Minimum Z

Because Y_1 retains a bilateral tolerance, and given that $\overline{\overline{X}} \neq T$, it was necessary to compute two Z values, Z_{min} and Z_{max}. The *minimum* mid-term limiting standard normal deviate ($Z_{MT\,min}$) was calculated using Eq. (6-20). The outcome was given as

$$Z_{MT_{min}} = Z_{ST} (1-k) = 2.92 (1-.307) = 2.02 \; .$$
$$\text{Eq. (7-8)}$$

As may be apparent, the degree of mean offset $(\delta\sigma)$ was given as

$$\delta\sigma = Z_{ST} k = 2.92 \times .307 = .90 \ . \quad \text{Eq. (7-9)}$$

The .90 standard deviation disparity between the short- and mid-term Z represents the influence of perturbing effects over a moderate amount of time. In other words, it is the degree to which the instantaneous reproducibility was degraded over time as a result of undesirable mean behavior of a static offset nature. Hence, it may be said that parameter Y_1 was only $C_R = (2.02/2.92) = .692$, or 69.2 percent robust to perturbing influences of a nonrandom temporal nature. Notice that Eq. (6-19) was employed to make the latter calculation.

The reader may also recognize that Z_{MTmin} could have been calculated as

$$Z_{MT_{min}} = Z_{ST} - \delta\sigma = 2.92 - .90 = 2.02 \ .$$
$$\text{Eq. (7-10)}$$

Step 4: Compute Maximum Z

Again, because the specification was symmetrical and bilateral, and given the fact that $k > 0$, it was necessary to compute the *maximum* limiting standard normal deviate (Z_{MTmax}). In this instance, Z_{LTmax} was associated with the lower specification limit (LSL). Such a determination was made and subsequently given as

$$Z_{MT_{max}} = Z_{ST} (1 + k) = 2.92 (1 + .307) = 3.82 \ .$$
$$\text{Eq. (7-11)}$$

As before, the reader may recognize that Z_{MTmax} could also have been calculated as

$$Z_{MT_{max}} = Z_{ST} + \delta\sigma = 2.92 + .90 = 3.82 \ .$$
$$\text{Eq. (7-12)}$$

Step 5: Establish Mid-Term Yield

From the resultant Z values, the mid-term parts per million above the USL was determined to be $ppm_{USL;MT} = 21,692$, while below the LSL was $ppm_{LSL;MT} = 67$. Hence, the total mid-term parts per million was reported as $ppm_{TOT;MT} = ppm_{USL;MT} + ppm_{LSL;MT} = 21,759$. Thus, the mid-term, first-time yield was calculated as $Y_{FT;MT} = 1 - (21,759/10^6) = .9782$.

Step 6: Compute Mid-Term Capability Ratio

Following this, the mid-term parameter capability ratio was calculated. The calculation was given as

$$C_{pk} = \frac{Z_{ST} (1 - k)}{3} = \frac{2.92 (1 - .307)}{3} = .675 \ .$$
$$\text{Eq. (7-13)}$$

7.3.3 Estimation of Long-Term Capability (Y_1)

Step 1: Establish Yield

Since the mid-term estimate of yield was predicated upon a static mean offset, as a result of fairly limited sampling (i.e., N = 100), the engineer reasoned that a different sampling period might reveal a mean shift in the opposite direction from what was originally observed. Consequently, the engineer elected to approximate the long-term performance under the assumption of dynamic mean behavior (i.e., $\delta\sigma_{EQ} = \pm .90$). Thus, $ppm_{USL;LT} = 21,692$, $ppm_{LSL;LT} = 21,692$, and $ppm_{TOT;LT} = 43,384$. Consequently, the expected long-term, first-time yield was given as $Y_{FT;LT} = .9566$. Such an estimate was considered to be "in-line" with historical knowledge of the process, due to the fact that defects had previously been known to occur on both ends of the bilateral tolerance.

Step 2: Establish Z

At this point, the equivalent long-term limiting standard normal deviate (Z_{LT}) was established by working backwards in the table of area under the normal curve (Appendix C). This is to say, the engineer first calculated $(1 - Y_{FT;LT})/2 = (1 - .9566)/2 = .0217$ and then used this value to ascertain the equivalent Z value. In this instance, .0217 area converted to $Z_{LT} = 2.02$.

At this time, the reader is invited for a comparison of the latter resultant and that obtained in Eq. (7-10). Notice that the Z values are identical; however, the given yields are not. This is due to the fact that $\delta\sigma = .90$ under the constraint of mid-term estimation versus $\delta\sigma = \pm .90$ for long-term. As a consequence, k did not change; hence, $C_{pk} = C_p^* = .675$ in this instance.

To test the rationality of the given assumptions, the engineer computed

$$c = \frac{1}{1 - k} = \frac{1}{1 - .307} = 1.443 \ . \quad \text{Eq. (7-14)}$$

Recognize that the general guideline for c, in ambiguous situations, was previously given within this booklet as $1.4 < c < 1.6$. Hence, the expected rate of inflation in the standard deviation, as applied to the observed instantaneous capability, would result in a yield value similar to that obtained under the assumption of $\pm \delta\sigma$ versus $\delta\sigma$ or $-\delta\sigma$. Thus, $Y_{FT;LT} = .9566$ was accepted as a rational approximation for a highly extended period of production.

7.4 MECHANICS RELATED TO RESPONSE PARAMETER Y_2 – CONTINUOUS DATA

7.4.1 Estimation of Short-Term Capability (Y_2)

Step 1: Organize Data

In the instance of Y_2, it was not possible to form "rational subgroups" because the order of production could not be retained. Because of this and other constraints, it was necessary to randomly sample product from within a single lot. After some discussion with an experienced practitioner, it was decided that the aforementioned random sampling strategy would significantly minimize the likelihood of estimation bias due to perturbing temporal influences.

In accordance to the prescribed sampling plan, the N = 1, n = 30 measurements were gathered. The individual measurements (X) were recorded and are located in Table 7-3.

Table 7-3.   Raw Data Associated with Parameter Y_2

10.3	9.0	9.5	8.1	7.5
9.4	8.9	8.2	7.3	6.8
8.6	7.8	7.1	6.5	6.1
10.1	9.4	8.5	8.0	7.9
8.9	7.7	7.2	6.9	6.8
9.2	8.4	8.1	7.2	6.9

Step 2: Compute Statistics

Next, the sample mean and standard deviation were computed using Eq. (5-2) and Eq. (5-4), respectively. The resulting calculations revealed that

$$\overline{X} = \sum_{i=1}^{30} X_i/n = 242.3/30 = 8.08 \quad \text{Eq. (7-15)}$$

and

$$S = \sqrt{\sum_{i=1}^{30} (X_i - \overline{X})^2/n\text{-}1}$$
$$= \sqrt{34.71/30\text{-}1} = 1.094 \ .$$
$$\text{Eq. (7-16)}$$

Step 3: Compute Z

Since the sampling objective associated with Y_2 was to surface instantaneous reproducibility, it was determined that the next activity should be the estimation of the short-term limiting standard normal deviate (Z_{ST}). This was accomplished via the generalization of Eq. (5-12). Based on the calculations, it was determined that

$$Z_{ST} = \frac{|SL - \overline{X}|}{S} = \frac{|11.80 - 8.08|}{1.094} = 3.40 \ .$$
$$\text{(Eq. (7-17))}$$

As before, the sample standard deviation (S) was substituted for the population standard deviation (σ). In addition, the sample mean ($\overline{X}$) was substituted for the target value (T) since no nominal specification value was given.

Step 4: Establish Yield

Once Z_{ST} had been calculated, the short-term parts per million (ppm_{ST}) estimate was made with the aide of Appendix C. By entering the table in the left-most column, the row Z value of 3.4 was located. Next, the .00 column was located. The Z value of 3.40 proved to be the intersect of the given row and column. Hence, it was determined that ppm_{ST} = 337. Since the specification was unilateral (one-sided), $ppm_{TOT:ST}$ = 337. Thus, the short-term, first-time yield was determined to be $Y_{FT:ST} = 1 - (337/10^6) = .99966$.

Step 5: Compute Capability Ratio

Continuing with the sequence of activity, the parameter capability ratio was calculated using Eq. (5-16) as a guide. The result was given as

$$C_p = \frac{Z_{ST}}{3} = \frac{3.40}{3} = 1.13 \ . \quad \text{Eq. (7-18)}$$

As may be apparent from this estimate of parameter capability, Y_2 exhibited a somewhat marginal level of performance. If the mean of this parameter were to appreciably change over time, it is obvious the overall yield would be degraded significantly.

7.4.2 Estimation of Long-Term Capability (Y_2)

Step 1: Estimate Z

In order to estimate the long-term capability of Y_2, the "yield method of analysis" was selected. In this instance, valid historical data revealed that the average first-time yield was approximately 99 percent. The reader must recognize that this yield was obtained only after a great many intervals of production; consequently, it was classified as "long-term." Hence, the assumption of dynamic mean behavior prevailed. As may be apparent, the historical yield translated to ppm_{LT} = 10,000. Using Appendix C as a guide, it was determined that the tail area equal to 10,000 ppm was approximately equivalent to Z = 2.325. Hence, the equivalent long-term limiting standard normal deviate (Z_{LT}) was ascertained by working backwards in the table of area under the normal curve.

Step 2: Establish k

Next, the equivalent degree of mean offset, or "equivalent mean shift" ($\delta\sigma_{EQ}$) was estimated to approximate a value for k. This was done by first calculating the disparity between Z_{ST} and Z_{LT}. In this instance

$$\delta\sigma_{EQ} = Z_{ST} - Z_{LT} = 3.400 - 2.325 = 1.075 .$$
$$\text{(Eq. (7-19))}$$

Following this, a value for k (in equivalent form) was computed using Eq. (6-18). This was done as follows:

$$k = \frac{|\delta\sigma_{EQ}|}{|Z_{ST}|} = \frac{|1.075|}{|3.400|} = .316 . \quad \text{Eq. (7-20)}$$

Be aware that k could have also been computed by generalizing Eq. (6-14). Such calculation would reveal

$$k = 1 - \frac{Z_{LT}}{Z_{ST}} = 1 - \frac{2.325}{3.400} = .316 . \quad \text{Eq. (7-21)}$$

As a consequence of this calculation, it was determined that approximately 32 percent of the pseudo-tolerance zone was consumed as a result of perturbing influences of a temporal nature. Thus, the 1.075σ equivalent mean shift represented the influence of perturbing effects over time. In other words, it was the degree to which the instantaneous reproducibility degraded over time, as a result of dynamic mean behavior. In this instance, it may be said that parameter Y_2 was only $C_R = (2.325/3.400) = .684$, or 68.4 percent robust to perturbing influences of a temporal nature. Again, this particular calculation was made by way of Eq. (6-19).

Step 3: Compute Capability Ratio

Following this, the long-term parameter capability ratio was calculated using Eq (6-21). This was given as

$$C_p^* = \frac{Z_{LT}}{3} = \frac{2.325}{3} = .775 . \quad \text{Eq. (7-22)}$$

By comparing the short-and long-term outcomes, it is quite apparent that temporal perturbations had a significant impact on producibility. Obviously, it was determined this parameter would be a likely candidate for subsequent long-term optimization of the mean.

7.5 MECHANICS RELATED TO RESPONSE PARAMETER Y₃ – DISCRETE DATA

7.5.1 Estimation of Long-Term Capability (Y₃)

Step 1: Estimate Yield

In the case of parameter Y_3, it was first necessary to estimate the overall level of quality. This was accomplished by instituting a sequential sampling plan for discrete data. Since it was generally known that defects were few and far

between, it was decided that sampling should be terminated once a single defect was discovered (e.g., r = 1 using the "best estimate" method).

After the production of N = 70,000 consecutive units, the first defect was observed. Such performance was considered "long-term" due to the fact that many intervals of production were required to generate N. Thus, the best estimate of long-term parts per million was $ppm_{LT} = 10$. This estimate was made with the assistance of Appendix D. The equivalent long-term, first-time yield was calculated as $Y_{FT:LT} = 1 - (10/10^6) = .99999$.

Step 2: Establish Z

By virtue of the knowledge gained during the execution of Step 1, the ppm_{LT} was converted to an equivalent long-term limiting standard normal deviate using Appendix C. The conversion revealed that $Z_{LT} = 4.27$. Notice that this is a one-tailed value.

Step 3: Calculate Capability Ratio

Next, the long-term parameter capability ratio was calculated via the generalization of Eq. (6-21). In this instance, the ratio was given as

$$C_p^* = \frac{Z_{LT}}{3} = \frac{4.27}{3} = 1.42 . \quad \text{Eq. (7-23)}$$

Obviously, this is a very good level of performance, especially in the case of dynamic long-term variation.

7.5.2 Estimation of Short-Term Capability (Y₃)

Step 1: Establish k

Once the capability ratio was computed, it was necessary to establish a value for k. Since no quantitative information was available from which to calculate k, it was decided that "best engineering and manufacturing judgment" would prevail. In this case, k was set at the recommended default value of .333.

Step 2: Estimate Z

It was now time to estimate the equivalent short-term limiting standard deviate. This was accomplished using Eq. (6-22). The result was given as

$$Z_{ST} = \frac{Z_{LT}}{1 - k} = \frac{4.27}{1 - .333} = 6.40 . \quad \text{Eq. (7-24)}$$

Needless to say, this represented an excellent instantaneous reproducibility; however, it must be recognized that the estimate was made on the basis of experience and judgment. Based upon the preceding calculations, it may be said that Y_3 was generally believed to be $C_R = (4.27/6.40) = .667$, or 66.7 percent robust to perturbing influences of a temporal nature.

Step 3: Calculate Capability Ratio

Proceeding under the metric guidelines, the short-term capability ratio was computed using Eq. (5-16). The computation was expressed as

$$C_p = \frac{Z_{ST}}{3} = \frac{6.40}{3} = 2.13 \; . \qquad \text{Eq. (7-25)}$$

Step 4: Establish Yield

Once Z_{ST} had been calculated, the short-term parts per million (ppm$_{ST}$) estimate was established with the aid of Appendix C. As before, the table was applied by entering in the left-most column. The row Z value of 6.4 was located. Next, the .00 column was located. The Z value of 6.40 proved to be the intersect of the given row and column. Hence, it was determined that ppm$_{ST}$ = .00012. Given this, the short-term, first-time yield was determined (on the basis of approximation) to be $Y_{FT;ST} = 1-(.00012/10^6) = .99999999988$.

This estimate is, of course, above Motorola's short-term standard for "Six Sigma" performance.

7.6 MECHANICS RELATED TO RESPONSE PARAMETER Y_4 – DISCRETE DATA

7.6.1 Estimation of Short-Term Capability (Y_4)

Step 1: Establish Yield

In the special instance of Y_4, it was necessary to establish the first-time, automated inspection yield. This was accomplished by instituting a sequential sampling plan. It was generally known that defects were fairly common; consequently, it was decided the sampling should continue until r = 10 to ensure a relatively high degree of estimate precision.

After the production of N= 2000 consecutive units, a total of 10 nonconformities were observed. Such performance was considered "short-term" due to the fact that N was obtained in a short production interval. Thus, the best estimate of short-term parts per million was estimated to be ppm$_{ST}$ = 5000. The estimate was made via a visual interpretation of the chart given in Figure 6-11. Hence, the short-term, first-time yield was calculated as $Y_{FT;ST} = 1-(5000/10^6) = .995$.

Again, it should also be noted that, because of the normally high volume associated with Y_4, the sample (e.g., N = 2000) was considered to be "short-term." That is to say, it was generally believed that perturbing influences could not significantly inflate the "instantaneous" ppm$_{ST}$ estimate during the time the sample was gathered.

Step 2: Establish Z

By virtue of the short-term ppm estimate made during the execution of Step 1, the equivalent short-term limiting standard normal deviate (Z_{ST}) was ascertained by applying Appendix C. However, the reader should recognize that the given ppm represents the total of those defects which exceeded the "Hi" and "Lo" gauge limits. As a consequence, the conversion to Z was based upon the bilateral case. Hence, conversion revealed that when ppm$_{ST}$/2 = .5000/2 = 2500, the equivalent short-term limiting standard normal deviate was approximately Z_{ST} = 2.81.

Step 3: Calculate Capability Ratio

Again, proceeding under the metric guidelines, the equivalent short-term capability ratio was computed using Eq. (5-16). The computation revealed that

$$C_p = \frac{Z_{ST}}{3} = \frac{2.81}{3} = .937 \; . \qquad \text{Eq. (7-26)}$$

7.6.2 Estimation of Long-Term Capability (Y_4)

Step 1: Establish k

At this point, it was necessary to establish a value for k. Since no quantitative information was available from which to calculate k, it was decided that "best engineering and manufacturing judgment" would prevail; however, in this instance, it was generally known that the process would often be run off-center so as to reap certain manufacturing efficiencies. In this case, the equivalent static mean offset or "shift" was set at $\delta\sigma_{EQ}$ = 1.5.

Here again, the engineer tested the rationality of this assumption by calculating c. In this instance, c = 2.15. Obviously, this far exceeds the general criterion range of 1.4 < c < 1.6; however, it was generally agreed that Y_4 deserved an overly conservative mean shift based on best manufacturing judgment and experience. So, K = 1 − 1/2.15 = .534.

Step 2: Compute Z

At this point, the equivalent long-term limiting standard deviate (Z_{LT}) was estimated by way of Eq. (6-24). The result was given as

$$Z_{LT} = Z_{ST} - |\delta\sigma_{EQ}| = 2.81 - 1.50 = 1.31 \; .$$
$$\text{(Eq. (7-27))}$$

Notice that this value could also have been obtained from Eq. (6-20) in the form of

$$Z_{LT} = Z_{ST}(1\text{-}k) = 2.81\,(1\text{-}.534) = 1.31 \qquad \text{Eq. (7-28)}$$

where,

$$k = \frac{|\delta\sigma_{EQ}|}{|Z_{ST}|} = \frac{|1.50|}{|2.81|} = .534 \ . \quad \text{Eq. (7-29)}$$

Also note that the robustness of parameter Y_4 was estimated to be $C_R = (1.31/2.81) = .466$, or 46.6 percent by way of Eq. (6-19).

Step 3: Compute Capability Yield

Next, the long-term parameter capability ratio was calculated using Eq. (6-21) as a guide. In this instance, the ratio was given as

$$C_p^* = \frac{Z_{LT}}{3} = \frac{1.31}{3} = .437 \ . \quad \text{Eq. (7-30)}$$

Step 4: Establish Yield

Once Z_{LT} was calculated (for the bilateral condition), it was determined that the long-term parts per million (ppm_{LT}) estimate should be made with the aid of Appendix C. Based on the Z_{LT} value of 1.31, it was determined that $ppm_{LT} = 95,100 \times 2 = 190,200$. Thus, the equivalent long-term, first-time yield was calculated as $Y_{FT;LT} = 1-(190,200/10^6) = .8098$.

7.7 MECHANICS FOR POOLING CHARACTERISTICS

7.7.1 Computation of the Short-Term Pool

Step 1: Organize Information

In this instance, it was first necessary to identify the response variables to be pooled; e.g., $Y_1 \ldots Y_4$. Once this was done, the short-term parts per million (ppm_{ST}) and first-time yield ($Y_{FT;ST}$) estimates for each respective parameter were tabulated. Table 7-4 displays the summary performance information.

Table 7-4. Short-Term Performance Information Related to Parameters $Y_1 \ldots Y_4$

	Y_1	Y_2	Y_3	Y_4
ppm_{ST}	3500	337	.00012	5000
$Y_{FT;ST}$	.99650	.99966	.99788	.99500

Note:1. $Y_{FT} = 1 - (ppm/10^6)$.

2. Raised digits represent the number of times the preceding digit is repeated; e.g., $.99^34$ would be .999994.

Step 2: Compute Rolled-Throughput Yield

Next, the short-term, rolled-throughput yield ($Y_{RT;ST}$) was estimated via the generalization of Eq. (2-1). The estimate was computed to be

$$Y_{RT;\,ST} = \prod_{i=1}^{m} Y_{FT;\,ST_i}$$
$$= .9965 \times .99966 \times .99^788 \times .995$$
$$= .9912 \quad \text{Eq. (7-31)}$$

Notice that .9912 is the joint probability of zero defects: i.e., $p(d = 0)$ with respect to $Y_1 \ldots Y_4$. This is the confidence that $d = 0$. On the flip side, $(1 - .9912) = .0088$ is the risk that $d > 0$: i.e., the probability of one or more nonconformities.

Step 3: Establish ppm

Following this, the short-term, rolled-throughput yield was converted to parts per million. In this instance, the short-term rolled ppm was given as $ppm_{RT;ST} = (1 - .9912)10^6 = .0088 \times 10^6 = 8800$.

Step 4: Normalize Rolled-Throughput Yield

This particular step involved estimating the normalized short-term, rolled-throughput yield ($Y_{RT;ST;N}$) in light of the total number of response parameters (m) in accordance with Eq. (2-2). This was given as

$$Y_{RT;\,ST;\,N} = \sqrt[m]{\prod_{i=1}^{m} Y_{FT;\,ST_i}}$$
$$= \sqrt[4]{.9912} = .9978 \ . \quad \text{Eq. (7-32)}$$

Note that $Y^{1/m} = .9912^{1/4} = .9978$ and $Y^m = .9978^4 = .9912$. Obviously, a parts-per-million conversion for such a yield estimate would reveal that $ppm_{RT;ST;N} = (1-.9978)10^6 = 2200$.

Step 5: Establish Z

Next, the normalized, equivalent, unilateral, short-term, limiting standard normal deviate ($Z_{RT;ST;N}$) was estimated by calibrating the normalized short-term, rolled-throughput yield ($Y_{RT;ST;N}$) to the equivalent one-tailed area under the standard normal curve. This was done by consulting Appendix C. In this instance, $Z_{RT;ST;N} = 2.85$.

At this point, the reader is strongly encouraged to recognize that the normalized Z value will always be related to the one-tailed case, even though the data is a composite of both the unilateral and bilateral cases. Since rolled-throughput yield is more closely associated with cumulative area under the normal curve, the one-tailed convention has been adopted.

Step 6: Compute Capability Ratio

After this, the normalized equivalent short-term capability ratio was computed after the generalization of Eq. (5-16). The computation was expressed as

$$C_p = \frac{Z_{RT;\,ST;\,N}}{3} = \frac{2.85}{3} = .95 \quad . \quad \text{Eq. (7-33)}$$

7.7.2 Computation of the Long-Term Pool

Step 1: Organize Data

This step involved defining the long-term parts per million (ppm_{LT}) and long-term, first-time yield ($Y_{FT;LT}$) values for each parameter. The appropriate values (actual or equivalent) were noted and are presented in Table 7-5.

Table 7-5. Long-Term Performance Information Related to Parameters $Y_1 \dots Y_4$

	Y_1	Y_2	Y_3	Y_4
ppm_{LT}	43384	10000	10	190,200
$Y_{FT;LT}$	.95662	.99000	.99999	.8098

NOTE: $Y_{FT} = 1 - (ppm/10^6)$.

Step 2: Compute Rolled-Throughput Yield

Next, the long-term, rolled-throughput yield ($Y_{RT;LT}$) was estimated via the generalization of Eq. (2-1). Doing so revealed that

$$Y_{RT;\,LT} = \prod_{i=1}^{m} Y_{FT;\,LT_i}$$
$$= .95662 \times .99 \times .99999 \times .8098$$
$$= .7669 \quad . \qquad \text{(Eq. 7-34)}$$

Step 3: Establish ppm

Following this, the long-term parts per million was calculated. In this instance, the long-term ppm was given as $ppm_{RT;LT} = (1-.7669)10^6 = .2331 \times 10^6 = 233,100$.

Step 4: Normalize Rolled-Throughput Yield

This step involved estimating the normalized long-term, rolled-throughput yield ($Y_{RT;LT;N}$) in view of the total number of response parameters (m) in accordance with Eq. (2-2). The result was given as

$$Y_{RT;\,LT;\,N} = \sqrt[m]{\prod_{i=1}^{m} Y_{FT;\,LT_i}}$$
$$= \sqrt[4]{.7669} = .9358 \quad . \quad \text{Eq. (7-35)}$$

Obviously, a parts-per-million conversion would reveal that $ppm_{RT;LT;N} = (1-.9358)10^6 = 64,200$.

Step 5: Establish Z

Next, the normalized, equivalent, unilateral, long-term, limiting standard normal deviate ($Z_{RT;LT;N}$) was estimated by calibrating the normalized long-term, rolled-throughput yield ($Y_{RT;LT;N}$) to the equivalent unilateral area under the standard normal curve. This was done by consulting Appendix C. In this instance, $Z_{RT;LT;N} = 1.52$.

Step 6: Compute Capability Ratio

Following this, the normalized equivalent long-term capability ratio was computed using Eq. (6-21). The computation was expressed as

$$C_p^* = \frac{Z_{RT;\,LT;\,N}}{3} = \frac{1.52}{3} = .51 \quad . \quad \text{Eq. (7-36)}$$

Step 7: Compute k

Next, the equivalent normalized long-term mean offset, or "equivalent mean shift ($\delta\sigma_{EQ}$)" was estimated to approximate a normalized value for k. This was done by first calculating the disparity between $Z_{RT;ST}$ and $Z_{RT;LT}$. In this instance

$$\delta\sigma_{EQ;\,N} = Z_{RT;\,ST} - Z_{RT;\,LT}$$
$$= 2.85 - 1.52 = 1.33 \quad . \quad \text{Eq. (7-37)}$$

Following this, a value for k (in equivalent mean shift form) was computed via the generalization of Eq. (6-18). This was done as follows

$$k = \frac{|\delta\sigma_{EQ;\,N}|}{|Z_{RT;\,ST}|} = \frac{|1.33|}{|2.85|} = .467 \quad . \quad \text{Eq. (7-38)}$$

As a consequence of this calculation, it was determined that approximately 46.7 percent of an equivalent tolerance zone was consumed by the normalized equivalent mean shift. Thus, the shift represented the influence of normalized perturbing effects per parameter over many manufacturing intervals. Hence, it may be said that the normalized response characteristic was only $C_R = 1 - (1.33/2.85) = 1 - .467$ or 53.3 percent robust to perturbing influences of a temporal nature.

7.8 REPORTING CAPABILITY METRICS

7.8.1 Summarizing the Performance of a Single Process

In many manufacturing situations (such as our example), multiple response characteristics are tied to a single process. Also, we often see a wide variety of design configurations being served by that single process. Obviously, this creates a myriad of potential capability indices, especially when some of the response characteristics are constrained via bilateral tolerances, while others are subject to unilateral tolerances. The situation becomes even more complex when we consider the nature of the data that emanates from the various measurement devices (e.g., discrete and continuous forms of data). Nonetheless, the question is asked: "What is the capability of this particular manufacturing process?"

As this question implies, one should be able to produce a single figure of merit; however, we all know that the application of classical SPC methodology precludes this from happening – so we are stuck with the answer: "Well, it depends on which characteristic you are talking about." When all has been said and done, the classical SPC practitioner is hard pressed to provide an answer in the context of the question. To the novice practitioner, the question is overwhelming, to say the least. Hence, the need for the characterization metrics presented in this booklet. Through such metrics, the engineer can reduce the overall performance of a given process to a single number, calibrated to the unilateral case.

Of course, all of the mathematical arguments related to such calibration and normalization are well understood by the authors; however, the need for a first-time composite process-performance metric most often outweighs the need for "seven-digit precision." After all, management does not profess to be the rank and file of who's who in statistics. They want simple and reasonably valid information from which to make sound decisions.

To facilitate the reporting of process-performance information, a standardized format has been defined in Table 7-6. Recognize that the table is flexible in that it can be further summarized, or expanded if need be. For example, the short- and long-term yield values may be listed on rows for N number of response characteristics. In turn, different (but similar) processes (e.g., wave soldering, IR reflow, vapor phase, etc.) could then be given as the column variable.

In this manner, the normalized rolled-throughput yields could be computed and subsequently listed on both margins. In turn, this would provide the information necessary to determine (a) which process is best overall, (b) which response parameter displays good performance regardless of process, and (c) which response parameters are most sensitive to process type. The possibilities are many; however, such flexibility can only be realized if the basic reporting structure will support it. Hence, we have the format given in Table 7-6.

Table 7-6. Standardized Reporting Table for Process Characterization Metrics
(Example Data Provided)

Response Parameter (Y)	Response Specification	Short-Term			Long-Term					Parameter Robustness (%)
		Z	C_p	ppm	Z	C_p^*	ppm	$\delta\sigma$	k	(C_R)
1	B	2.92	0.97	3500	**2.02**	**0.68**	**43384**	**± .90**	**.307**	69.3
2	U	3.40	1.13	337	2.33	0.78	10000	1.08	.316	68.4
3	U	*6.40*	*2.13*	*~ 0*	4.27	1.42	10	*2.13*	*.333*	66.7
4	B	2.81	0.94	5000	*1.31*	*0.44*	*190200*	*± 1.50*	*.534*	46.6
Norm	U	2.85	0.95	2200	1.52	0.51	64200	1.33	.467	53.3
Rolled	NA	NA	NA	8800	NA	NA	233100	NA	NA	NA

B = Bilateral   U = Unilateral

NOTE 1. *Italicized values have been predicated on certain rational assumptions*
2. *Bold values are based upon mid-term empirical data*

In our example, all four response parameters were originated by the ABC process. Consequently, it may be stated that the normalized short-term performance per parameter was approximately 2.85σ, as evidenced in the standardized reporting table displayed in Table 7-6. The normalized long-term capability per parameter was given as 1.31σ. If the four response parameters had each displayed 6σ short-term capability, the normalized short-term benchmark per parameter would have been 6.0σ. In reference to long-term capability, the normalized benchmark per parameter would have been 4.5σ.

In general, the inherent reproducibility of the normalized response (as related to our example ABC process) was only 53.3 percent robust to systematic nonrandom variations within the underlying cause system. If each of the individual response parameters conformed to Motorola's Six Sigma standard, the normalized robustness benchmark would have been 75 percent. Note that the *robustness* metric reflects the relative extent of control exerted over the manufacturing process across many intervals of production.

Such performance benchmarking criteria can be better visualized in the context of Figure 7-1. This figure presents a standard reporting format for the presentation of characterization data. In the instance of Figure 7-1, the ABC process parameters ($Y_1 \ldots Y_4$) are given and so noted. Recognize that the benchmarking format could also be used to plot the normalized values for multiple processes therein, allowing the viewer to immediately detect "best-in-class" performance.

As a final point, it should be recognized that the average cost of quality per nonconformance (i.e., $/d) may be computed, assuming the appropriate information is available, or can be rationally postulated. Following this, the cost savings per fractional sigma improvement may then be studied via the quadratic loss function, or any other financial model, for that matter. In addition, the $/d value may be weighted on the basis of some criteria (e.g., criticality in terms of customer satisfaction, cycle time, reliability, serviceability, etc.). Such information can, of course, then be used as a basis for further decision making.

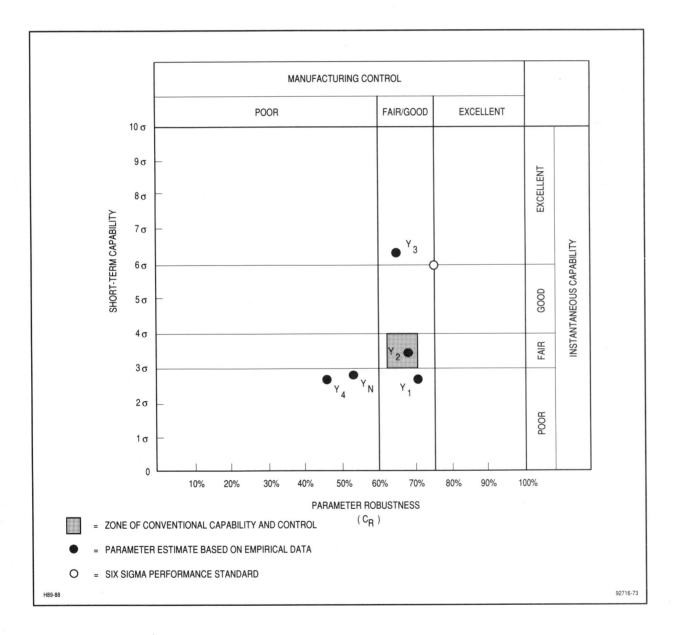

Figure 7-1. Standard Benchmarking Chart for the Presentation of Characterization Data

SECTION 8
PROCESS CHARACTERIZATION
CASE STUDY[1]

8.1 INTRODUCTION

This particular case study addresses two fundamental issues with regard to the production of printed circuit boards (PCBs). First, it focuses on a statistically based, four-phase strategy aimed at better organizing and facilitating the characterization of a manufacturing process. The fact that the case addresses copper plating thickness of PCBs is secondary to the characterization strategy. The second intent is to provide analytical insight into a statistical methodology aimed at establishing coupon-to-board correlation.

Essentially, the case analysis systematically progresses through all four phases of the parameter characterization strategy, highlighting the key aspects of each phase. In addition, the aforementioned technique for assessing coupon-to-board correlation is given substantiative discussion; however, it should be pointed out that a thorough narration pertaining to many of the statistical and engineering details of the case analysis have been deliberately omitted for the sake of brevity and reading ease. As a result of such considerations, it is assumed that the reader has a working knowledge of descriptive and inferential statistics, as well as experiment design. The benefit to this approach is simple – focus can easily be given to the analytical strategy and order of execution without the usual clouding of mathematical explanations.

8.2 CASE STUDY BACKGROUND INFORMATION

Perhaps the best place to start the case analysis is by introducing various background information and considerations. In specific, we shall first consider the historical state-of-affairs from a business perspective. Following this, we will discuss how the company organized itself to tackle the problem. Finally, the mechanics associated with implementing the characterization strategy will be presented.

8.2.1 Nature of the Problem

In essence, the case originated at a major corporation involved in the manufacture of large computer systems. It should be noted that this particular organization has always

had an exceptional reputation for delivering high-quality products, on time, at the right price; however, at some point in time, the organization began to experience a major problem within one of its PCB manufacturing facilities. More specifically, the problem was declining first-time yield related to the XYZ family of PCBs. Figure 8-1 displays the basic XYZ PCB configuration and Figure 8-2 displays the state-of-affairs for this family of boards over a 12-month production period.

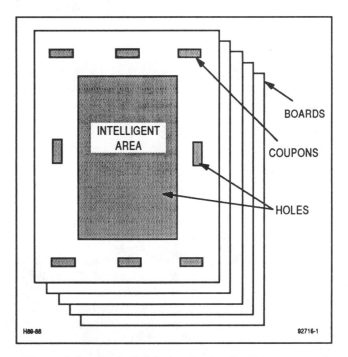

Figure 8-1.   Basic Configuration for the XYZ Family of Printed Circuit Boards

As may be apparent, the first-time yield of the XYZ boards was moderately low, on the average, and fairly unstable for the given time interval. Upon further analysis of the situation, a severe scrap problem was revealed. In this instance, the scrap analysis focused on the XYZ boards. Figure 8-3 displays the costs associated with the scrap problem over the same 12-month production interval given in Figure 8-2. Notice the correlation between the total factory scrap cost and that of the XYZ family of boards. It is intuitively apparent that the XYZ family possessed a significant amount of leverage in the total scheme of things.

---

[1] Section 8 of the booklet has been reprinted with the expressed permission of WELA Publications Ltd. registered in England No. 1184908. Registered office: 2A Highfield Road, Dartford Kent EA12JY. Portions of this section appeared in "Circuit World," Vol. 16, No. 1, 1989, Published by WELA Publications Ltd., Ayr, Scotland. The paper was authored by Mikel J. Harry, Ph.D. under the title "PCB Plated Through-Hole Optimization: A Case Study in SPC."

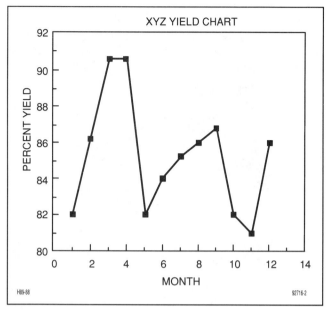

Figure 8-2. *Factory Yield for the XYZ Family of Printed Circuit Boards*

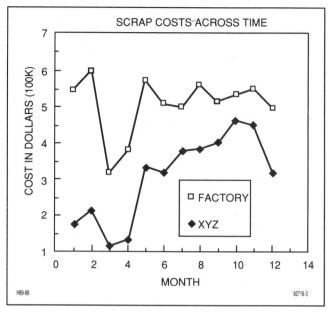

Figure 8-3. *Comparison of Factory and XYZ Scrap Costs*

8.2.2 *Defining the Problem*

With these facts in mind, the facility manager called all of the department managers together for a "problem solving" meeting. Needless to say, the meeting went as one might expect – finger pointing, excuses, etc. At one point during the meeting, the manufacturing manager boldly suggested that,

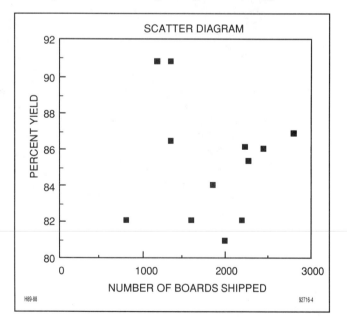

Figure 8-4. *Scatter Diagram Relating Yield to Production Volume*

in reality, there was nothing to be concerned about, simply because the production schedule had dramatically increased and, as a consequence, one could expect proportionally higher scrap costs; therefore, the problem was not "real." In fact, the manager indicated that the problem was a "mere illusion." Based on this line of reasoning, the notion of a "tolerable scrap level" was introduced and discussed with much enthusiasm.

Up to this point, the problem rationale seemed quite plausible to almost everyone present; however, a lone voice faintly asked, "What is the correlation between XYZ yield and production schedule?" No one responded. In order to provide an answer to the latter question, additional data were gathered and subsequently plotted on a scatter diagram. The resulting diagram is displayed in Figure 8-4. It is quite interesting to note that the association between yield and production volume was quite low. It goes without saying that this information was convincing enough to "shoot the sacred cow," so to speak.

Fresh out of cows, management decided to dig a little deeper by conducting a Pareto analysis. After constructing the appropriate Pareto charts, it was discovered that the defect category called "Thin CU" was dominant over the many other categories of nonconformance. After some additional manufacturing and engineering reconnaissance and subsequent discussions, the following problem statement was rendered:

Our factory yield has varied from 55 percent to 86 percent over the production period extending from July through November. The average yield is approximately 80 percent for this time period. Initial investigation has revealed that this particular problem is due primarily to unsatisfactory yields within the XYZ family of printed circuit boards.

A Pareto analysis revealed that the K4 and L1 categories of nonconformance account for virtually all of the defects recorded during the previously mentioned time frame. In specific, the problem is related to inadequate copper (CU) plating thickness within through-holes of the XYZ boards. The product specification lists the lower limit (LSL) at 1.25 mils and the upper limit (USL) at 2.80 mils. with the nominal value being centrally located between the two limits. It is apparent that the problem is constrained to the lower specification; i.e., the problem is related to thin copper.

Currently, there is no estimate of the plating thickness mean or variance; hence, the probability of nonconformance can not be determined at this time. In addition, the validity and reliability of the measurement system is unknown, in a quantitative sense. It should be pointed out that the previously mentioned estimates of nonconformance are based on test coupon number 6. It is currently assumed that the test coupon is representative of the intelligent area of the PCB; therein, driving reasonably accurate estimates of nonconformance with respect to the various defect categories which we monitor.

Based on the problem statement and prevailing business circumstances, it was determined that the copper plating process and related measurement systems should be statistically characterized. Furthermore, management indicated that if the estimates of existing capability proved to be unsatisfactory, the response characteristics would be optimized. In addition, it was agreed that if the given response characteristics could not be statistically optimized, a technological solution would be sought.

8.3 PHASE I: PARAMETER DEFINITION

By this point, it was quite clear that excessive variation in copper plating thickness (within the XYZ through-holes) was the primary enemy. In preparation for a direct confrontation with the enemy, management prioritized the problem, organized resources, and formed a process characterization team. The process characterization team immediately started to work on the issue after the careful formulation of an action plan based on the generic steps described in Section 4.0 of this booklet.

8.3.1 Activity 1: Measurement Error Analysis

As a first step, the team decided to fully analyze all of the related measurement systems, methodologies, and accept/reject criteria. They knew that if the existing measurement system did not provide valid and reliable data, subsequent characterization and optimization could be in vain. The reader should note that the existing measurement methodology embodied the following steps:

1. Select a single through-hole on coupon number 6 (XYZ PCBs).

2. Micro-section the coupon through-hole.

3. Measure the through-hole at the top, middle, and bottom (left and right sides).

4. Record the measurements in Block 8 of form ABC-123.

5. Isolate the point of minimum plating and measure.

6. Record the measurement in Block 9 of form ABC-123.

7. Verify that the minimum measurement is within specification.

8. If minimum is within specification, accept PCB; otherwise, reject.

It is interesting to note that step 2 of this particular measurement strategy employed a micro-sectioning procedure known as the "Y grind method." It is referred to as such because the resulting cross-section reveals the copper wall thickness along the longitudinal or "Y" axis of the hole. Figure 8-5 illustrates the locations where each of the response measurements were taken. Since the locations were fixed, this procedure became known as the "fixed-location Y grind" method. These measurements were then tallied and subsequently used to study various plating phenomenon such as tapering, dogboning, etc.

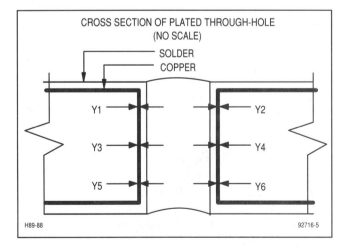

Figure 8-5. Illustration of Fixed-Location Y Grind Micro-Section

Following a cursory analysis of the methods and procedures, the team began to question the validity of the measurement system due to an apparent potential for measurement bias. In this instance, it was reasoned that the fixed-location measurements would not be representative of the total plating area within any given through-hole, statistically speaking that is. Consequently, estimates of central tendency and variability based on such measurements would not provide valid nor reliable data. Hence, inaccurate estimates of capability would be very likely. Because of this, it was determined that an experiment should be conducted so as to quantitatively benchmark the fixed-location Y grind method in terms of measurement validity and reliability.

Testing the Existing Measurement Method

In order to accomplish the latter aim, a single-variable comparative experiment was statistically designed. The purpose of this experiment was to determine if the fixed-location Y grind method of measurement was significantly different from some control condition. Of course, the control condition had to be created due to the absence of an internal standard. In this case, the control group was based on a method of cross-sectioning known as a "Z grind," so called because the cutting plane passes through the Z axis of the through-hole.

The reader must recognize that the Z grind method, as employed by the characterization team, also entailed cross-sectioning the Y axis. In this manner, all axes could be concurrently sampled. It should also be pointed out that specific points of measurement were randomly selected from along the circumference of the copper ring and through-hole wall. Hence, the random-location Z grind method (Figure 8-6) could provide a statistically reliable benchmark from which to study the relative accuracy of the fixed-location Y grind method.

From a data analysis point of view, focus was given to testing the null hypothesis of no statistically significant difference (H_o), as relating to the means and variances of both measurement methods. This was done using analysis-of-variance (ANOVA) and various post-hoc tests. The type I (alpha) and type II (beta) thresholds were established *a priori* at .05 with n_1 and n_2 degrees of freedom, respectively. Test sensitivity was established at .5 standard deviations. The error variance (for sample size calculations) was estimated from historical response data. In addition, the data were evaluated, in both distributional instances, for conformance to the normal density function. Specific tests of homogeneity-of-variance were also undertaken.

In some instances, data transformations were utilized so as to comply with the requisite statistical and mathematical assumptions surrounding ANOVA. Furthermore, all such data transformations were verified for correlation via simple regression. Note that several nonparametric statistics were also employed; e.g., chi-square analysis, median testing, and sign testing. As a final point, all calculations were made using a well-recognized statistical software package in conjunction with an electronic spreadsheet.

The outcomes of the measurement experiment are displayed in Figures 8-7 and 8-8 in the form of histograms. By contrasting the two histograms, it is more than apparent that the fixed-location Y grind method (Figure 8-7) exhibited far greater variation than the random-location Z grind method (Figure 8-8). The differences were subsequently confirmed as statistically and practically significant. This meant that there was at least 95 percent confidence that the observed differences (between sample means and variances) did not occur as a result of random sampling error; therefore, the differences could be attributed to the experimental variable called "measurement method."

In short, the alternate hypothesis of statistically significant difference (H_a) was accepted with greater than 95 percent decision confidence. Because of this, it was determined that the fixed-location Y grind method would not provide valid information from which to conduct a process characterization study.

Even though the random-location Z grind method displayed superiority in terms of validity, it was more than apparent that such an approach, on a production basis, would be both cost and time prohibitive. With this in mind, the characterization team set out to devise yet another measurement scheme. This time, the alternative was a random-location Y grind method. Essentially, this method relied on the random selection of measurement points within several Z axis strata. In this manner, the strength of statistical sampling could be overlayed on the production benefits associated with the Y grind method of micro-sectioning.

On the basis of this logic, a second measurement experiment was undertaken. This particular experiment was based on the hypothesis that there would be no statistically significant difference between the random-location Z grind method and the random-location Y grind method, in terms of central tendency and variability.

Let it suffice to say that the second measurement experiment revealed mean and variance differences which were not statistically significant. As a consequence, the team had substantiative evidence to support the use of existing measurement technology (Y axis micro-section) in conjunction with stratified random sampling; i.e., random selection of measurement points within each Y axis strata. The importance of this point can not be overly emphasized, as we shall later see.

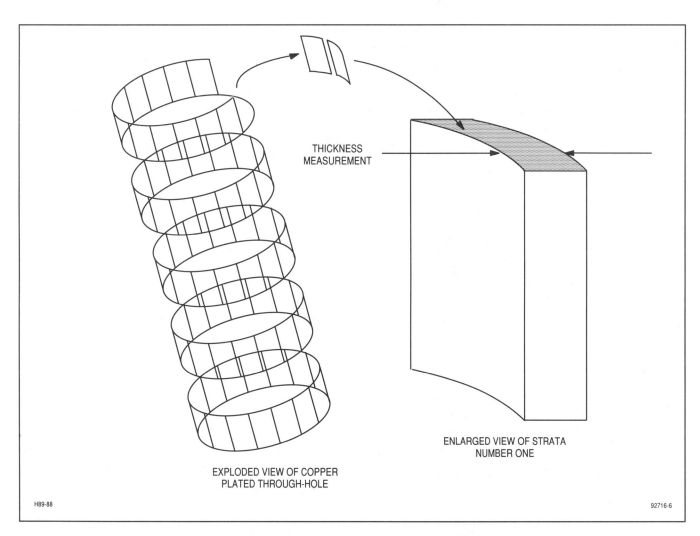

THICKNESS
MEASUREMENT

ENLARGED VIEW OF STRATA
NUMBER ONE

EXPLODED VIEW OF COPPER
PLATED THROUGH-HOLE

H89-88

92716-6

Figure 8-6. Breakdown of the Random-Location Z Grind Method

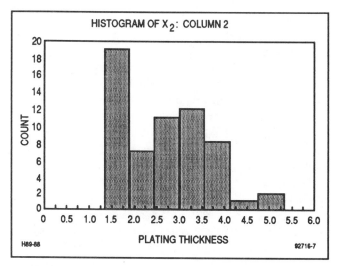

HISTOGRAM OF X_2: COLUMN 2

COUNT

PLATING THICKNESS

H89-88

92716-7

*Figure 8-7. Histogram Associated with the
Fixed-Location Y Grind Method*

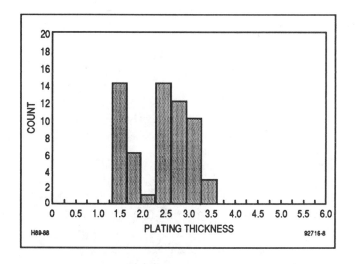

COUNT

PLATING THICKNESS

H89-88

92716-8

*Figure 8-8. Histogram Associated with the
Random-Location Z Grind Method*

Testing the Man-Machine Interface

A final experiment was designed and conducted so as to establish the proportion of measurement error attributable to differences between raters, or "inspectors" as they are most often called. Obviously, the intent was to establish the degree to which the measurement scheme was sensitive to variations within and between inspectors.

The results of this experiment revealed that only 1.5 percent of the total observed variation could be explained by the independent variable called "rater." The results have been summarized in Figure 8-9. Note that the difference proved to be statistically insignificant. Therefore, it was concluded that inspectors could be changed or rotated during the course of production, characterization, or experimentation without fear of contaminating the data to such an extent that unacceptable distortion in the statistical parameters would occur.

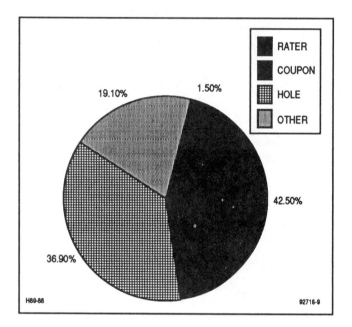

Figure 8-9. Experimental Outcomes of the Inspector (Rater) Error Analysis

8.3.2 Activity 2: Coupon-to-Board Correlation

For many organizations involved in the manufacture of PCBs, the degree of correlation between the intelligent area of a given PCB and its related test coupon(s) is of major concern. If the correlation is high, the coupons are said to be "representative of the intelligent area" and thus reflect the true state-of-affairs. On the other hand, when the correlation is low, the test coupons do not adequately describe the intelligent area.

As may be apparent, when PCB test coupons are used as a basis for decision making, the extent of correlation translates to some likelihood of decision error in terms of what is loosely referred to as "board buy-off." If the correlation is

high, the probability of buy-off decision error is low. The implications of this issue should be self-evident.

The Historical Method

Historically, the primary method for establishing coupon-to-board correlation has focused on statistical regression. Using this method, several PCBs would be randomly selected for analysis. Once selected, each of the PCBs would be tagged for purposes of identification.

Next, several plated through-holes within the intelligent area would be micro-sectioned (via the Y grind method) and subsequently measured for plating thickness. At this point, the minimum thickness measurement would be noted (Y_{min}). The same procedure would be repeated for the corresponding test coupon (X_{min}). Following this, the paired measurements, or "XY pairs" as they are often called, would be plotted on a scatter diagram, such as the one illustrated in Figure 8-10.

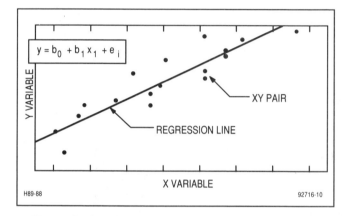

Figure 8-10. Scatter Diagram Depicting Coupon-to-Board Correlation (Minimum Measurements)

After plotting the data, statistical analysis would ensue. Again, this would most often be done using linear regression. From such an analysis, a general linear model would be constructed along with statistical statements of correlation and goodness-of-fit. With such information, an organization could proclaim the extent to which test coupons represent intelligent board area. As may already be noted, such an approach has very strong intuitive appeal; however, such appeal is short-lived upon closer examination.

To begin our detailed examination, let us again consider the historical XYZ PCB data displayed in Figure 8-10. At first glance, it would appear that a fairly high statistical correlation existed between the minimum intelligent area measurements ($Y_1 ... Y_{18}$) and the corresponding minimum coupon measurements ($X_1 ... X_{18}$). In fact, the correlation coefficient (r) was computed (by someone) to be .90; hence, r^2 was given as .81.

On the basis of this reasoning, the organization concluded that 81 percent of the variation in minimum intelligent area measurements could be predicted by the test coupons;

therefore, the extent of prediction error $(1 - r^2)$ was minimal, for all practical purposes. So what was wrong with this approach and subsequent conclusion? The answer to this question will unfold as we discuss the recommended method for establishing coupon-to-board association.

The Recommended Method

What the organization really wanted to know was the extent to which a test coupon could report on the overall state-of-affairs within the intelligent board area, not just the minimum condition. Because they were "mentally locked in" to the use of regression, however, they could not see any other way of establishing correlation. In other words, the analytical tools shaped the problem definition. From a different perspective, we might say that the problem was made to conform to their knowledge of statistics. The implications of this point can not be overstressed – tools must conform to the situation, not the other way around.

In this case, they needed to know how well the test coupon mean and variance agreed with the mean and variance of the corresponding intelligent board area, within- and across-boards. In statistical terminology, we would say that they were concerned with studying a certain product state in which the null condition would be desirable, relative to certain indices of central tendency and variability, for all comparative populations, regardless of performance standards.

To better understand this concept, let us consider the actual XYZ state displayed in Figure 8-11. From this figure, it can be reasoned that the most desirable condition is 100 percent overlap, regardless of where the overlapped distributions may be on the measurement scale. The condition displayed in Figure 8-11 does not represent a state of extensive overlap. In fact, the extent of agreement is quite small; consequently, it may be concluded that the given coupon distribution does not represent the intelligent board area.

In the instance of this case study, test coupon number 6 was designated as the "buy-off" vehicle for the XYZ PCBs. As already indicated, there is little agreement between this particular test coupon and its corresponding intelligent area; however, the left-most tail areas do somewhat coincide (see Figure 8-11). Thus, we can now see how the organization erroneously concluded that test coupon number 6 was representative of the intelligent board area; e.g., the minimum coupon-board values displayed correlation across-boards even though the within-board means and variances were significantly different. As a direct result of this, the likelihood of buy-off decision error was exceptionally high.

As the reader can well imagine, the business implications of such concepts prompted many heated discussions within the organization. For example, much debate was given to the possibility of reworking/scrapping good PCBs and the likelihood of shipping bad ones. Obviously, such issues related to producer's and consumer's risk.

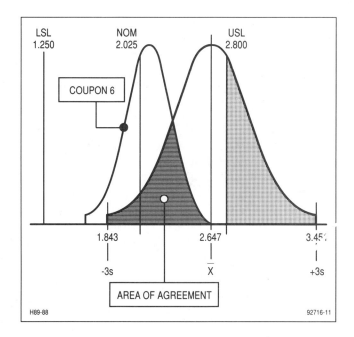

Figure 8-11. Comparison of Coupon and Intelligent Area Distributions

Even if one were to consider values other than the minimum, linear regression could not be used (in the classical sense) to establish coupon-to-board correlation simply because there is no logical basis for creating XY pairs. For example, let us consider through-hole number 24 within test coupon number 6. Which intelligent area hole should it be paired with for purposes of regression? Better yet, if some coupon measurement, say X_{24}, was to be paired with a given intelligent area measurement, say Y_{78}, what would be the logical basis of classification for such pairing? Who is to say that Y_{78} shouldn't be tied to X_{14}, or X_{85} for that matter? As you can see, there is no logical basis for pairing.

If regression is inappropriate in such a situation, what is to be done? Well, the solution to the latter dilemma is quite simple, statistically speaking, that is. In essence, the solution involves the concepts associated with tests of significance; more specifically, a two-group comparison of means and variances.

Through such techniques, the null condition (H_o) can be tested for statistical significance. If the data reveal substantive evidence for supporting the null condition, we may say that coupon and intelligent area distributions are indistinguishable from each other. Given the null condition, we could further say the likelihood of nonconformance, with respect to the intelligent board area, could be given by the test coupon. Hence, the coupons would be considered representative of their respective intelligent areas; therein, providing the producer and consumer with a high degree of buy-off confidence.

Of course, it is recognized that a test of significance would only be valid on a board-by-board basis. Therefore, it would be necessary to expand the analysis via the inclusion of a blocking variable called "board." Naturally, this infers that more than one board would need to be included in the study. In fact, enough boards should be selected so as to ensure the presence of perturbing nonrandom influences. During data analysis, the sums-of-squares (SS) could be adjusted to account for the block effect. Thus, the null condition could be tested independent of board differences. The end result of such analysis would reveal the extent of coupon-to-board association within certain limits of decision error.

The reader must recognize that the aforementioned strategy can be further expanded to include other potential blocking variables, as we shall see later on in the case analysis. The principal advantage associated with such an expansion is related to statistical precision and decision making confidence.

In the instance of this particular case analysis, use of the aforementioned approach (e.g., tests of significance) revealed that the extent of agreement between the various test coupons and corresponding intelligent board areas was not satisfactory within or across boards. As a consequence, the team determined that the ensuing characterization and optimization study should rely only upon the intelligent area of the XYZ PCB until such time that the coupon-to-board association could be remedied via an engineering solution.

Further discussion on this topic is far beyond the scope and intent of this case analysis; therefore, let it suffice to say that with some sound engineering logic and rigorous statistical reasoning, the details of an appropriate strategy can be readily surfaced to fit almost any situation involving coupon-to-board correlation.

8.4   PHASE II: PARAMETER ANALYSIS

As you may recall, the purpose of this phase is to gather baseline data so as to estimate the instantaneous reproducibility of the response characteristic; e.g, copper plating thickness within PCB through-holes. In addition, this phase also focuses on identifying leverage within the network of causation.

By executing this phase, the characterization team was able to establish the extent to which the plating process was capable of meeting the given product quality standards. Once the copper plating capability was established, the key process variables ($X_1 ... X_N$) were identified. In this fashion, engineering and manufacturing leverage was realized. Let us now consider the specific activities which were executed by the team.

8.4.1   Activity 1: Parameter Capability Analysis

Within this phase, the first step taken by the characterization team was to plan the capability study. In this instance, it was determined that the instantaneous reproducibility or "short-term capability" should be estimated using $n_1 = 5$ sequentially produced PCBs. The rational for $n_1 = 5$ will be discussed later on. Relative to the intelligent area on each board, $n_2 = 16$ sub-sections were identified. Within each of the sub-sections, $n_3 = 5$ hole locations were identified. Within each hole, $n_4 = 6$ measurements were made using the random-location Y grind method. Thus, the total number of measurements was $N = n_1 \times n_2 \times n_3 \times n_4 = 2400$. In all instances, the same rater was used to take the N measurements.

Once the sampling methodology was established, data collection sheets were devised and appropriate data collection training was conducted. Following this, data were gathered and subsequently analyzed in such a manner so as to derive the arithmetic mean and variance. With this information, the various indices of capabilities were computed.

Existing Capability Data

In summary, the team determined that, at the board level, the sample standard deviation was .000268 inches (.268 mils) and the sample mean was .002647 inches (2.647 mils). Based on this information, the board-level process capability ratios were given as $C_p = .9639$ and $C_{pk} = .1903$. The limiting standard normal deviates related to the upper and lower specification limits, at the board level, were computed as $Z_{USL} = .571$ and $Z_{LSL} = 5.2$ respectively.

Using a table of area under the normal curve, it was determined that the probability of exceeding the USL was approximately 28.4 percent. The probability of exceeding the lower specification was virtually zero, for all practical purposes. Thus, the total probability of nonconformance, in the short term, was approximately 28.4 percent; however, it must be recognized that, due to known inconsistencies within the plating tank at the time of data collection, a slight mean offset was expected.

Without regard to centering, we would expect a symmetric value of $Z_{SL} = 2.70$. This translated to a .70 percent probability of nonconformance to standard. Inversely stated, there was a short-term, board-level yield expectation of $(1 - .007)100 = 99.30$ percent. Naturally, this assumes the distribution to be centered within the specification limits; hence, it is a measure of instantaneous reproducibility.

Since the intelligent area of each XYZ PCB contained approximately 4000 plated through-holes, it was determined that the "typical" short-term, through-hole yield could be given by $(.9930^{1/4000})100 = 99.99982$ percent. In the same manner as before, the yield was translated to a bilateral Z deviate using the table of area under the standard normal curve. In this case, the short-term bilateral Z deviate, at the through-hole level of analysis, was determined to be $Z_{SL} = 4.78$. Using this information, the short-term, through-hole capability ratio was calculated as $C_p = 4.78/3 = 1.59$. The reader must recognize that this particular estimate of capability represents a mathematically normalized value. In this sense, it provides a "typical" through-hole estimate.

Following the later estimates, the characterization team decided to approximate the long-term, through-hole capability, taking into account nonrandom sources of manufacturing and material variation. To do this, it was necessary to "back compute" through-hole capability on the basis of historical board-level yield data.

In this instance, the long-term, board-level yield was determined to be approximately 86 percent (reference original problem statement). Given this, the normalized long-term, through-hole yield was estimated to be $(.86^{1/4000})100 = 99.9962$ percent. Translating this yield value to area under the standard normal curve revealed an approximate bilateral Z value of 4.12. Thus, the long-term, through-hole capability ratio was calculated as $C_{p*} = 4.12/3 = 1.37$.

Based on the long- and short-term bilateral Z values, 4.12 and 4.78 respectively, the characterization team computed the extent of parameter robustness. In this case, the robustness metric was given as $C_R = (4.12/4.78)100 = 86.19$ percent. This would be to say that the instantaneous reproducibility was degraded by only $(1 - .8619)100 = 13.81$ percent; hence, it was concluded that the problem of low long-term plating yield was primarily due to inadequate short-term capability rather than the cumulative effects of long-term variations in the mean. Further investigations, as yet to be discussed, supported this conclusion.

Target Capability Data

In order to establish a quantitative objective, it was first necessary for management to set a long-term target with respect to plating yield. In this instance, it was resolved that the existing yield of 86 percent (reference problem statement) should be elevated to 96 percent in order to meet the business objectives pertaining to the XYZ family of PCBs. Given this, it was readily determined that the typical long-term, through-hole yield would need to be $.96^{1/4000} = .99999$ in order to achieve the long-term target yield of 96 percent (at the board level). Consulting a table of area under the standard normal curve revealed that the bilateral Z value associated with .99999 area was $Z = 4.42$.

In order to reverse the effects of perturbing nonrandom influences, the long-term Z value was multiplied by the inverse of the robustness metric. In this case, the short-term limiting standard normal deviate was given as $Z_{SL} = 4.42(1/.8619) = 5.13$. Thus, the short-term, through-hole capability ratio (target value) was stipulated to be $5.13/3 = 1.71$.

As a final point on this topic, the reader should note that the capability goal was set on a standard 12-month learning curve so as to better manage the improvement cycle. Information related to the capability study has been located in Table 8-1.

Table 8-1. Summary Capability Information Related to the XYZ Circuit Board Family

Metric	Time Frame	Board Level		Through-Hole	
		Short-Term	Long-Term	Short-Term	Long-Term
μ	Current	2.647	NA	NA	NA
σ	Current	.287	.718	.162	.188
Z_{SL}	Current	2.70	1.08	4.78	4.12
Y_{FT}	Current	.9930	.8600	.993 82	.992 62
μ	Goal	NA	NOM.	NA	NOM.
σ	Goal	.241	.443	.150	.175
Z_{SL}	Goal	3.22	1.75	5.13	4.42
Y_{FT}	Goal	.9935	.9600	.994 84	.99 3

NOTE: 1. Tabulated values for μ and σ are expressed in mils.

2. Raised digits represent number of times preceding digit is repeated: example, .99³4 would be .999994.

Perhaps the most important point related to the capability exercise is one of recognition. Once the data were in plain view, the management alarm was triggered, thereby setting the stage for goal setting and resource allocation. Remember, in the beginning, one of the managers tried to "write the problem off." Only by adhering to the philosophy of "let the data do the talking" did this situation change. By applying this philosophy, the organization was able to formulate clear direction and purpose.

8.4.2 Activity 2: Multi-Vari Analysis

At this point in the game, the team decided it would be necessary to conduct a multi-vari study. The intent of this particular study was to: (a) identify the major family of variation responsible for the undesirably low short-term and long-term capability estimates and (b) further analyze potential causes of low coupon-to-board association. In this manner, the team was able to simultaneously study two unique, but interrelated issues. As the old saying goes, they could "get more bang for the buck."

Preparing for the Multi-Vari Study

To accomplish the latter aim, it was determined that the problem had to be further classified so as to "set the stage" for a multi-vari study. This was done by defining certain physical boundaries relative to the plating tank, intelligent board area, coupons, and through-hole locations. First, the various rack positions within the plating tank were defined via a numbering system. In abstract form, the various rack positions have been illustrated in Figure 8-12. Notice that one of the tank locations was labeled "NA." This particular position was not included in the multi-vari study for certain constraining reasons (presumedly of an engineering nature).

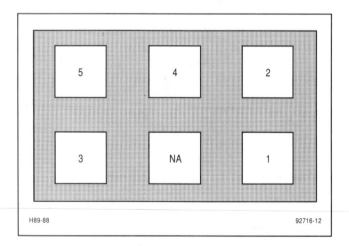

Figure 8-12. Breakdown of the Plating Tank Rack Positions (Multi-Vari Study)

Second, the intelligent area of the basic board configuration was subdivided into four regions approximately equal in size (i.e., quadrants). Figure 8-13 illustrates the breakdown. Such a device was used to provide a basis for studying within-board variations. In addition, each of the quadrants was divided into four subsections (see Figure 8-14). This was done to achieve additional analytical resolution, if need be. The reader should be aware that the numbering scheme progressed from left to right, starting at the top of the PCB.

Third, each coupon was segregated into various regions (see Figure 8-15). Finally, the intelligent area and coupon through-hole sampling locations were defined. By introducing such boundaries and constraints into the data analysis scheme, the characterization team was able to hierarchically study the response variations; e.g., looking for patterned variations within through-holes, across through-holes, within quadrants, across quadrants, within board, across boards, within rack, and so on. In this instance, the process of classification made it possible to concurrently study many different relationships, therein allowing a determination to be made as to where "the problem was and was not," so to speak.

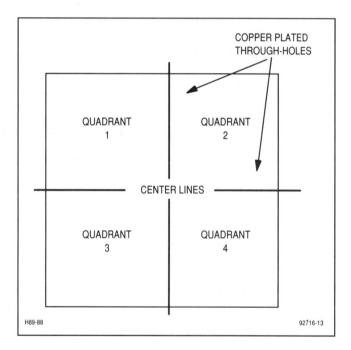

Figure 8-13. Breakdown of XYZ Intelligent Board Area (Multi-Vari Study)

Outcomes of the Multi-Vari Study

The results of the multi-vari study proved to be quite profound. For instance, it was determined that the problem of low board-level capability was, to a large extent, primarily due to within-board and board-to-board (within rack) variance differences. Interestingly, the within-board and board-to-board averages were relatively uniform.

This particular piece of quantitative evidence gave the team much insight into why previous experimentation (conducted months earlier) failed to yield substantiative answers. Such failures resulted because board-level means were used as a basis of analysis – the multi-vari study revealed that the problem was constrained to the variance in certain areas of the PCB and plating tank. Second, the experimental factors historically used for experimentation were temporal in nature (i.e., time related) – the multi-vari study suggested that the problem was positional in nature (e.g., focused within and between boards). Consequently, the experiments were improperly vectored with respect to the problem parameters and performance metrics. Not only did the multi-vari study surface the major sources of variation, it provided a vital base for brainstorming potentially influential process variables.

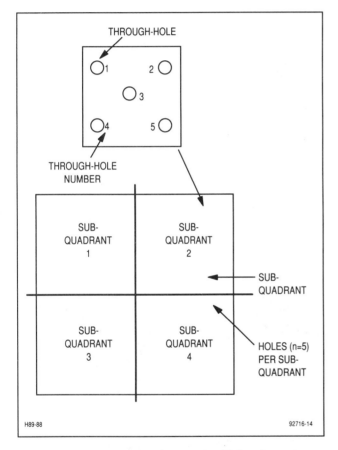

Figure 8-14. Expanded View of XYZ Quadrant Area (Multi-Vari Study)

Figures 8-16 and 8-17 display the actual multi-vari charts developed by the characterization team. It should be pointed out that each of the datum within Figure 8-16 and Figure 8-17 consisted of N = 120 individual plating-thickness measurements.

As you can see from Figure 8-16, the within-board and across-board averages were relatively consistent.

Interestingly, Figure 8-17 reveals a strong, repeatable pattern in the subquadrant means. Obviously, this means that the lower portion of each board received more copper, on the average, than the upper portion, irrespective of rack position. In addition, it is interesting to note that those boards with largest plating averages (e.g., boards 1 and 3) occupied rack positions within the lower portion of the plating tank.

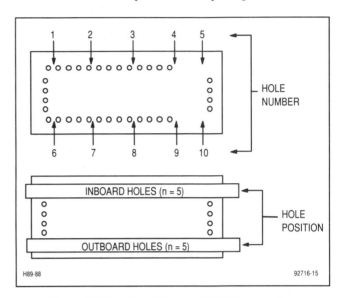

Figure 8-15. Breakdown of XYZ Coupon Area (Multi-Vari Study)

Given the multi-vari charts presented in Figures 8-18 and 8-19, it quickly became apparent to the team that copper plating uniformity was the major problem. A careful analysis of Figure 8-19 revealed that the problem was primarily constrained to the lower half of boards 1 and 3. Board number 2 also displayed the same symptom, but to a lesser extent. Again, the problem appeared to be focused in those rack positions within the lower portion of the plating tank.

In terms of the test coupons, it is interesting to note that the averages were highly repeatable from board-to-board, but not within board; however, several of the test coupons were reasonably representative in terms of the standard deviation. Remember, coupon 6 was the buy-off vehicle. Given this, it was readily apparent (see Figures 8-16 through 8-19) that the buy-off coupon was not representative of the intelligent board area.

In a nutshell, the team drew three major conclusions from the multi-vari exercise. First, it was determined that greatest leverage could be gained by focusing on the reduction of within-board and within-rack variation (i.e., positional variation). Second, the primary performance metric for subsequent investigations should be the response variance. Third, the lack of coupon-to-board agreement was primarily a design issue; therein, removing it from their "immediate span of control."

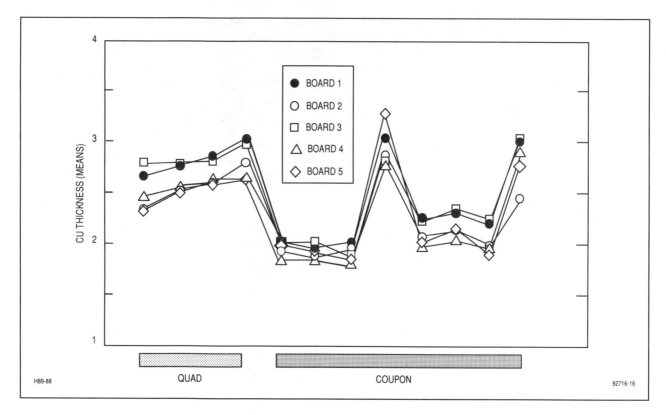

Figure 8-16.   Multi-Vari Chart of Quadrant and Coupon Averages

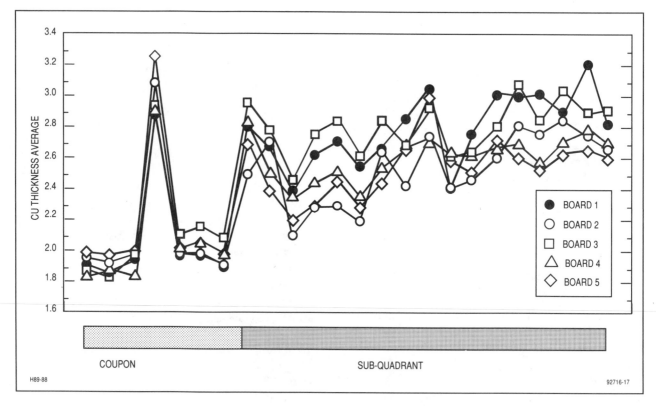

Figure 8-17.   Multi-Vari Chart of Subquadrant and Coupon Averages

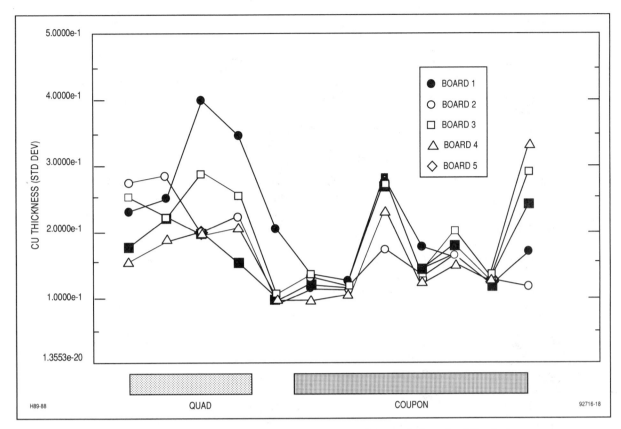

Figure 8-18. *Multi-Vari Chart of Quadrant and Coupon Standard Deviations*

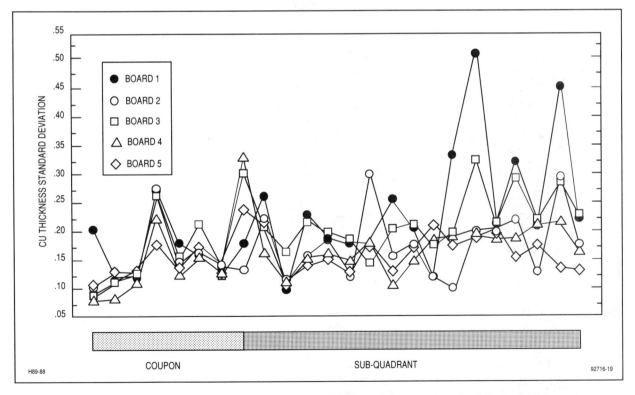

Figure 8-19. *Multi-Vari Chart of Subquadrant and Coupon Standard Deviations*

In terms of the variance, it is quite obvious that a severe problem existed (see Figure 8-19). Not only was there a wide range of standard deviations from board-to-board, in terms of the intelligent area, the problem appeared to be particularly acute within the low half of the PCBs (e.g., quadrants 3 and 4). Given Figure 8-19, it would appear that the change was in the form of a sudden shift. It is also quite apparent that the standard deviation was not very repeatable across boards; however, this did not hold true for all of the PCBs. Using Figure 8-19 as a guide, we can see that the standard deviation was quite consistent across the intelligent area of board number 4. This particular observation stirred much controversy within the team.

As before, the characterization team reasoned it was quite possible that the undesirably low capability ratio was, in large part, due to the wide range of pooled through-hole measurements. Obviously, when compiled into a single data set, the board-level standard deviation would be consistently higher than the individual through-hole standard deviations, therein, driving a low capability ratio.

In terms of the coupons, it is interesting to note that repeatability is fairly good across boards; such repeatability is absent from coupon-to-coupon within a board. The reader should take note of the buy-off coupon; e.g., coupon number 6. The board-to-board stability of this particular coupon is high; however, it is not representative of the intelligent area standard deviation. Again, coupon 8 seems to be the most representative.

Based on these observations, the team concluded that coupon number 6 was generally not representative of the intelligent board area in terms of central tendency or variability; hence, the coupon-to-board correlation would expectedly be low. The team further concluded that the given composite intelligent area capability was controlled primarily by within-board variations and not board-to-board variations. Furthermore, they agreed that the problem of nonconformance was more related to the variance than the mean.

As a consequence of these conclusions, the characterization team determined that the variance should be the primary statistical response during variable identification and optimization. Furthermore, it was decided that the optimization effort should focus on the individual subquadrants within the intelligent board area. In other words, the team determined that if the optimization study was to bear fruit, they would have to optimize each of the subquadrants individually, but in a collective fashion. As a final point, it was believed that if the key process variables were related to each of the subquadrants, leverage could be realized in terms of yield enhancement at the board level.

8.4.3 Activity 3: Variable Identification Via Experimentation

Once the multi-vari study was completed, the team was again assembled. The purpose of the meeting was to statistically design an experiment which would identify the leverage-independent variables. The first step in this process was to freely brainstorm all of the variables which could potentially impact the variance within the intelligent board area of a PCB and from board-to-board within a rack. Remember, the multi-vari study revealed that the problem was related to the variance and not the mean.

The brainstorming matrix presented in Figure 8-20 was used to help the team stay focused during brainstorming. In this case, focus was given to those factors which were not formally controlled on an ongoing basis; e.g., those variables which did not have formal control mechanisms, or "knobs" as some would say.

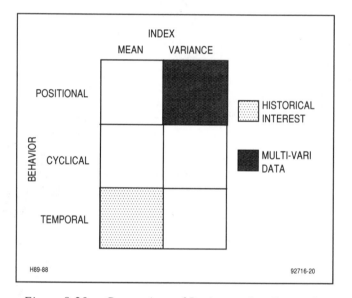

Figure 8-20. *Comparison of Brainstorming Categories*

Selecting the Experimental Factors

When the brainstorming process was complete, 36 variables had been identified as potentially causal in terms of the variance. The reader is encouraged to focus on Figure 8-20. As you can well imagine, the increased focus in brainstorming, as a result of knowing the matrix intersect, can not be expressed enough. This was the principal key to successful experimentation.

This writer has seen numerous skillfully executed experiments "bite the dust" because the wrong class of variables were considered. Remember, the most powerful statistical methods known to the human race can not rescue an experiment that did not manipulate the right variables — a word to the wise and a caveat to the impatient. Perhaps such discussion is best summarized in the axiom: "Penny wise (not conducting a multi-vari study) and pound foolish (unproductive experiments)."

Following the brainstorming sessions, the team developed a rigorous method of variable selection and prioritization. The key activity relating to this method involved rank ordering all of the variables on several unique multi-point rating scales. Such scales were inclusive of, but not limited to: (a) likelihood of causation, (b) extent of existing control, (c) measureability, (d) controllability, and (e) cost of manipulation. By weighting the various scales and making the necessary computations, it was possible for the team to quickly prioritize the 36 variables.

The experimental variables are listed in Figure 8-21. The control variables are defined in Figure 8-22. Notice that the experimental levels or "test settings" are also defined, as well as level tolerances. It should be pointed out that the team spent almost two full days getting to this point.

While many individuals might consider this excessive, it must be remembered that an experiment is only as good as its inputs and assumptions. In other words, "trash in, trash out." This point can not be overly emphasized. An experiment is only as good as its input. Shall we say it again?

CASE STUDY VARIABLES					
FACTOR DESCRIPTION	UNITS	LOW LEVEL	TOL +/-	HIGH LEVEL	TOL +/-
A: CURRENT DENSITY	USF	8	1	12	1
B: PLATE BATH TEMP	F	68	3	76	3
C: SPLINE TO BUS	NA	CONTAM	NA	CLEAN	NA
D: ANODE TO CATHODE X - N/S	IN	0.000	0.125	0.375 (N-O)	0.125
E: ANODE TO CATHODE Y - E/W	IN	0.000	0.125	1.000 (E-O)	0.125
F: CATHODE POSITION Z - T/B	NA	BOTTOM	NA	TOP	NA
G: SHARED ANODES	NA	UNSHARED	NA	SHARED	NA
H: ANODE BAR CONNEC-TION	NA	CON W/O CLAMP	NA	CLN W/ CLAMP	NA

H89-88   92716-21

Figure 8-21. Experimental Factors and Test Levels Identified During the Brainstorming Process

Designing the Experiment

Following the brainstorming sessions, an estimate of sample size was rendered on the basis of a two-level design model. In this instance, the sample size was computed using a type I (alpha) and type II (beta) error probability of 5 percent. It should be noted that the error term used in the sample size calculation was based on the outcomes of the initial process capability study. Test sensitivity was tentatively established at one standard deviation.

CASE STUDY CONTROL VARIABLES	
CONTROL FACTOR	ASSURANCE CRITERIA
FLIGHTBAR STRAIGHTNESS	SUPPORT BAR SPACING 17" ± 0.250"
FLIGHTBAR ISOLATION	BUS-BUS AND BUS-S. BAR >50k OHMS
CATHODE MASK POSITION	CENTERED ± 0.250" IN X,Y, AND Z
MECH. AGIT. STRK./FRQ.	0.500" ± 0.0625" LONG AND 18 ± 1 SPM
AIR AGITATION	ON AND EVEN SPARGING (VISUAL)
ANODE CHUNK SETTLING	SHAKE BEFORE EACH RUN
RECTIFIER CALIBRATION	BEFORE AND AFTER ENTIRE EXPERIMENT
NON-EXP. CONNECTIONS	NOM ± 5% ON BAR OR SADDLE TOT.
FILTER FUNCTION	ON AND MOVING SOLUTION (VISUAL)
SOLUTION LEVEL	4.000" -6.000" BELOW TANK RIM
PRECLN. AND INOR. CHEM.	CHEMISTRY IN SPEC. STD. PROC.
HULL CELL/CRAC CHK.	HCD BURN @ 40-80 ASF/CC PASS

H89-88   92716-22

Figure 8-22. Control Variables and Test Levels Identified During the Brainstorming Process

Given the required levels of decision confidence and test sensitivity, the team discovered they would not be able to execute a screening experiment and then follow on with a higher-resolution design – the testing costs were much too high. As a consequence, trade-offs were made. In this case, test sensitivity and beta risk were adjusted to reduce total sample size (N). After making all of the necessary compromises, it was determined that 16 experimental runs could be made (with minimum replication). Of course, the objective at this point was to test as many variables as possible.

After some general discussion, the team decided to employ a 2^{8-4} design (resolution IV fractional factorial). This particular type of design ensured that second-order and higher interactions were clear of the main effects; however, the second-order effects were aliased together in certain combinations. Recognize that the potential interactive effects were carefully evaluated. After such evaluation, the experimental factors were assigned to the appropriate design matrix columns. The reader should be aware that the aforementioned process provided an experiment design which represented the practical balance between such things as experimental precision, decision risk, manufacturing objectives, and cost, just to mention a few. The design matrix is located in Figure 8-23.

CASE STUDY 2^{8-4} EXPERIMENT DESIGN

	A	B	C	D	E	F	G	H
1	-	-	-	+	+	+	-	+
2	+	-	-	-	-	+	+	+
3	-	+	-	-	+	-	+	+
4	+	+	-	+	-	-	-	+
5	-	-	+	+	-	-	+	+
6	+	-	+	-	+	-	-	+
7	-	+	+	-	-	+	-	+
8	+	+	+	+	+	+	+	+
9	-	+	+	-	-	-	+	-
10	+	+	+	+	+	-	-	-
11	-	-	+	+	-	+	-	-
12	+	-	+	-	+	+	+	-
13	-	+	-	-	+	+	-	-
14	+	+	-	+	-	+	+	-
15	-	-	-	+	+	-	+	-
16	+	-	-	-	-	-	-	-

92716-23

Figure 8-23. Fractional Factorial Design Matrix

The characterization team spent a lot of time preparing for the experiment. Over a two-week period, they developed and tested all of the test instructions and data collection sheets. To do this, the test instructions were "proof read" by several employees. Next, fictitious data were recorded on the data sheets and transferred to a computer file for subsequent analysis using the selected software. This was done to ensure compatibility between all of the various "subsystems." After working out all of the kinks, a short workshop was conducted for those employees designated for participation.

The primary purpose for this workshop was to ensure that everyone was "on the same wavelength." This approach is often not taken by novice experimenters. Let it suffice to say that all it takes to "throw a wrench in the experimental machinery" is one person who arbitrarily decides to do something beyond the scope and intent of the test plan; e.g., changing test settings in the middle of a run, throwing away data, iterating an operation, etc. Many times, a well-intentioned worker inadvertently crashes an experiment naively thinking that someone would highly appreciate their unplanned contribution.

Outcomes of the Experiment

The experimental results revealed that the main effects of factor B (plating bath temperature), factor G (shared anodes), and factor H (anode bar connection) were very important; i.e., statistically and practically significant. In fact, the independent contributions of these three main effects accounted for nearly 60 percent of the observed variation. In addition, it was quite apparent that several of the second-order effects were also very important. In Pareto terminology, it was concluded that the "vital few" effects had been successfully isolated from the "trivial many" in terms of XYZ copper plating thickness variability.

A graphic presentation of the overall results is shown in Figure 8-24. Notice that the horizontal axis of the bar chart displays a number. In order of sequence, 1 = factor A, 2 = factor B, 3 = factor C, and so on. The vertical axis of the bar chart reflects the percent contribution that the related effect had in the total scheme of things. For example, it is apparent that bar 8 (factor H, or "anode bar connection") extends to the 20 percent mark on the vertical scale. This would be to say that the anode bar connection accounted for approximately 20 percent of the observed experimental variation.

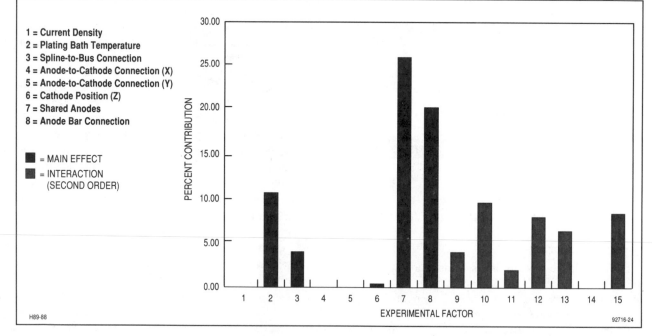

Figure 8-24. Display of Relative Effects Related to the Experimental Factors and Interactions

The reader is reminded that all such proportions were calculated from the sums-of-squares (SS) associated with the analysis-of-variance procedure. Also note that, where appropriate, mathematical transformations were used to ensure compliance to the underlying assumptions.

8.5   PHASE III: PARAMETER OPTIMIZATION

Since the experimental data and design vectors were previously entered into an electronic spreadsheet, it was possible for the team to further explore the data via systematic sorting and stratification. It should be pointed out that the team spent an entire day planning the flow of analysis. Again, this may initially seem excessive; however, as those that have been involved in massive data analyses will testify, it is very easy to get lost exploring the many trivial analytical tributaries that periodically spring from the data.

To avoid this pitfall, a plan of attack must be carefully developed in the light of realistic objectives – and then adhered to. This is not to say that the tributaries be avoided because they often yield valuable information; however, it is to say that if one decides to "canoe down the Amazon," the procurement of a map is highly recommended. Simply stated, the data analysis must be planned prior to executing the experiment.

In accordance to plan, the first activity involved sorting the entire experimental matrix and related row-wise response measures by design vector (see Figure 8-25). Essentially, this had the advantage of separating the positive design vectors of any given column factor from its negative design vectors.

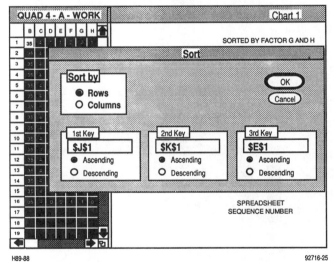

Figure 8-25.   Example of Systematic Sorting for Data Analysis

Next, the data were stratified by quadrant, coupon, sub-quadrant, hole, etc. In this manner, the data could be plotted by line number. The many resultant graphs provided a basis from which to visualize the main effects and potential interactions at various analytical and product strata.

By following this strategy, the team was able to assess the consistency of effects across the intelligent area of each board, as well as the related coupons. This is an extremely important point for the reader to recognize. If the experimental effects were not consistent, it would have been highly likely that the problem could have been resolved in one portion of the PCB or rack and subsequently magnified in some other area, thereby neutralizing the gains. Even worse, it might have been possible to narrow the range of variability within a certain board location, but throw the mean far off target in some other location. Remember, the purpose of experimentation was to reduce the variance without impacting overall mean location – a tall order indeed.

Figures 8-26 and 8-27 illustrate the sequential plot of standard deviations associated with the two most important main effects; namely, factors G and H. It should be pointed out that the horizontal axis of this graph is tied to the spreadsheet line number and that the vertical axis reflects the corresponding standard deviation. In this manner, the data could be sorted in any given fashion and then subsequently plotted in a manner such that the negative design vectors graphically appear before the positive vectors. Line markers 1 through 8 within Figure 8-26 display the standard deviations when factor G was set at its low test level. Line markers 9 through 16 illustrate the behavior of the standard deviation when factor G was at its high test level. From this graph, it is more than apparent that, when factor G was held at its low test level, the response standard deviation was smaller, on the average, than when the high test level was considered.

In the context of the experimental objectives, the smaller standard deviation was more desirable. It is also apparent that factor G interacts with some other factor because the response standard deviation is more stable at the low test level than at the high test level. This was confirmed when the ANOVA tables were individually considered along with several other graphs.

Based on the experimental outcomes, realistic tolerances and/or operating conditions were established for factors B, G, and H. As a caveat, the reader must recognize that it is far beyond the scope of this particular case study to present the outcomes of the entire data analysis. One must recognize that only a small portion of the total analytical picture is given. Again, the most important thing to be gained is an understanding of the analytical strategy and approach, not the physics associated with plating PCB through-holes.

The reader is highly cautioned not to attempt replication of this experiment on the basis of the information given in this case study – the data is incomplete. Again, the strategy, tactics, and tools can be replicated, but the data cannot be used "as is" to make improvements within an existing process – the outcomes are unique to the XYZ process.

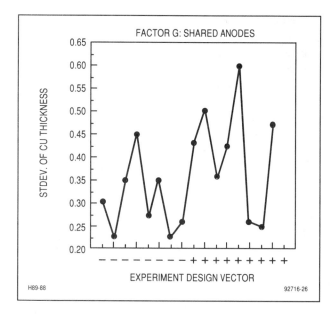

Figure 8-26. *Sequential Plot of Experimental Standard Deviations After Sorting on Factor G*

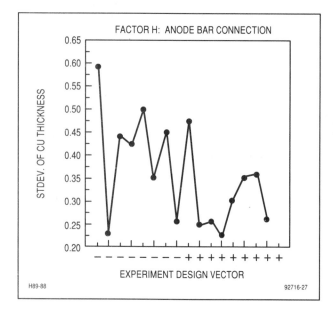

Figure 8-27. *Sequential Plot of Experimental Standard Deviations After Sorting on Factor H*

8.6 PHASE IV: PARAMETER CONTROL

After completing the statistically designed experiments, the team set out to establish a parameter control scheme. In order to do this, several things needed to occur. First, it was necessary to define the most efficient and economic means of control for each of the candidate variables. Next, all necessary administrative and logistical arrangements were made.

Such things as data collection sheets, maintenance schedules, and control charts were created. Following this, all necessary training was conducted. Finally, the control scheme was implemented and periodically audited.

In the final analysis, the team was very successful. Within a matter of days, the XYZ PCB yield increased dramatically and the scrap decreased in a corresponding manner. In fact, the scrap cost associated with the XYZ family of PCBs was reduced from approximately $500,000 per month to $72,000. This represented a seven-fold improvement. The cost of solving the problem was estimated to be approximately $250,000. Based on this information, it was determined that the annual cost savings was approximately $5,000,000.

On a more micro level, a follow-on, board-level capability study was undertaken after implementing the parameter control scheme and coupon-to-board solution. The histogram associated with that study is shown in Figure 8-28. Notice that the variability associated with the intelligent area was significantly reduced. Also notice that the centering and spread of the intelligent area and buy-off coupon are approximately the same. Overall, this represented a higher level of agreement than previously established. In turn, this constituted higher customer confidence and lower manufacturing costs.

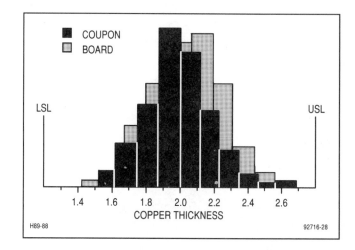

Figure 8-28. *Post-Study Comparison of the Histograms Related to the Intelligent Board Area and Test Coupon*

In short, it could be said that the process was much more predictable due to the higher level of producibility. The reader should note that over a six-month period, several additional follow-on capability analyses were conducted. The results of those studies revealed consistently high performance. As a consequence, the problem was considered solved.

ABOUT THE AUTHORS

Mikel J. Harry

Mikel Harry is currently Director of the Six Sigma Research Laboratory and Senior Member of Technical Staff within Motorola University, Schaumburg, Illinois. In this capacity, he is directly responsible for the research and development of advanced engineering tools as applied to product and process design, as well as manufacturing activities. Such endeavor is aimed at the concurrent optimization of quality, producibility, and performance. Prior to this assignment, he served as Chief Statistician and Member of Technical Staff, Group Operations, Government Electronics Group, Motorola, Inc. Before this, Dr. Harry was a Principal Staff Engineer within the Advanced Quantitative Research Laboratory, Government Electronics Group, Motorola, Inc. He received his B.S. degree in Industrial Technology (electronics) from Ball State University in 1973. His M.A. degree was awarded in 1981, also from Ball State. In 1984, he was awarded his Ph.D. degree from Arizona State University. Dr. Harry has published numerous technical papers, is the author of a reference book, and is a contributing author to two textbooks. He is chairperson of the Product Design Subcommittee for Design Producibility Metrics sponsored by the United States Navy, and is a member of the Statistics Division, American Society of Quality Control. Dr. Harry is also an Associate Member of the Motorola Science Advisory Board. He may be reached for consultation at (602) 441-2227.

J. Ronald Lawson

J. Ronald Lawson is a Principal Staff Engineer with the Communications Division, Government Electronics Group, Motorola, Inc., Scottsdale, Arizona. As a member of the Quality and Reliability Engineering Staff and the Advanced Quantitative Research Laboratory, he is responsible for the application of statistical methods in achieving and controlling product reliability and high-quality manufacturing processes. He has also served as Manager of Process Development and Device Engineering in the Motorola Integrated Circuits Research Laboratory. Dr. Lawson has over twenty years of industrial experience in semiconductors and system electronics. His M.S. and Ph.D. degrees in Solid-State Physics are from Case Western Reserve University. His B.S. degree in Physics is from the University of Notre Dame. Currently, Dr. Lawson is Chairperson of the Statistics Policy Advisory Board of the Government Electronics Group, as well as President of the Motorola Phoenix-Area Six-Sigma Special Interest Group. He has also been awarded membership in the Motorola Scientific and Technical Society for his technical contributions to the Motorola Government Electronics Group. Dr. Lawson is a member of the American Physical Society and the Institute of Environmental Sciences. He may be reached for consultation at (602) 441-2183.

ACKNOWLEDGMENTS

Contributors

The authors gratefully recognize the following individuals for their contribution toward the development and publication of this booklet. Their assistance has significantly enhanced the overall quality of the booklet.

John Frei, Chief Engineer, Integrated Circuits Facility, Government Electronics Group, Motorola, Inc.

John Hathaway, Principal Staff Engineer, Advanced Quantitative Analysis Laboratory, Government Electronics Group, Motorola, Inc.

Randy Jameson, Manager, Group Quality and Audit, Government Electronics Group, Motorola, Inc.

Cyrus Kotval, Ph.D., Manager, Central Manufacturing Facility, Government Electronics Group, Motorola, Inc.

Jerry Norley, Manager, Group Manufacturing, Government Electronics Group, Motorola, Inc.

Ralph Ponce de Leon, Vice President and Director, Group Operations, Government Electronics Group, Motorola, Inc.

Reigle Stewart, Senior Engineering Specialist, Group Mechanical Design Technology, Government Electronics Group, Motorola, Inc.

Dick White, Manager, Quality Assurance, Government Electronics Group, Motorola, Inc.

David Yee, Processing Engineering Manager, Integrated Circuits Facility, Government Electronics Group, Motorola, Inc.

Doug Mader, Graduate Student, Colorado School of Mines, Masters program in Mathematics.

Members of the Process Standardization Committee, Government Electronics Group, Motorola, Inc.

Wela Publications Ltd. for allowing the reprinting of the material in Section 8 of this booklet.

U.S. Navy Producibility Measurement and Guidelines Program.

For contribution of the plasma cleaning case study, the authors would like to recognize members of the Integrated Circuits Facility Process Characterization Team, Government Electronics Group, Motorola, Inc.: Kim Bertagnolli, Process Engineer; Russell Fiorenzo, Process Engineer; Jeff Galvin, Process Engineer; Dick Gross, Manufacturing Manager; Claudia Jensen, Process Technician; and Dan Knuth, Process Engineer.

Special acknowledgment is given to the members of Information Services, Government Electronics Group, Motorola, Inc., who contributed many hours of work and gave close attention to detail. Such effort was very instrumental in assuring a publication deserving of Corporate distribution.

Gail Levinson, Publications Administrator, Information Services, Government Electronics Group, Motorola, Inc.

Peter Bordow, Publications Specialist, Information Services, Government Electronics Group, Motorola, Inc.

Referees

Many thanks go to the distinguished referees for their technical review of this booklet. Their judicious consideration, meaningful guidance, and insightful recommendations greatly assisted the authors.

J. Bert Keats, Ph.D., P.E., Director of SEAQL, CIM Systems Research Center, College of Engineering and Applied Sciences, Arizona State University, Tempe, Arizona.

Kenneth Chase, Ph.D., Professor of Engineering, Mechanical Engineering Department, Brigham Young University, Provo, Utah.

Vijay A. Tipnis, Sc.D., Professor; and Morris M. Bryan, Jr. Chair for Advanced Manufacturing Systems, School of Mechanical Engineering, Georgia Institute of Technology.

Col. Steven R. Schmidt, Ph.D., Professor and Deputy Head, Department of Mathematical Sciences, USAF Academy, Colorado Springs, Colorado.

Philip Barkan, Ph.D., Professor, Mechanical Engineering Department, Design Division, Stanford University, Stanford, California.

Carl Sorensen, Ph.D., Professor of Engineering, Mechanical Engineering Department, Brigham Young University, Provo Utah.

REFERENCES

Bender, A. (1975). "Statistical Tolerancing as it Relates to Quality Control and the Designer." Automotive Division Newsletter of ASQC.

Bowker, A., and G. Lieberman. (1972). *Engineering Statistics*. New Jersey: McGraw-Hill Book Co.

Brownlee, K.A. (1965). *Statistical Theory and Methodology in Science and Engineering*. (Second Edition). New York: John Wiley and Sons, Inc.

Burr, I. (1953). *Engineering Statistics and Quality Control*. New York: McGraw-Hill Book Co.

Department of the Army Materials and Mechanics Research Center. (1984). *MIL-HDBK-727 Design Guidance for Producibility*. Washington, D.C.: Government Printing Office, April.

Dixon, W., and F. Massey. (1969). *Introduction To Statistical Analysis*. (Third Edition). New York: McGraw-Hill book Co.

Evans, David H. (1975). "Statistical Tolerancing: The State of the Art, Part III: Shifts and Drifts." *Journal of Quality and Technology*; 7(2), pp. 72-76.

Ford Motor Company. (1984). "Continuing Process Control and Process Capability Improvement." *Statistical Methods Office*. Operation Support Staffs, Ford Motor Co.

Gilson, J. (1951). *A New Approach to Engineering Tolerances*. London, England: Machinery Publishing Co. Ltd.

Grant, E.L., and R.S. Leavenworth. (1974). *Statistical Quality Control*. (Fifth Edition). New York: McGraw-Hill Book Co.

Gunter, B.H. (1989). "The Use and Abuse of C_{pk}, Part 2." *Quality Progress;* March, 1989, pp 108.

Gunter, B.H. (1989). "The Use and Abuse of C_{pk}, Part 3." *Quality Progress;* May, 1989, pp. 79.

Guralnk, D.B., editor. (1986). *Webster's New World Dictionary*. (Second Edition). New York: Simon and Schuster Inc.

Hald, A. (1952). *Statistical Theory with Engineering Applications*. New York: John Wiley and Sons.

Harry, M.J. (1989). "PCB Plated Through-Hole Optimization: A Case Study in SPC." *Circuit World*; 16, No. 1, 1989, pp. 33-43.

Harry, M., and R. Stewart. (1988). *Six Sigma Mechanical Design Tolerancing*. Motorola, Inc.

Hillier, F.S., and G.J. Lieberman. (1980). *Operations Research*. (Second Edition). San Francisco: Holden-Day, Inc.

Hillkirk, John, Editor. (1989). "Top Quality Is Behind Comeback." *USA Today*. Cover Story.

Juran, J.M., F.M. Gryna, and R.S. Bingham. (1979). *Quality Control Handbook*. New York: McGraw-Hill Book Co.

Kane, V.E. (1986). "Process Capability Indices." *Journal of Quality Technology*; 18(1), pp. 41-52.

Kelvin, W.T. (1891). *Popular Lectures and Addresses*.

Mendenhall, W., and R. Schaeffer. (1973). *Mathematical Statistics with Applications*. Massachusetts: Duxbury Press. pp. 185-188.

Motorola, Inc. (1986). *Design for Manufacturability: Eng 123 (Participant Guide)*. Motorola Training and Education Center, Motorola, Inc., Illinois.

Nelson. (1988). "Control Charts: Rational Subgroups and Effective Applications." *Journal of Quality Technology*; 20(1), pp. 73-75.

Ott, L. (1977). *An Introduction to Statistical Methods and Data Analysis*. Massachusetts: Duxbury Press.

Pearson, C. (1983). *Handbook of Applied Mathematics*. (Second Edition). New York: Van Nostrand Reinhold Co.

Shewhart, W.A. (1931). *Economic Control of Manufactured Product*. New Jersey: Van Nostrand Book Co.

Stoll, H., A. Kumar, and D. Maas. (Date Unknown). *Producibility Management: Key to the Design of Producible Products*. Industrial Technology Institute. Michigan: Unpublished.

Taylor. (1982). *An Introduction to Error Analysis – The Study of Uncertainties in Physical Measurements*. California: University Science Books.

Webster's New Collegiate Dictionary. (1976). Massachusetts: Merriam-Webster.

BIBLIOGRAPHY

Design Applications

Andreasen, M., S. Kahler, and T. Lund. (1983). *Design for Assembly*. IFS Publications, Ltd.

Bancroft, C. (1988). "Overlooked Aspects of Design for Manufacturability." *IEEE Circuits Devices Mag.* USA;Vol. 4, No. 6, Nov. pp. 15-19.

Barker, Paul A. (1989). "Design for Manufacturability." *Printed Circuit Design,* Vol. 6, No. 1, Jan. pp 37-38.

Battin, L. (1988). "Six Sigma Process by Design." *Design and Dimensions, a Publication of Group Mechanical Technology*; Vol. 1, No. 1, p. 4, Government Electronics Group, Motorola Inc.

Becker, David. (1988). "Flex Circuitry: Designing for Manufacturability." *Printed Circuit Design;* Vol. 5, No. 8, Aug. pp. 54-57.

Bender, A. (1962). "Benderizing Tolerances – A Simple Practical Probability Method of Handling Tolerances for Limit-Stack-Ups." *Graphic Science.* Dec.

Bender, A. (1968). "Statistical Tolerancing as it Relates to Quality Control and the Designer." *Society of Automotive Engineers*; SAE Paper No. 680490, May.

Boothroyd, Geoffrey, and Peter Dewhurst. (1983). *Design for Assembly: A Designer's Handbook*. Rhode Island: Boothroyd Dewhurst, Inc.

Boothroyd, G., and Dewhurst. (1986). *Product Design for Assembly*. Rhode Island: Boothroyd Dewhurst, Inc.

Box, G., and S. Bisgaard. (1988). "Statistical Tools for Improving Designs." *Mechanical Engineering*, Jan.

Bralla, J.G. (1986). *Handbook of Product Design for Manufacturing*. New York: McGraw-Hill Book Co.

Brayton, R.K., S.W. Director, and G.D. Hachtel. (1980). "Yield Maximization and Worst-Case Design with Arbitrary Statistical Distributions." *IEEE Transactions on Circuits and Systems*; Vol. 27, No. 9, pp. 756-764.

Burgess, John A. (1984). *Design Assurance for Engineers and Managers*. New York: Marcel Dekker, pp. 166-182.

Chase, K.W., and W.H. Greenwood. (1987). "Design Issues in Mechanical Tolerance Analysis." *ASME Conference Paper*. Winter Annual Meeting of the American Society of Mechanical Engineers. Dec. 13-18. pp. 11-26.

Cooke, et. al. (1984). *A Guide to Design for Production*. Institution of Production Engineers.

Dao-Thien, My. (1981). "Approach for Optimum Tolerancing of the Design Components." *CANCAM Proceedings*. Canadian Congress of Applied Mechanics 8th, Vol. 1, pp. 333-334.

DeVor, R.E. (1987). "Role of Parameter Design in the Simultaneous Engineering of Products and Processes." *American Society of Mechanical Engineers, Production Engineering Division*. New York: Vol. 27. pp 131-135.

Evans, David H. (1958). "Optimum Tolerance Assignment to Yield Minimum Manufacturing Cost." *Bell System Technical Journal*; 37(2).

Evans, David H. (1970). "Statistical Tolerancing Formulation." *Journal of Quality and Technology*; 2(4), pp. 226-231.

Evans, David H. (1972). "Application of Numerical Integration Techniques to Statistical Tolerancing – III." *Technometrics;* 14(1), pp. 23-35.

Evans, David H. (1974). "Statistical Tolerancing: The State of the Art, Part I: Background." *Journal of Quality and Technology*; 6(4), pp. 188-195.

Evans, David H. (1975). "Statistical Tolerancing: The State of the Art, Part II: Methods for Estimating Moments." *Journal of Quality and Technology*; 7(1), pp. 1-12.

Greenwood, G. (1986). "Manufacturability and Testability Issues Increase Design Creativity." *Automated Design and Engineering for Electronics West*. Proceedings of the Technical Sessions, 209-11. 11-13 Mar., Illinois: Cahners Exposition Group.

Greenwood, W.H., and K.W. Chase. (1987). "A New Tolerance Analysis Method for Designers and Manufacturers." *Journal of Engineering for Industry*; Vol. 109, pp. 112-116.

Harry, M.J. (1987). *Electrical Engineering Application of the Taguchi Design Philosophy*. Government Electronics Group, Motorola, Inc.

Heath, H.H. (1979). "Statistical Tolerancing of Engineering Components: Is It Worth It?" *Precision Engineering*; 1(3), pp. 153-156.

Hunter, J.S. (1985). "Statistical Design Applied to Product Design." *Qual. Technol.*; Vol. 17, No. 4, Oct. 210(21).

Jones, S.W. (1973). *Product Design and Process Selection*. London, England: Butterworts.

Joshi, Dileep C. (1985). *Advantages of Simultaneous Design of Product and Processes*. Proceedings of the National Electronics Conference; Vol. 39, Professional Education Int. Inc. pp 650-657.

Kelly Sines, R. (1988). *Integrating Simultaneous Engineering Into New Product Introduction*. Sponsor: Troy Conferences; Boothroyd & Dewhurst. Proceedings of the 3rd International Conference on Product Design for Manufacture and Assembly. Michigan: Troy Conferences. 10 pp.

Knauer, Karl, and Hans Joerg Pfleiderer. (1982). "Yield Enhancement Realized for Analogue Integrated Filters by Design Techniques." *IEEE Proceedings, Part I: Solid-State and Electron Devices*; 129(2), pp. 67-71.

Langford, T. (1986). "Design or Manufacturability-Cooperation+CAD+CIM." *Automated Design and Engineering for Electronics*. – East. Proceedings of the Technical Sessions, NCR, Corp; Illinois: Cahners Exposition Group, Sep.-Oct., pp. 45-54.

Mansoor, E.M. (1963). "The Application of Probability to Tolerances Used in Engineering Design." *Proceedings, Institute of Mechanical Engineering*; 1781(1).

Melander, Wes, and Kim Mast. (1986). "Design for Manufacturability: It's Not Just Design Rules Anymore." ATE East – E.I. Conference #10327, Hewlett-Packard Co., Massachusetts: MG Expositions Group. June, pp. IV 11-IV. 21.

Mercadante, M. (1986). "The Hewlett Packard Company's Approach to Design for Manufacturability." *Automated Design and Engineering for Electronics* – East. Proceedings of the Technical Sessions. Illinois: Cahners Exposition Group, Sep.-Oct., pp. 437.

Oh, H.L. (1987). "Variation Tolerant Design." *American Society of Mechanical Engineers – PED*, General Motors. New York: ASME. Vol. 27, pp. 137-146.

Olivera, R. (1988). *Sigma/Fit Tolerance Analysis*. Communications Sector, Motorola, Inc., Illinois.

Phadke, Madhav S. (1986). "Design Optimization Case Studies." *AT&T Tech. J.,* AT&T Bell lab. New Jersey: Vol. 65, No. 2, Mar.-Apr., pp. 51-68.

Pike, E.W., and T.R. Silverberg. (1953). "Assigning Tolerances for Maximum Economy." *Machine Design;* Sep. pp. 139-146.

Russell, G.A. (1985). "Design for Manufacturability of Printed Circuit Board Assemblies." *CIRP Annuals*. Berne, Switzerland: Technische Rundschau, Vol. 34, No. 1, Aug. pp. 37-40.

Shigley, Joseph E. (1972). *Mechanical Engineering Design*. (Second Edition). New York: McGraw-Hill Book Co.

Singhal, K., and J.F. Pinel. (1981). "Statistical Design Centering and Tolerancing Using Parametric Sampling." *IEEE Transactions on Circuits and Systems*; 28(7), pp. 692-701.

Starkey, John M., and Gregory J. Florin. (1986). " Design for Manufacturability." *American Society of Mechanical Engineers (Paper)*. New York: ASME. Pap 86-DET-121, 6p.

Tietjen, Gary L., and Mark E. Johnson. (1979). "Exact Statistical Tolerance Limits for Sample Variances." *Technometrics*; 21(1), pp. 107-110.

Trucks, H.E. (1974). *Designing for Economical Production*. Michigan: Society of Manufacturing Engineers, 1974.

Wade, Oliver R. (1967). *Tolerance Control in Design and Manufacturing*. New York: Industrial Press, Inc.

Wallace, J.R., and J.L. Grant. (1977). "Least Squares Method for Computing Statistical Tolerance Limits." *Water Resources Research*; 13(5), pp. 819-823.

Computer-Aided Engineering

Afifi, A.A., and S.P. Azen. (1979). *Statistical Analysis, A Computer Oriented Approach.* (Second Edition), Academic Press.

Bohling, D.M., and L.A. O'Neill. (1970). "Interactive Computer Approach to Tolerance Analysis." *IEEE Trans Comput*; C-19(1), pp. 10-16.

Hennessey, Mike, and Gary Krutz. (1986). "Expert CAD System for Statistical Tolerancing Internal Hydraulic Components." *Proceedings of the National Conference on Fluid Power*; Annual Meeting 41st, pp. 115-120.

Ramalingam, Subbiah. (1985). "Expert Systems for Manufacturing: Examples of Tools to Assess Manufacturability." *SME*; 13th NAMRC Proceedings. Michigan: pp. 411-417.

Mathematical Statistics

Abramovitz, M., and Stegun, I.A., Editors. (1964). *Handbook of Mathematical Functions.* National Bureau of Standards Applied Mathematics Series 55, Washington, D.C., p. 955ff and references.

Box, G.E.P., W.G. Hunter, and J.S. Hunter. (1978). *Statistics for Experimenters.* New York: John Wiley and Sons, Inc.

Cowden, Dudley, J. (1957). *Statistical Methods in Quality Control.* New Jersey: Prentice-Hall.

Cramer, H. (1964). *Mathematical Methods of Statistics.* New Jersey: Princeton University Press.

Daniel, C. (1976). *Applications of Statistics To Industrial Experimentation.* New York: John Wiley and Sons.

Guenther, W. (1973). *Concepts of Statistical Interference.* New York: McGraw-Hill Book Co.

Hadley, G. (1967). *Introduction to Probability and Statistical Decision Theory.* California: Holden-Day, Inc.

Hahn, G., and S. Shapiro. (1967). *Statistical Models In Engineerings.* New York: John Wiley and Sons.

Hald, A. (1952). *Statistical Theory with Engineering Applications.* New York: John Wiley and Sons.

Hicks, T.G. (1972). *Standard Handbook of Engineering Calculations.* New York: McGraw-Hill Book Co.

Kendall, M.G., and A. Stuart. (1963). *The Advanced Theory of Statistics.* New York: Hafner Publishing Co.

King, James R. (1971). *Probability Charts for Decision Making.* New York: The Industrial Press.

Mendenhall, W., and R. Schaeffer. (1973). *Mathematical Statistics With Applications.* Massachusetts: Duxbury Press.

Miller, Irwin, and John E. Freund. (1965). *Probability and Statistics for Engineers.* New Jersey: Prentice-Hall, Inc.

Mood, A., and F. Graybill. (1963). *Introduction To The Theory of Statistics.* (Second Edition). New York: McGraw-Hill Book Co.

Moses, L.E. (1959). *Elementary Decision Theory.* New York: John Wiley and Sons.

Natrella, Mary G. (1963). *Experimental Statistics.* Washington, D.C.: National Bureau of Standards Handbook 91, Government Printing Office.

Neville, A.M., and J.B. Kennedy. (1964). *Basic Statistical Methods for Engineers and Scientists.* International Textbook Co.

Nie, N.N., C.H. Hull, J.G. Jenkins, K. Steinbrenner, and D.H. Bent. (1975). *Statistical Package for the Social Sciences.* (Second Edition). New York: McGraw-Hill Book Co.

Pearson, C. (1983). *Handbook of applied Mathematics,* (Second Edition). New York: Van Nostrand Reinhold Co.

Pearson, E.S., and H.O. Hartley. (1972). *Biometrika Tables for Statisticians*; Vol. 2. Cambridge, Eng.: Cambridge University Press.

Snedecor, G.W., and W.G. Cochran (1967). *Statistical Methods.* (Sixth Edition). Iowa State University Press.

Spotts, M.F. (1978). "Fast Dimensional Checks With Statistics." *Machine Design*; Oct. pp. 171-173.

Wallis, W.A., and H.V. Roberts. (1956). *Statistics: A New Approach.* The Free Press.

Ward, J., and E. Jennings. (1973). *Introduction to Linear Models.* New Jersey: Prentice-Hall

Design of Experiments

Anderson, V.L., and R.A. McLean. (1974). *Design of Experiments*. New York: Marcel Dekker.

Cochran, W., and G. Cox. (1957). *Experimental Designs*. (Second Edition). New York: John Wiley and Sons.

Hicks, C.R. (1964). *Fundamental Concepts in the Design of Experiments*. New York: McGraw-Hill Book Co.

John, P.W.M. (1971). *Statistical Design and Analysis of Experiments*. New York: The MacMillan Company.

Kempthrone, O. (1952). *The Design and Analysis of Experiments*. New York.

Kwok-Leung, Tsui. (1988). "Strategies for Planning Experiments Using Orthogonal Arrays and Confounding Tables." *Qual. Reliab: Eng. Int.* AT&T Bell Lab., New Jersey (UK), Vol. 4, No. 2, Apr.-Jun. 113-22.

Lichtenberg, L.R., M. Sleiman, and M.J. Harry. (1986). "Statistics, Designed Experiments Assembly." *Circuit World, Journal of the Institute of Circuit Technology*; 12(4), pp. 34-39.

Lipson, C., and N. Sheth. (1973). *Statistical Design and Analysis of Engineering Experiments*. New York: McGraw-Hill Book Co.

Montgomery, D.C. (1984). *Design and Analysis of Experiments*. (Second Edition). John Wiley and Sons.

Myers, R.H. (1971). *Response Surface Methodology*. Massachussets: Allyn and Bacon, Inc.

Patel, M.S. (1962). "Group Screening with More Than Two Stages." *Technometrics;* 4(2), pp. 209-217.

Plackett, R.L., and J.P. Burman. (1946). "The Design of Optimum Multifactorial Experiments." *Biometrika*; Vol. 33, pp. 305-325.

Ryan, Thomas P. (1988). "Taguchi's Approach to Experimental Design: Some Concerns." *Quality Progress*. ABI/Inform. Vol. 21, No. 5, May, pp. 34-36.

Shoemaker, Anne C., and Raghu N. Kacker. (1988). "Methodology for Planning Experiments in Robust Product and Process Design." *Quality and Reliability Engineering Intn'l.* New Jersey: AT&T Bell lab. Vol. 4, No. 2, Apr.-Jun. pp. 95-103.

Watson, G.S. (1961). "A Study of the Group Screening Method." *Technometrics;* 3(3), pp. 371-388.

Wheeler, D.J., Ph.D. *(1988). Understanding Industrial Experimentation*. Tennessee: Statistical Process Control Inc.

Statistical Process Control

Duncan, Acheson, J. (1965). *Quality Control and Industrial Statistics*. (Third Edition). Illinois: Richard D. Irwin, Inc.

Grant, E.L., and R.S. Leavenworth. (1972). *Statistical Quality Control*. (Fourth Edition). New York: McGraw-Hill Book Co.

Johnson, L.G. (1964). *Theory and Techniques of Variation Research*. Elsevier Publishing Co.

Kackar, R.N. (1985). "Off Line Quality Control, Parameter Design, and the Taguchi Method." *Journal of Quality Technology*; 17(4), pp. 176-188.

Ott, Ellis R. (1975). *Process Quality Control*. New York: McGraw-Hill Book Co.

Shewhart, W.A. (1931). *Economic Control of Manufactured Product*. New Jersey: Van Nostrand Book Co.

Standard IPC-PC-90. (1989). *General Requirements for Implementation of Statistical Process Control*. Illinois: Institute for Interconnecting and Packaging Electronic Circuits.

Western Electric Company. (1956). *Statistical Quality Control Handbook*. Pennsylvania: Mack Printing Co.

Producibility

Billatos, Samir B. (1988). "Guidelines for Productivity and Manufacturability Strategy." *Manufacturing Review,* Univ. of Connecticut, Storrs, CT., Vol. 1, No. 3, Oct. pp. 164-167.

Boltz, Roger W. (1977). *Production Processes — The Producibility Handbook*. North Carolina: Conquest Publications.

Boothroyd, G., C. Poli, and L. Murch. (1982). *Automatic Assembly*. New York: Marcel Decker, Inc.

Boyer, David E., and John W. Nazemetz. (1985). "Introducing Statistical Selective Assembly – A Means of Producing High Precision Assemblies from Low Precision Components." *Proceedings, American Institute of Industrial Engineers*. Annual Conference and Convention, pp. 562-570.

Brown, John O. (1987). "Producibility Problem Solving or the Supplier Quality Paradox – A Fix?" *Annual Quality Congress Transactions*. (Fourty-First Edition). Wisconsin: ASQC.

Bunselmeyer, K. (1987). "Manufacturability Checklist for Printed Wiring Assemblies." *Printed Circuit Des*. Missouri: Manuf. Eng. Srvcs. Vol. 4, No. 6, Jun. pp. 23-4.

Deming, W. Edwards. (1982). *Quality, Productivity and Competitive Position*. Massachusetts Institute of Technology, Center for Advanced Engineering Study.

Dwivedi, Suren N., and Barry R. Klein. (1986). "Design for Manufacturability Makes Dollars and Sense." *CIM Rev;* Vol. 2, No. 3, pp. 53-59.

Fortini, E.T. (1967). *Dimensioning for Interchangeable Manufacture*. New York: Industrial Press.

Kackar, R.N., and A.C. Shoemaker. (1986). *Robust Design: A Cost-effective Method for Improving Manufacturing Processes*. New Jersey: AT&T Bell Labs. Vol. 65, No. 2, Mar.-Apr. pp. 39-50.

King, Robert. (1987). "Listening to the Voice of the Customer: Using the Quality Function Deployment System." *National Productivity Review;* Vol. 6, No. 3, pp. 277-281.

Lewis, G.M. (1988). "Design for Manufacturability Applying the Methodology." *Proceedings of the 3rd International Conference on the Product Design for Manufacture and Assembly*. Michigan: Troy Conferences.

Lin, K.M., and R.N. Kacker. (1986). "Optimizing the Wave Soldering Process." *Packaging and Production;* Feb., pp. 108-115.

Maddoux, K.C., and S.C. Jain. (1986). "CAE for the Manufacturing Engineer: The Role of Process Simulation In Concurrent Engineering." *American Society of Mechanical Engineers. Production Engineering Division*. New York: ASME, Vol. 20, Dec. pp. 1-15.

McGregory, Jim, and Hal Conklin. (1986). "Analyzing Manufacturability and the Effects of Design Changes." *Printed Circuit Des.;* Vol. 3, No. 5, May, pp. 25-27, 31.

Phadke, M.S., and K. Dehnad. (1988). "Optimization of Product and Process Design for Quality and Cost." *Quality and Reliability Engineering International*. AT&T Bell Lab. New Jersey: Vol. 4, No. 2, Apr.-Jun. pp. 105-112.

Priest, J.W. *(1988). Engineering Design for Producibility and Reliability*. New York: Marcel Dekker.

Spotts, M.F. (1977). "Running the Risk of Interference Fits." *Machine Design;* 49(17), pp. 106-111.

Miscellaneous

Baldwin, L.V. (1983). "New Modes for Advanced Engineering Study." *Journal of Engineering Education;* Vol. 31, pp. 384-386.

Baumeister, T., and L.S. Marks. (1967). *Standard Handbook for Mechanical Engineers*. New York: McGraw-Hill Book Co.

Charbonneau, Harvey C., and Gordon L. Webster. (1978). *Industrial Quality Control*. New Jersey: Prentice-Hall.

Coffman, Cathy. (1987). "Make Me A Match: Getting Design and Manufacturing Together – Simultaneously." *Automotive Industries;* Vol. 167, No. 12, Dec. pp 62-64.

Daetz, D. (1987). "The Effect of Product Design on Product Quality and Product Cost." *Manuf. Res. Center*. California: Hewlett-Packard Labs. Vol. 20, No. 6, 64(7), Jun.

DeGarmo, Paul. (1974). *Materials and Processes in Manufacturing*. (Fourth Edition). New York: MacMillan.

Department of the Navy. (1986). *Best Practices for Transitioning from Development to Production*. NAVSO P-6071. Washington.

Doyle, L.E., C.A. Keyser, J.L. Leach, G.F. Schrader, and M.B. Singer. (1969). *Manufacturing Processes and Materials for Engineers*. New Jersey: Prentice-Hall, Inc.

Farag, M.M. (1979). *Materials and Process Selection in Engineering*. London, England: Applied Science Publishers Ltd.

Feigenbaum, A.V. (1961). *Total Quality Control.* New York: McGraw-Hill Book Co.

Gardiner, Paul, and Roy Rothwell. (1985). "Tough Customers: Good Designs." *Design Studies;* Vol. 6, No. 1, Jan. pp 7-17.

Harry, Mikel J. (1987). *The Nature of Six Sigma Quality.* Government Electronics Group, Motorola, Inc.

Ishikawa, Kaoru. (1976). *Guide to Quality Control.* Asian Productivity Organization, Revised Edition.

Juran, J.M., and Frank M. Gryna Jr. (1970). *Quality Planning and Analysis.* New York: McGraw-Hill Book Co.

Little, R.E. (1980). "Statistical Tolerance Limits for Censored Log-Normal Data (Tolerance Limit Computations: Fatigue Life Applications.)" *Journal of Testing and Evaluation;* 8(2), pp. 80-84.

Osborn, A. (1957). *Applied Imagination.* New York: Charles Scribner's Sons.

Parry, G.W., P. Shaw, and D.H. Worledge. (1981). "Statistical Tolerance in Safety Analysis." *Nuclear Safety;* 22(4), pp. 459-463.

Pignatiello, J.J., and J.S. Ramberg. (1985). "Discussion." *Journal of Quality Technology;* 17(4) pp. 198-206.

APPENDIX A
GENERAL CHECKLIST RELATED TO EACH OF THE GENERIC PROBLEM-SOLVING ACTIVITIES

1. CONDUCT SITUATION ANALYSIS

1.1. Form problem solving team if appropriate or required.

1.2. Conduct first problem solving team meeting

1.3. Review all available sources of information related to the situation

1.4. Define the historical state of the situation

1.5. Define the current situation in general terms

1.6. Establish the improvement objective(s) relative to the current situation

1.7. Identify all driving and restraining forces

1.8. Establish the nature of the information required to satisfy the objective(s)

1.9. Determine what type of performance measure meets the information needs

1.10. Select an appropriate index of variability for the given performance measure

2. CONDUCT LITERATURE REVIEW

2.1. Examine experimental objective

2.2. Examine dependent variable(s)

2.3 Examine measurement methodology

2.4. Examine experimental factor(s)

2.5. Examine blocking variables

2.6. Examine covariates

2.7. Evaluate author bias

2.8. Evaluate clarity of content

2.9. Evaluate recent references and bibliography

2.10. Evaluate assumptions of research methods and related activities

2.11. Study analytical methods

2.12. Study degree to which conclusions are supported by numerical evidence

2.13. Study sampling methodology

2.14. Assess referee status

2.15. Assess background of author

2.16. Consider text books

2.17. Consider journal articles

2.18. Consider periodicals

2.19. Consider white papers

2.20. Consider video tapes

2.21. Consider audio tapes

2.22. Consider seminar materials

3. CONDUCT TRAINING ACTIVITIES

3.1. Establish training and education need

3.2. Identify target population

3.3. Identify knowledge requirements

3.4. Identify skill requirements

3.5. Devise training and education action plan

3.6. Prepare initial cost estimate

3.7. Obtain management approval for further development

3.8. Develop training materials

3.9. Conduct necessary training

4. SYNTHESIZE AND FOCUS

4.1. Revise problem statement as necessary to reflect new information

4.2. Write technical report if appropriate or required

4.3. Write management report if appropriate or required

4.4. Disseminate reports and information to all concerned

4.5. Prepare technical level presentation if appropriate or required

4.6. Prepare management level presentation if appropriate or required

4.7. Make presentation if appropriate or required

4.8. Obtain management approval for continued investigation

4.9. Prepare a preliminary agenda for next team meeting

4.10. Schedule next problem solving team meeting

4.11. Disseminate the preliminary agenda to team members and resource personnel

4.12. Conduct problem solving team meeting

5. **DEFINE DEPENDENT VARIABLES(S)**

   5.1. Review carefully the phenomenon under investigation

   5.2. Identify potential response variable(s) to be studied

   5.3. Describe the unique properties of each response variable

   5.4. Describe the constraining properties of each variable

   5.5. Describes the desirable properties of each variable

   5.6. Select the most viable response variable for each phenomenon

6. **DEFINE INDEPENDENT VARIABLES**

   6.1. Construct a Cause and Effect matrix (C&E) for use during brainstorming

   6.2. Integrate literature search results into the C&E matrix

   6.3. Identify all individuals whom could make a contribution to brainstorming

   6.4. Prepare a working copy of the C&E matrix for each individual

   6.5. Distribute copies of the C&E matrix to all participating individuals

   6.6. Record respondent's C&E inputs as they are gathered

   6.7. Schedule first group level brainstorming session and notify all participants

   6.8. Conduct group level brainstorming session

7. **DEFINE CONTROL VARIABLES**

   7.1. Identify the key independent variable(s) to be controlled

   7.2. Define the control objectives for each variable

   7.3. Determine technical feasibility for controlling with SPC methods

   7.4. Prepare initial cost estimate

   7.5. Obtain management approval and support

8. **IDENTIFY MEASUREMENT SYSTEM**

   8.1. Brainstorm potential measurement scales for each response variable

   8.2. Establish a methodology for each measurement scale

   8.3. Identify all practical cost/time/resource constraints related to each scale

   8.4. Study data analysis implications of the various measurement scales

   8.5. Establish selection criteria

   8.6. Select the top rated measurement system based on the criteria

9. **IDENTIFY DATA VEHICLE**

   9.1. Define the primary objective of the data vehicle

   9.2. Identify all characteristics which the data vehicle must possess

   9.3. Review all data requirements in relation to the data vehicle characteristics

   9.4. Define all process performance specifications in relation to the data vehicle

   9.5. Devise final list of characteristics, requirements, and specifications

   9.6. Establish degree of compatibility between criteria and existing vehicle(s)

   9.7. Make engineering decision related to feasibility of using existing vehicle(s)

10. **DESIGN MEASUREMENT VALIDATION STUDY**

    10.1. Devise a test to study measurement sensitivity in relation to data vehicle

    10.2. Prepare initial cost estimate for the study

    10.3. Obtain management approval and funding for the study

    10.4. Develop measurement sensitivity test

    10.5. Study measurement sensitivity, validity, and reliability

    10.6. Modify the measurement methodology as required

    10.7. Document all pertinent information related to the methodology

11. **DESIGN HIERARCHICAL PARETO STUDY**

    11.1. Establish objectives related to study

    11.2. Review the product quality parameter(s) subject to study

    11.3. Devise defect/failure coding system if necessary

    11.4. Select the most appropriate type of format in which to display the data

12. DESIGN PARAMETER CAPABILITY STUDY

12.1. Review the variables to be included in the study

12.2. Identify the specification(s) related to the study

12.3. Define operating limits of the specification

12.4. Define model distribution parameters if appropriate or required

12.5. Establish criterion capability indices if appropriate or required

12.6. Identify all pertinent conditions to which the study is restricted

12.7. Select representative personnel for participation in the study

12.8. Make necessary administrative and logistical arrangements

13. DESIGN MULTI-VARI STUDY

13.1. Establish objectives for the study

13.2. Review the response characteristics to be investigated

13.3. Define all major categories of variation worthy of investigation

13.4. Design Multi-Vari chart format based on defined categories of variation

13.5. Circulate MV format among colleagues for critical review

13.6. Revise MV chart format as necessary

14. DESIGN EXPERIMENTAL STUDY

14.1. Define experimental objectives

14.2. Establish the number of factors to be studied

14.3. Make initial selection of factors based on the objective(s) and constraints

14.4. Determine the degree of experimental confounding considered to be tolerable

14.5. Define levels for the experimental factors to be used

14.6. Revise system components

14.7. Designate primary control variables

14.8. Establish testing conditions for each primary control variable

14.9. Revise system components

14.10. Identify blocking variables

14.11. Define how each blocking variable must be handled

14.12. Revise system components

14.13. Identify background variables which could contaminate experimental results

14.14. Define how the effects of uncontrolled background variables must be handled

14.15. Revise system components

14.16. Finalize the list of experimental factors and related variables

14.17. Construct an appropriate statistical model if appropriate

14.18. Develop statistical hypotheses based on the model, objectives, and constraints

14.19. Define criteria for the selecting an appropriate experiment design

14.20. Select an appropriate experiment design

14.21. Evaluate rationality of all underlying assumptions related to the design

14.22. Revise system components

14.23. Prepare initial cost estimate for the experiment

14.24. Conduct a dry run of the experiment

14.25. Document all related aspects of the experiment design

14.26. Obtain management approval and support for continued investigation

14.27. Revise system components

15. DESIGN PARAMETER CONTROL STUDY

15.1. Review the system variables under consideration

15.2. Select the statistical parameters to be controlled relative to each variable

15.3. Establish the degree of sensitivity each variable parameter must display

15.4. Select appropriate types of charts based on parameters and sensitivity

15.5. Define an appropriate control chart format for each variable parameter

15.6. Determine type of centerline to be used for each parameter

15.7. Select the statistical control limits to be used on each chart

15.8. Establish basis for calculating control limits for each parameter

15.9. Evaluate all pertinent assumptions underlying the selected charts

16. DEVELOP DATA ANALYSIS SYSTEM

16.1. Define data analysis objectives

16.2. Establish the level of analytical precision required

16.3. Identify output format(s) which will satisfy the objectives

16.4. Identify specific methods which will drive the output format(s)

16.5. Select specific data analysis method(s) to be used

16.6. Study all assumptions underlying the selected method(s)

16.7. Devise plan to insure compliance with all relevant assumptions

16.8. Establish required test sensitivity and confidence/risk levels

16.9. Identify experimental error source if appropriate or required

16.10. Derive sample size based on appropriate equation(s) or tables

16.11. Identify practical constraints surrounding the sample size

16.12. Adjust risk and sensitivity parameters based on constraints

16.13. Revise sample size as necessary

16.14. Obtain management approval and support for continued investigation

16.15. Revise system components

16.16. Identify the most efficient computational strategy

16.17. Define hardware requirements

16.18. Define software requirements

16.19. Estimate costs related to the data analysis system

16.20. Obtain management funding

16.21. Conduct a complete dry run of the analytical system

16.22. Revise system components

16.23. Prepare all necessary written instructions

17. DEVELOP DATA TRACKING SYSTEM

17.1. Define tracking requirements

17.2. Establish data gates within the process

17.3. Devise sample coding/labeling system

17.4. Design tracking system

17.5. Estimate costs related to tracking system

17.6. Obtain management approval and funding

17.7. Conduct dry run of the tracking system

17.8. Revise system components

17.9. Document all related aspects of the tracking system

18. DEVELOP DATA COLLECTION SYSTEM

18.1. Establish a data format consistent with data analysis requirements

18.2. Identify all pertinent information which must be attached to the data

18.3. Devise method for establishing data accuracy and validity

18.4. Establish data collection points/gates within the process

18.5. Devise data collection form(s)

18.6. Provide for independent evaluation of data collection form(s)

18.7. Conduct dry run of the data collection devices and aids

18.8. Evaluate results of the dry run

18.9. Revise system components

18.10. Document all related aspects of the data collection system

18.11. Prepare cost estimates

18.12. Obtain management approval for continued development

18.13. Write detailed sample preparation instructions

18.14. Write detailed data collection instructions

18.15. Review instructions by appropriate persons

18.16. Revise data collection instructions as required

18.17. Document all related aspects of the data collection system

19. CONDUCT DATA COLLECTION

19.1. Insure that all required test and measurement apparatus are calibrated

19.2. Prepare sample in accordance to instructions

19.3. Subject samples to the process

19.4. Record response data on data collection form(s)

19.5. Verify accuracy of data recording

20. CONDUCT DATA ANALYSIS

20.1. Review data analysis plan

20.2. Construct data summary tables

20.3. Display data in accordance to the data analysis plan

20.4. Study data displays for potential distortion as a function of scale

20.5. Verify accuracy of the information

20.6. Interpret graphical outcomes

20.7. Compute defined summary indices

20.8. Compute defined statistics

20.9. Consider all pertinent underlying assumptions and test if necessary

20.10. Interpret statistical outcomes

20.11. Rationalize statistical outcomes against data display

20.12. Construct statistical summary table(s) if appropriate or required

20.13. Conduct secondary exploratory data analysis activities

20.14. Verify computational accuracy

20.15. Draw conclusions strictly based on the data

20.16. Establish implications based on the data and interpretations

20.17. Document conclusions and implications

20.18. Translate all analytical outcomes into costs and percentages

20.19. Construct technical level summary tables, charts, and graphs

20.20. Construct management level summary tables, charts, and graphs

21. ESTABLISH SAMPLE SIZE

21.1. Establish sampling objectives

21.2. Preliminary considerations

21.3. Classify the response measurement scale

21.4. Establish required test sensitivity (delta sigma)

21.5. Establish type I error probability (alpha risk – producer's risk)

21.6. Establish type II error probability (beta risk – consumer's risk)

21.7. Identify experimental error source (residual)

21.8. Define number of required runs

21.9. Establish the degree of replication necessary at each run

21.10. Identify practical constraints surrounding the sample size

21.11. Adjust risk and sensitivity parameters based on constraints

21.12. Revise system components

21.13. Document all related aspects of the sample size determination

21.14. Obtain management approval and support for continued investigation

21.15. Revise system components

22. ESTABLISH SAMPLING METHODOLOGY

22.1. Random

22.2. Sequential

22.3. Systematic (based on specified classification variable)

22.4. Time based

22.5. Stratified sequential

22.6. Stratified random

22.7. Stratified systematic

22.8. Establish sampling interval

22.9. Rational subgrouping

23. DESIGN TEST VEHICLE

23.1. Establish design criteria

23.2. Conduct necessary design activities

23.3. Prepare initial cost estimate

23.4. Obtain management approval for further development

23.5. Construct prototype test vehicle

23.6. Verify test vehicle performance in relation to design criteria

23.7. Revise test vehicle design as required

23.8. Document all pertinent aspects of the test vehicle

APPENDIX B
TABLE OF d_2 AND d_2^* VALUES

N \ n →	2	3	4	5	6	7	8	9	10	11	12	13	14	15	16	17	18	19	20
1	1.414	1.906	2.237	2.474	2.669	2.827	2.961	3.076	3.178	3.268	3.348	3.423	3.490	3.552	3.610	3.663	3.713	3.760	3.805
2	1.276	1.806	2.149	2.405	2.603	2.767	2.905	3.024	3.129	3.221	3.304	3.380	3.449	3.513	3.571	3.626	3.677	3.725	3.770
3	1.227	1.767	2.120	2.379	2.580	2.746	2.886	3.006	3.112	3.205	3.289	3.365	3.435	3.499	3.558	3.613	3.665	3.713	3.759
4	1.206	1.749	2.105	2.365	2.569	2.736	2.876	2.997	3.104	3.197	3.281	3.358	3.428	3.492	3.552	3.607	3.659	3.707	3.753
5	1.189	1.738	2.096	2.353	2.562	2.729	2.870	2.992	3.098	3.192	3.276	3.354	3.424	3.488	3.548	3.603	3.655	3.704	3.749
6	1.179	1.731	2.090	2.353	2.557														
7	1.172	1.726	2.086	2.349	2.554														
8	1.167	1.722	2.082	2.346	2.552														
9	1.163	1.718	2.080	2.344	2.550														
10	1.159	1.716	2.078	2.342	2.548														
11	1.157	1.714	2.076	2.339	2.547														
12	1.154	1.712	2.075	2.339	2.546														
13	1.152	1.711	2.073	2.338	2.545														
14	1.151	1.709	2.072	2.337	2.544														
15	1.149	1.708	2.071	2.337	2.543														
16	1.148	1.707	2.071	2.336	2.543														
17	1.147	1.707	2.070	2.335	2.542														
18	1.145	1.706	2.069	2.335	2.542														
19	1.145	1.705	2.069	2.334	2.541														
20	1.144	1.705	2.068	2.334	2.541														
21	1.143	1.704	2.068	2.333	2.541														
22	1.143	1.704	2.068	2.333	2.540														
23	1.142	1.703	2.067	2.333	2.540														
24	1.141	1.703	2.067	2.333	2.540														
25	1.141	1.702	2.066	2.332	2.540														
∞	*1.128*	*1.693*	*2.059*	*2.326*	*2.534*	*2.704*	*2.847*	*2.970*	*3.078*	*3.173*	*3.258*	*3.336*	*3.407*	*3.472*	*3.532*	*3.588*	*3.64*	*3.689*	*3.735*

N = Number of subgroups
n = Number of samples in a subgroup
d_2 = Limiting value for d_2^* (note: d_2 values are italicized.)

N \ n →	21	22	23	24	25	30
1	3.846	3.886	3.923	3.959	3.994	4.147
2	3.812	3.853	3.891	3.927	3.963	4.116
3	3.801	3.841	3.880	3.917	3.952	4.106
4	3.795	3.836	3.875	3.911	3.947	4.101
5	3.792	3.833	3.871	3.908	3.944	4.098
∞	*3.788*	*3.819*	*3.858*	*3.895*	*3.931*	*4.086*

APPENDIX C
TABLE OF UNILATERAL TAIL AREA
UNDER THE NORMAL CURVE BEYOND SELECTED Z VALUES

Z	0.00	0.01	0.02	0.03	0.04	0.05	0.06	0.07	0.08	0.09
0.00	5.000E-01	4.960E-01	4.920E-01	4.880E-01	4.840E-01	4.801E-01	4.761E-01	4.721E-01	4.681E-01	4.641E-01
0.10	4.602E-01	4.562E-01	4.522E-01	4.483E-01	4.443E-01	4.404E-01	4.364E-01	4.325E-01	4.286E-01	4.247E-01
0.20	4.207E-01	4.168E-01	4.129E-01	4.090E-01	4.052E-01	4.013E-01	3.974E-01	3.936E-01	3.897E-01	3.859E-01
0.30	3.821E-01	3.783E-01	3.745E-01	3.707E-01	3.669E-01	3.632E-01	3.594E-01	3.557E-01	3.520E-01	3.483E-01
0.40	3.446E-01	3.409E-01	3.372E-01	3.336E-01	3.300E-01	3.264E-01	3.228E-01	3.192E-01	3.156E-01	3.121E-01
0.50	3.085E-01	3.050E-01	3.015E-01	2.981E-01	2.946E-01	2.912E-01	2.877E-01	2.843E-01	2.810E-01	2.776E-01
0.60	2.743E-01	2.709E-01	2.676E-01	2.643E-01	2.611E-01	2.578E-01	2.546E-01	2.514E-01	2.483E-01	2.451E-01
0.70	2.420E-01	2.389E-01	2.358E-01	2.327E-01	2.297E-01	2.266E-01	2.236E-01	2.207E-01	2.177E-01	2.148E-01
0.80	2.119E-01	2.090E-01	2.061E-01	2.033E-01	2.005E-01	1.977E-01	1.949E-01	1.922E-01	1.894E-01	1.867E-01
0.90	1.841E-01	1.814E-01	1.788E-01	1.762E-01	1.736E-01	1.711E-01	1.685E-01	1.660E-01	1.635E-01	1.611E-01
1.00	1.587E-01	1.562E-01	1.539E-01	1.515E-01	1.492E-01	1.469E-01	1.446E-01	1.423E-01	1.401E-01	1.379E-01
1.10	1.357E-01	1.335E-01	1.314E-01	1.292E-01	1.271E-01	1.251E-01	1.230E-01	1.210E-01	1.190E-01	1.170E-01
1.20	1.151E-01	1.131E-01	1.112E-01	1.093E-01	1.075E-01	1.056E-01	1.038E-01	1.020E-01	1.003E-01	9.853E-02
1.30	9.680E-02	9.510E-02	9.342E-02	9.176E-02	9.012E-02	8.851E-02	8.691E-02	8.534E-02	8.379E-02	8.226E-02
1.40	8.076E-02	7.927E-02	7.780E-02	7.636E-02	7.493E-02	7.353E-02	7.214E-02	7.078E-02	6.944E-02	6.811E-02
1.50	6.681E-02	6.552E-02	6.426E-02	6.301E-02	6.178E-02	6.057E-02	5.938E-02	5.821E-02	5.705E-02	5.592E-02
1.60	5.480E-02	5.370E-02	5.262E-02	5.155E-02	5.050E-02	4.947E-02	4.846E-02	4.746E-02	4.648E-02	4.551E-02
1.70	4.457E-02	4.363E-02	4.272E-02	4.182E-02	4.093E-02	4.006E-02	3.920E-02	3.836E-02	3.754E-02	3.673E-02
1.80	3.593E-02	3.515E-02	3.438E-02	3.363E-02	3.288E-02	3.216E-02	3.144E-02	3.074E-02	3.005E-02	2.938E-02
1.90	2.872E-02	2.807E-02	2.743E-02	2.680E-02	2.619E-02	2.559E-02	2.500E-02	2.442E-02	2.385E-02	2.330E-02
2.00	2.275E-02	2.222E-02	2.169E-02	2.118E-02	2.068E-02	2.018E-02	1.970E-02	1.923E-02	1.876E-02	1.831E-02
2.10	1.786E-02	1.743E-02	1.700E-02	1.659E-02	1.618E-02	1.578E-02	1.539E-02	1.500E-02	1.463E-02	1.426E-02
2.20	1.390E-02	1.355E-02	1.321E-02	1.287E-02	1.255E-02	1.222E-02	1.191E-02	1.160E-02	1.130E-02	1.101E-02
2.30	1.072E-02	1.044E-02	1.017E-02	9.903E-03	9.642E-03	9.387E-03	9.137E-03	8.894E-03	8.656E-03	8.424E-03
2.40	8.198E-03	7.976E-03	7.760E-03	7.549E-03	7.344E-03	7.143E-03	6.947E-03	6.756E-03	6.569E-03	6.387E-03
2.50	6.210E-03	6.036E-03	5.868E-03	5.703E-03	5.543E-03	5.386E-03	5.234E-03	5.085E-03	4.940E-03	4.799E-03
2.60	4.661E-03	4.527E-03	4.396E-03	4.269E-03	4.145E-03	4.024E-03	3.907E-03	3.792E-03	3.681E-03	3.572E-03
2.70	3.467E-03	3.364E-03	3.264E-03	3.167E-03	3.072E-03	2.980E-03	2.890E-03	2.803E-03	2.718E-03	2.635E-03
2.80	2.555E-03	2.477E-03	2.401E-03	2.327E-03	2.256E-03	2.186E-03	2.118E-03	2.052E-03	1.988E-03	1.926E-03
2.90	1.866E-03	1.807E-03	1.750E-03	1.695E-03	1.641E-03	1.589E-03	1.538E-03	1.489E-03	1.441E-03	1.395E-03
3.00	1.350E-03	1.306E-03	1.264E-03	1.223E-03	1.183E-03	1.144E-03	1.107E-03	1.070E-03	1.035E-03	1.001E-03
3.10	9.676E-04	9.354E-04	9.042E-04	8.740E-04	8.447E-04	8.163E-04	7.888E-04	7.622E-04	7.364E-04	7.114E-04
3.20	6.871E-04	6.637E-04	6.410E-04	6.190E-04	5.977E-04	5.770E-04	5.571E-04	5.378E-04	5.191E-04	5.010E-04
3.30	4.835E-04	4.665E-04	4.501E-04	4.343E-04	4.189E-04	4.041E-04	3.898E-04	3.759E-04	3.625E-04	3.495E-04
3.40	3.370E-04	3.249E-04	3.132E-04	3.019E-04	2.909E-04	2.804E-04	2.702E-04	2.603E-04	2.508E-04	2.416E-04
3.50	2.327E-04	2.242E-04	2.159E-04	2.079E-04	2.002E-04	1.927E-04	1.855E-04	1.786E-04	1.719E-04	1.655E-04
3.60	1.592E-04	1.532E-04	1.474E-04	1.418E-04	1.364E-04	1.312E-04	1.262E-04	1.214E-04	1.167E-04	1.123E-04
3.70	1.079E-04	1.038E-04	9.974E-05	9.587E-05	9.214E-05	8.855E-05	8.509E-05	8.175E-05	7.854E-05	7.545E-05
3.80	7.248E-05	6.961E-05	6.685E-05	6.420E-05	6.165E-05	5.919E-05	5.682E-05	5.455E-05	5.236E-05	5.025E-05
3.90	4.822E-05	4.627E-05	4.440E-05	4.260E-05	4.086E-05	3.920E-05	3.760E-05	3.606E-05	3.458E-05	3.316E-05
4.00	3.179E-05	3.048E-05	2.921E-05	2.800E-05	2.684E-05	2.572E-05	2.465E-05	2.362E-05	2.263E-05	2.168E-05
4.10	2.076E-05	1.989E-05	1.905E-05	1.824E-05	1.747E-05	1.672E-05	1.601E-05	1.533E-05	1.467E-05	1.404E-05
4.20	1.344E-05	1.286E-05	1.231E-05	1.177E-05	1.126E-05	1.077E-05	1.031E-05	9.857E-06	9.426E-06	9.014E-06
4.30	8.619E-06	8.240E-06	7.878E-06	7.530E-06	7.198E-06	6.879E-06	6.574E-06	6.282E-06	6.002E-06	5.734E-06
4.40	5.478E-06	5.233E-06	4.998E-06	4.773E-06	4.558E-06	4.353E-06	4.156E-06	3.968E-06	3.787E-06	3.615E-06
4.50	3.451E-06	3.293E-06	3.143E-06	2.999E-06	2.861E-06	2.730E-06	2.604E-06	2.484E-06	2.369E-06	2.259E-06
4.60	2.154E-06	2.054E-06	1.959E-06	1.867E-06	1.780E-06	1.697E-06	1.617E-06	1.541E-06	1.469E-06	1.399E-06
4.70	1.333E-06	1.270E-06	1.210E-06	1.153E-06	1.098E-06	1.046E-06	9.956E-07	9.480E-07	9.026E-07	8.593E-07
4.80	8.181E-07	7.787E-07	7.411E-07	7.054E-07	6.712E-07	6.387E-07	6.077E-07	5.782E-07	5.500E-07	5.232E-07
4.90	4.976E-07	4.733E-07	4.501E-07	4.280E-07	4.070E-07	3.869E-07	3.678E-07	3.496E-07	3.323E-07	3.159E-07

Table of Unilateral Tail Area Under the Normal Curve Beyond Selected Z Values (Cont)

Z	0.00	0.01	0.02	0.03	0.04	0.05	0.06	0.07	0.08	0.09
5.00	3.002E-07	2.853E-07	2.711E-07	2.575E-07	2.447E-07	2.324E-07	2.208E-07	2.097E-07	1.991E-07	1.891E-07
5.10	1.796E-07	1.705E-07	1.619E-07	1.537E-07	1.459E-07	1.385E-07	1.314E-07	1.247E-07	1.184E-07	1.123E-07
5.20	1.066E-07	1.011E-07	9.591E-08	9.098E-08	8.629E-08	8.184E-08	7.762E-08	7.360E-08	6.979E-08	6.617E-08
5.30	6.273E-08	5.947E-08	5.637E-08	5.343E-08	5.064E-08	4.799E-08	4.548E-08	4.309E-08	4.083E-08	3.868E-08
5.40	3.664E-08	3.471E-08	3.288E-08	3.114E-08	2.949E-08	2.792E-08	2.644E-08	2.503E-08	2.370E-08	2.244E-08
5.50	2.124E-08	2.010E-08	1.903E-08	1.801E-08	1.704E-08	1.613E-08	1.526E-08	1.444E-08	1.366E-08	1.292E-08
5.60	1.222E-08	1.156E-08	1.093E-08	1.034E-08	9.776E-09	9.244E-09	8.741E-09	8.264E-09	7.812E-09	7.385E-09
5.70	6.980E-09	6.598E-09	6.235E-09	5.893E-09	5.568E-09	5.262E-09	4.971E-09	4.697E-09	4.437E-09	4.191E-09
5.80	3.959E-09	3.739E-09	3.532E-09	3.335E-09	3.150E-09	2.974E-09	2.808E-09	2.651E-09	2.503E-09	2.363E-09
5.90	2.230E-09	2.105E-09	1.987E-09	1.875E-09	1.769E-09	1.670E-09	1.576E-09	1.487E-09	1.402E-09	1.323E-09
6.00	1.248E-09	1.177E-09	1.110E-09	1.047E-09	9.876E-10	9.314E-10	8.783E-10	8.281E-10	7.808E-10	7.361E-10
6.10	6.940E-10	6.542E-10	6.166E-10	5.812E-10	5.478E-10	5.163E-10	4.865E-10	4.585E-10	4.320E-10	4.070E-10
6.20	3.835E-10	3.613E-10	3.403E-10	3.206E-10	3.020E-10	2.844E-10	2.679E-10	2.523E-10	2.376E-10	2.237E-10
6.30	2.107E-10	1.983E-10	1.867E-10	1.758E-10	1.655E-10	1.558E-10	1.466E-10	1.380E-10	1.299E-10	1.223E-10
6.40	1.151E-10	1.083E-10	1.019E-10	9.586E-11	9.020E-11	8.486E-11	7.983E-11	7.510E-11	7.064E-11	6.645E-11
6.50	6.250E-11	5.878E-11	5.529E-11	5.199E-11	4.889E-11	4.597E-11	4.323E-11	4.065E-11	3.821E-11	3.593E-11
6.60	3.377E-11	3.175E-11	2.984E-11	2.805E-11	2.637E-11	2.478E-11	2.329E-11	2.189E-11	2.057E-11	1.933E-11
6.70	1.816E-11	1.706E-11	1.603E-11	1.506E-11	1.415E-11	1.329E-11	1.249E-11	1.173E-11	1.102E-11	1.035E-11
6.80	9.719E-12	9.127E-12	8.572E-12	8.049E-12	7.559E-12	7.097E-12	6.664E-12	6.257E-12	5.874E-12	5.515E-12
6.90	5.178E-12	4.860E-12	4.562E-12	4.283E-12	4.020E-12	3.773E-12	3.541E-12	3.323E-12	3.119E-12	2.927E-12
7.00	2.747E-12	2.577E-12	2.418E-12	2.269E-12	2.129E-12	1.997E-12	1.874E-12	1.758E-12	1.649E-12	1.547E-12
7.10	1.451E-12	1.361E-12	1.277E-12	1.198E-12	1.123E-12	1.053E-12	9.879E-13	9.264E-13	8.688E-13	8.147E-13
7.20	7.639E-13	7.163E-13	6.716E-13	6.297E-13	5.904E-13	5.535E-13	5.189E-13	4.864E-13	4.560E-13	4.275E-13
7.30	4.007E-13	3.756E-13	3.520E-13	3.300E-13	3.092E-13	2.898E-13	2.716E-13	2.546E-13	2.386E-13	2.235E-13
7.40	2.095E-13	1.963E-13	1.839E-13	1.723E-13	1.615E-13	1.513E-13	1.417E-13	1.328E-13	1.244E-13	1.166E-13
7.50	1.092E-13	1.023E-13	9.581E-14	8.975E-14	8.407E-14	7.874E-14	7.375E-14	6.908E-14	6.470E-14	6.060E-14
7.60	5.675E-14	5.315E-14	4.977E-14	4.661E-14	4.365E-14	4.087E-14	3.827E-14	3.584E-14	3.356E-14	3.142E-14
7.70	2.942E-14	2.755E-14	2.579E-14	2.415E-14	2.261E-14	2.116E-14	1.981E-14	1.855E-14	1.736E-14	1.625E-14
7.80	1.522E-14	1.424E-14	1.333E-14	1.248E-14	1.168E-14	1.093E-14	1.023E-14	9.579E-15	8.965E-15	8.391E-15
7.90	7.853E-15	7.349E-15	6.878E-15	6.437E-15	6.024E-15	5.637E-15	5.275E-15	4.937E-15	4.620E-15	4.323E-15
8.00	4.045E-15	3.785E-15	3.542E-15	3.314E-15	3.101E-15	2.901E-15	2.715E-15	2.540E-15	2.376E-15	2.223E-15
8.10	2.080E-15	1.946E-15	1.821E-15	1.703E-15	1.593E-15	1.491E-15	1.395E-15	1.305E-15	1.220E-15	1.142E-15
8.20	1.068E-15	9.991E-16	9.346E-16	8.742E-16	8.177E-16	7.649E-16	7.155E-16	6.692E-16	6.260E-16	5.855E-16
8.30	5.477E-16	5.122E-16	4.791E-16	4.481E-16	4.191E-16	3.920E-16	3.666E-16	3.429E-16	3.207E-16	2.999E-16
8.40	2.805E-16	2.624E-16	2.454E-16	2.295E-16	2.146E-16	2.007E-16	1.877E-16	1.755E-16	1.642E-16	1.535E-16
8.50	1.436E-16	1.342E-16	1.255E-16	1.174E-16	1.098E-16	1.027E-16	9.601E-17	8.978E-17	8.395E-17	7.851E-17
8.60	7.341E-17	6.865E-17	6.419E-17	6.003E-17	5.613E-17	5.249E-17	4.908E-17	4.589E-17	4.291E-17	4.013E-17
8.70	3.752E-17	3.508E-17	3.281E-17	3.068E-17	2.868E-17	2.682E-17	2.508E-17	2.345E-17	2.193E-17	2.050E-17
8.80	1.917E-17	1.792E-17	1.676E-17	1.567E-17	1.465E-17	1.370E-17	1.281E-17	1.198E-17	1.120E-17	1.047E-17
8.90	9.792E-18	9.155E-18	8.560E-18	8.004E-18	7.484E-18	6.998E-18	6.543E-18	6.118E-18	5.720E-18	5.349E-18
9.00	5.001E-18	4.676E-18	4.372E-18	4.088E-18	3.823E-18	3.574E-18	3.342E-18	3.125E-18	2.922E-18	2.732E-18
9.10	2.555E-18	2.389E-18	2.234E-18	2.089E-18	1.953E-18	1.826E-18	1.707E-18	1.597E-18	1.493E-18	1.396E-18
9.20	1.305E-18	1.221E-18	1.141E-18	1.067E-18	9.979E-19	9.332E-19	8.726E-19	8.160E-19	7.630E-19	7.135E-19
9.30	6.672E-19	6.239E-19	5.834E-19	5.456E-19	5.102E-19	4.771E-19	4.462E-19	4.172E-19	3.902E-19	3.649E-19
9.40	3.412E-19	3.191E-19	2.984E-19	2.791E-19	2.610E-19	2.441E-19	2.283E-19	2.135E-19	1.996E-19	1.867E-19
9.50	1.746E-19	1.633E-19	1.527E-19	1.428E-19	1.336E-19	1.250E-19	1.169E-19	1.093E-19	1.022E-19	9.562E-20
9.60	8.943E-20	8.365E-20	7.824E-20	7.318E-20	6.845E-20	6.402E-20	5.988E-20	5.601E-20	5.240E-20	4.901E-20
9.70	4.584E-20	4.288E-20	4.011E-20	3.752E-20	3.510E-20	3.284E-20	3.072E-20	2.873E-20	2.688E-20	2.515E-20
9.80	2.352E-20	2.201E-20	2.059E-20	1.926E-20	1.802E-20	1.686E-20	1.577E-20	1.476E-20	1.381E-20	1.292E-20
9.90	1.209E-20	1.131E-20	1.058E-20	9.898E-21	9.262E-21	8.666E-21	8.108E-21	7.587E-21	7.099E-21	6.643E-21
10.00	6.216E-21	5.817E-21	5.443E-21	5.093E-21	4.766E-21	4.460E-21	4.174E-21	3.906E-21	3.655E-21	3.421E-21

APPENDIX D
STATISTICAL ESTIMATES OF PARTS PER MILLION DEFECTIVE FOR VARIOUS DEFECT COUNTS AND UNITS

N \ r →	1	2	3	4	5	6	7	8	9	10
10	70233	168484	267886	367584	467402	567280	667193	767127	867076	967036
20	35117	84242	133943	183792	233701	283640	333596	383564	433538	483518
30	23411	56161	89295	122528	155801	189093	222398	255709	289025	322345
40	17558	42121	66971	91896	116850	141820	166798	191782	216769	241759
50	14047	33697	53577	73517	93480	113456	133439	153425	173415	193407
60	11706	28081	44648	61264	77900	94547	111199	127855	144513	161173
70	10033	24069	38269	52512	66772	81040	95313	109590	123868	138148
80	8779	21061	33486	45948	58425	70910	83399	95891	108385	120879
90	7804	18720	29765	40843	51934	63031	74133	85236	96342	107448
100	7023	16848	26789	36758	46740	56728	66719	76713	86708	96704
150	4682	11232	17859	24506	31160	37819	44480	51142	57805	64469
200	3512	8424	13394	18379	23370	28364	33360	38356	43354	48352
250	2809	6739	10715	14703	18696	22691	26688	30685	34683	38681
300	2341	5616	8930	12253	15580	18909	22240	25571	28903	32235
350	2007	4814	7654	10502	13354	16208	19063	21918	24774	27630
400	1756	4212	6697	9190	11685	14182	16680	19178	21677	24176
450	1561	3744	5953	8169	10387	12606	14827	17047	19268	21490
500	1405	3370	5358	7352	9348	11346	13344	15343	17342	19341
600	1171	2808	4465	6126	7790	9455	11120	12785	14451	16117
700	1003	2407	3827	5251	6677	8104	9531	10959	12387	13815
800	878	2106	3349	4595	5843	7091	8340	9589	10838	12088
900	780	1872	2977	4084	5193	6303	7413	8524	9634	10745
1,000	702	1685	2679	3676	4674	5673	6672	7671	8671	9670
1,100	638	1532	2435	3342	4249	5157	6065	6974	7883	8791
1,200	585	1404	2232	3063	3895	4727	5560	6393	7226	8059
1,300	540	1296	2061	2828	3595	4364	5132	5901	6670	7439
1,400	502	1203	1913	2626	3339	4052	4766	5479	6193	6907
1,500	468	1123	1786	2451	3116	3782	4448	5114	5781	6447
1,600	439	1053	1674	2297	2921	3546	4170	4795	5419	6044
1,700	413	991	1576	2162	2749	3337	3925	4513	5100	5688
1,800	390	936	1488	2042	2597	3152	3707	4262	4817	5372
1,900	370	887	1410	1935	2460	2986	3512	4038	4564	5090
2,000	351	842	1339	1838	2337	2836	3336	3836	4335	4835
2,200	319	766	1218	1671	2125	2579	3033	3487	3941	4396
2,400	293	702	1116	1532	1948	2364	2780	3196	3613	4029
2,600	270	648	1030	1414	1798	2182	2566	2950	3335	3719
2.800	251	602	957	1313	1669	2026	2383	2740	3097	3454
3,000	234	562	893	1225	1558	1891	2224	2557	2890	3223
3,200	219	527	837	1149	1461	1773	2085	2397	2710	3022
3,400	207	496	788	1081	1375	1668	1962	2256	2550	2844
3,600	195	468	744	1021	1298	1576	1853	2131	2409	2686
3,800	185	443	705	967	1230	1493	1756	2019	2282	2545
4,000	176	421	670	919	1169	1418	1668	1918	2168	2418
4,200	167	401	638	875	1113	1351	1589	1826	2064	2302
4,400	160	383	609	835	1062	1289	1516	1743	1971	2198
4,600	153	366	582	799	1016	1233	1450	1668	1885	2102
4,800	146	351	558	766	974	1182	1390	1598	1806	2015
5,000	140	337	536	735	935	1135	1334	1534	1734	1934
5,500	128	306	487	668	850	1031	1213	1395	1577	1758
6,000	117	281	446	613	779	945	1112	1279	1445	1612

N = a unit of product, an opportunity for nonconformities, etc.

r = the number of nonconformities.

Statistical Estimates of Parts Per Million Defective for Various Defect Counts and Units (Cont)

N	r → 1	2	3	4	5	6	7	8	9	10
6,500	108	259	412	566	719	873	1026	1180	1334	1488
7,000	100	241	383	525	668	810	953	1096	1239	1381
7,500	94	225	357	490	623	756	890	1023	1156	1289
8,000	88	211	335	459	584	709	834	959	1084	1209
8,500	83	198	315	432	550	667	785	903	1020	1138
9,000	78	187	298	408	519	630	741	852	963	1074
9,500	74	177	282	387	492	597	702	808	913	1018
10,000	70	168	268	368	467	567	667	767	867	967
11,000	64	153	244	334	425	516	607	697	788	879
12,000	59	140	223	306	390	473	556	639	723	806
13,000	54	130	206	283	360	436	513	590	667	744
14,000	50	120	191	263	334	405	477	548	619	691
15,000	47	112	179	245	312	378	445	511	578	645
16,000	44	105	167	230	292	355	417	479	542	604
17,000	41	99	158	216	275	334	392	451	510	569
18,000	39	94	149	204	260	315	371	426	482	537
19,000	37	89	141	193	246	299	351	404	456	509
20,000	35	84	134	184	234	284	334	384	434	484
25,000	28	67	107	147	187	227	267	307	347	387
30,000	23	56	89	123	156	189	222	256	289	322
35,000	20	48	77	105	134	162	191	219	248	276
40,000	18	42	67	92	117	142	167	192	217	242
45,000	16	37	60	82	104	126	148	170	193	215
50,000	14	34	54	74	93	113	133	153	173	193
55,000	13	31	49	67	85	103	121	139	158	176
60,000	12	28	45	61	78	95	111	128	145	161
65,000	11	26	41	57	72	87	103	118	133	149
70,000	10	24	38	53	67	81	95	110	124	138
75,000	9.4	22	36	49	62	76	89	102	116	129
80,000	8.8	21	33	46	58	71	83	96	108	121
85,000	8.3	20	32	43	55	67	78	90	102	114
90,000	7.8	19	30	41	52	63	74	85	96	107
95,000	7.4	18	28	39	49	60	70	81	91	102
100,000	7.0	17	27	37	47	57	67	77	87	97
105,000	6.7	16	26	35	45	54	64	73	83	92
110,000	6.4	15	24	33	42	52	61	70	79	88
120,000	5.9	14	22	31	39	47	56	64	72	81
130,000	5.4	13	21	28	36	44	51	59	67	74
140,000	5.0	12	19	26	33	41	48	55	62	69
150,000	4.7	11	18	25	31	38	44	51	58	64
160,000	4.4	10.5	17	23	29	35	42	48	54	60
170,000	4.1	9.9	16	22	27	33	39	45	51	57
180,000	3.9	9.4	15	20	26	32	37	43	48	54
190,000	3.7	8.9	14	19	25	30	35	40	46	51
200,000	3.5	8.4	13	18	23	28	33	38	43	48
210,000	3.3	8.0	12.8	18	22	27	32	37	41	46
220,000	3.2	7.7	12.2	17	21	26	30	35	39	44
230,000	3.1	7.3	11.6	16	20	25	29	33	38	42
240,000	2.9	7.0	11.2	15	19	24	28	32	36	40
250,000	2.8	6.7	10.7	14.7	18.7	23	27	31	35	39

N = a unit of product, an opportunity for nonconformities, etc.
r   = the number of nonconformities.

Statistical Estimates of Parts Per Million Defective for Various Defect Counts and Units (Cont)

N	r → 1	2	3	4	5	6	7	8	9	10
260,000	2.7	6.5	10.3	14.1	18.0	22	26	30	33	37
270,000	2.6	6.2	9.9	13.6	17.3	21	25	28	32	36
280,000	2.5	6.0	9.6	13.1	16.7	20	24	27	31	35
290,000	2.4	5.8	9.2	12.7	16.1	19.6	23	26	30	33
300,000	2.3	5.6	8.9	12.3	15.6	18.9	22	26	29	32
310,000	2.27	5.4	8.6	11.9	15.1	18.3	22	25	28	31
320,000	2.19	5.3	8.4	11.5	14.6	17.7	21	24	27	30
330,000	2.13	5.1	8.1	11.1	14.2	17.2	20	23	26	29
340,000	2.07	5.0	7.9	10.8	13.7	16.7	19.6	23	26	28
350,000	2.01	4.8	7.7	10.5	13.4	16.2	19.1	22	25	28
360,000	1.95	4.7	7.4	10.2	13.0	15.8	18.5	21	24	27
370,000	1.90	4.6	7.2	9.9	12.6	15.3	18.0	21	23	26
380,000	1.85	4.4	7.0	9.7	12.3	14.9	17.6	20.2	23	25
390,000	1.80	4.3	6.9	9.4	12.0	14.5	17.1	19.7	22	25
400,000	1.76	4.2	6.7	9.2	11.7	14.2	16.7	19.2	22	24
450,000	1.56	3.7	6.0	8.2	10.4	12.6	14.8	17.0	19	21
500,000	1.40	3.4	5.4	7.4	9.3	11.3	13.3	15.3	17	19
550,000	1.28	3.1	4.9	6.7	8.5	10.3	12.1	13.9	16	18
600,000	1.17	2.8	4.5	6.1	7.8	9.5	11.1	12.8	14	16
650,000	1.08	2.6	4.1	5.7	7.2	8.7	10.3	11.8	13	15
700,000	1.00	2.4	3.8	5.3	6.7	8.1	9.5	11.0	12.4	14
750,000	0.94	2.2	3.6	4.9	6.2	7.6	8.9	10.2	11.6	13
800,000	0.88	2.1	3.3	4.6	5.8	7.1	8.3	9.6	10.8	12
850,000	0.83	2.0	3.2	4.3	5.5	6.7	7.8	9.0	10.2	11
900,000	0.78	1.9	3.0	4.1	5.2	6.3	7.4	8.5	9.6	10.7
950,000	0.74	1.8	2.8	3.9	4.9	6.0	7.0	8.1	9.1	10.2
1,000,000	0.70	1.7	2.7	3.7	4.7	5.7	6.7	7.7	8.7	9.7

N = a unit of product, an opportunity for nonconformities, etc.

r = the number of nonconformities.

APPENDIX E
PERCENTILES OF THE t DISTRIBUTIONS

ν \ $1-\alpha$	0.60	0.70	0.80	0.90	0.95	0.975	0.99	0.995
1	0.325	0.727	1.376	3.078	6.314	12.706	31.821	63.657
2	0.289	0.617	1.061	1.886	2.920	4.303	6.965	9.925
3	0.277	0.584	0.978	1.638	2.353	3.182	4.541	5.841
4	0.271	0.569	0.941	1.533	2.132	2.776	3.747	4.604
5	0.267	0.559	0.920	1.476	2.015	2.571	3.365	4.032
6	0.265	0.553	0.906	1.440	1.943	2.447	3.143	3.707
7	0.263	0.549	0.896	1.415	1.895	2.365	2.998	3.499
8	0.262	0.546	0.889	1.397	1.860	2.306	2.896	3.355
9	0.261	0.543	0.883	1.383	1.833	2.262	2.821	3.250
10	0.260	0.542	0.879	1.372	1.812	2.228	2.764	3.169
11	0.260	0.540	0.876	1.363	1.796	2.201	2.718	3.106
12	0.259	0.539	0.873	1.356	1.782	2.179	2.681	3.055
13	0.259	0.538	0.870	1.350	1.771	2.160	2.650	3.012
14	0.258	0.537	0.868	1.345	1.761	2.145	2.624	2.977
15	0.258	0.536	0.866	1.341	1.753	2.131	2.602	2.947
16	0.258	0.535	0.865	1.337	1.746	2.120	2.583	2.921
17	0.257	0.534	0.863	1.333	1.740	2.110	2.567	2.898
18	0.257	0.534	0.862	1.330	1.734	2.101	2.552	2.878
19	0.257	0.533	0.861	1.328	1.729	2.093	2.539	2.861
20	0.257	0.533	0.860	1.325	1.725	2.086	2.528	2.845
21	0.257	0.532	0.859	1.323	1.721	2.080	2.518	2.831
22	0.256	0.532	0.858	1.321	1.717	2.074	2.508	2.819
23	0.256	0.532	0.858	1.319	1.714	2.069	2.500	2.807
24	0.256	0.531	0.857	1.318	1.711	2.064	2.492	2.797
25	0.256	0.531	0.856	1.316	1.708	2.060	2.485	2.787
26	0.256	0.531	0.856	1.315	1.706	2.056	2.479	2.779
27	0.256	0.531	0.855	1.314	1.703	2.052	2.473	2.771
28	0.256	0.530	0.855	1.313	1.701	2.048	2.467	2.763
29	0.256	0.530	0.854	1.311	1.699	2.045	2.462	2.756
30	0.256	0.530	0.854	1.310	1.697	2.042	2.457	2.750
40	0.255	0.529	0.851	1.303	1.684	2.021	2.423	2.704
60	0.254	0.527	0.848	1.296	1.671	2.000	2.390	2.660
120	0.254	0.526	0.845	1.289	1.658	1.980	2.358	2.617
∞	0.253	0.524	0.842	1.282	1.645	1.960	2.326	2.576

APPENDIX F
TABLE OF CHI-SQUARE VALUES

ν \ α	.005	.01	.025	.05	.10	.25	.50
1	$.0^4393$	$.0^3157$	$.0^3982$	.00393	.0158	.102	.455
2	.0100	.0201	.0506	.103	.211	.575	1.386
3	.0717	.115	.216	.352	.584	1.213	2.366
4	.207	.297	.484	.711	1.064	1.923	3.357
5	.412	.554	.831	1.145	1.610	2.675	4.351
6	.676	.872	1.237	1.635	2.204	3.455	5.348
7	.989	1.239	1.690	2.167	2.833	4.255	6.346
8	1.344	1.646	2.180	2.733	3.490	5.071	7.344
9	1.735	2.088	2.700	3.325	4.168	5.899	8.343
10	2.156	2.558	3.247	3.940	4.865	6.737	9.342
11	2.603	3.053	3.816	4.575	5.578	7.584	10.341
12	3.074	3.571	4.404	5.226	6.304	8.438	11.340
13	3.565	4.107	5.009	5.892	7.042	9.299	12.340
14	4.075	4.660	5.629	6.571	7.790	10.165	13.339
15	4.601	5.229	6.262	7.261	8.547	11.036	14.339
16	5.142	5.812	6.908	7.962	9.312	11.912	15.338
17	5.697	6.408	7.564	8.672	10.085	12.792	16.338
18	6.265	7.015	8.231	9.390	10.865	13.675	17.338
19	6.844	7.633	8.907	10.117	11.651	14.562	18.338
20	7.434	8.260	9.591	10.851	12.443	15.452	19.337
21	8.034	8.897	10.283	11.591	13.240	16.344	20.337
22	8.643	9.542	10.982	12.338	14.041	17.240	21.337
23	9.260	10.196	11.688	13.091	14.848	18.137	22.337
24	9.886	10.856	12.401	13.848	15.659	19.037	23.337
25	10.520	11.524	13.120	14.611	16.473	19.939	24.337
26	11.160	12.198	13.844	15.379	17.292	20.843	25.336
27	11.808	12.879	14.573	16.151	18.114	21.749	26.336
28	12.461	13.565	15.308	16.928	18.939	22.657	27.336
29	13.121	14.256	16.047	17.708	19.768	23.567	28.336
30	13.787	14.953	16.791	18.493	20.599	24.478	29.336
40	20.707	22.164	24.433	26.509	29.051	33.660	39.335
50	27.991	29.707	32.357	34.764	37.689	42.942	49.335
60	35.535	37.485	40.482	43.188	46.459	52.294	59.335
70	43.275	45.442	48.758	51.739	55.329	61.698	69.334
80	51.172	53.540	57.153	60.391	64.278	71.145	79.334
90	59.196	61.754	65.647	69.126	73.291	80.625	89.334
100	67.328	70.065	74.222	77.929	82.358	90.133	99.334

ν = Degrees of freedom

Table of Chi-Square Values (Cont)

α ν	.75	.90	.95	.975	.99	.995	.999
1	1.323	2.706	3.841	5.024	6.635	7.879	10.828
2	2.773	4.605	5.991	7.378	9.210	10.597	13.816
3	4.108	6.251	7.815	9.348	11.345	12.838	16.266
4	5.385	7.779	9.488	11.143	13.277	14.860	18.467
5	6.626	9.236	11.070	12.832	15.086	16.750	20.515
6	7.841	10.645	12.592	14.449	16.812	18.548	22.458
7	9.037	12.017	14.067	16.013	18.475	20.278	24.322
8	10.219	13.362	15.507	17.535	20.090	21.955	26.125
9	11.389	14.684	16.919	19.023	21.666	23.589	27.877
10	12.549	15.987	18.307	20.483	23.209	25.188	29.588
11	13.701	17.275	19.675	21.920	24.725	26.757	31.264
12	14.845	18.549	21.026	23.337	26.217	28.300	32.909
13	15.984	19.812	22.362	24.736	27.688	29.819	34.528
14	17.117	21.064	23.685	26.119	29.141	31.319	36.123
15	18.245	22.307	24.996	27.488	30.578	32.801	37.697
16	19.369	23.542	26.296	28.845	32.000	34.267	39.252
17	20.489	24.769	27.587	30.191	33.409	35.718	40.790
18	21.605	25.989	28.869	31.526	34.805	37.156	43.312
19	22.718	27.204	30.144	32.852	36.191	38.582	43.820
20	23.828	28.412	31.410	34.170	37.566	39.997	45.315
21	24.935	29.615	32.671	35.479	38.932	41.401	46.797
22	26.039	30.813	33.924	36.781	40.289	42.796	48.268
23	27.141	32.007	35.172	38.076	41.638	44.181	49.728
24	28.241	33.196	36.415	39.364	42.980	45.558	51.179
25	29.339	34.382	37.652	40.646	44.314	46.928	52.620
26	30.434	35.563	38.885	41.923	45.642	48.290	54.052
27	31.528	36.741	40.113	43.194	46.963	49.645	55.476
28	32.620	37.916	41.337	44.461	48.278	50.993	56.892
29	33.711	39.087	42.557	45.722	49.588	52.336	58.302
30	34.800	40.256	43.773	46.979	50.892	53.672	59.703
40	45.616	51.805	55.758	59.342	63.691	66.766	73.402
50	56.334	63.167	67.505	71.420	76.154	79.490	86.661
60	66.981	74.397	79.082	83.298	88.379	91.952	99.607
70	77.577	85.527	90.531	95.023	100.425	104.215	112.317
80	88.130	96.578	101.879	106.629	112.329	116.321	124.839
90	98.650	107.565	113.145	118.136	124.116	128.299	137.208
100	109.141	118.498	124.342	129.561	135.807	140.169	149.449

ν = Degrees of freedom

APPENDIX G
SIMULATION OF THE EFFECT OF MEAN PERTURBATIONS ON THE STANDARD DEVIATION

The purpose of this Appendix is to demonstrate how the effects of dynamic mean behavior will inflate the standard deviation of a given parameter over many intervals of manufacturing. The Appendix is intended to increase understanding of the aforementioned phenomenon, not to provide a mathematical definition of it. Such a definition will follow in subsequent publications. To facilitate discussion of this phenomenon, let us first list out assumptions:

- $Y=f(X_1 \ldots X_N)$ where Y is the product response parameter of interest and X_i is an independent variable within the underlying cause system.

- Some variables within a manufacturing cause system are deliberately controlled while others are free to vary.

- Those variables that are controlled tend to change the mean location of Y.

- Those variables that are not controlled tend to determine the variance of Y.

- In many instances, the variables may interact in such a manner that the mean and/or variance is affected.

- A sampling methodology can be developed which will significantly minimize nonrandom perturbing influences resulting from the "Vital Few" independent variables.

- The sampling methodology will reveal a collection of N rational subgroups, each of which consists of n independent parameter measurements.

- The response mean and variance are not correlated within or across subgroups.

- Homogeneity of variance exists across all possible pair-wise subgroups.

- The response parameter of interest is normally distributed.

- Dynamic mean variation is evidenced by nonrandom perturbations in the parameter mean.

- Over many intervals of manufacturing, the response mean will tend toward the nominal specification.

In compliance with the previously mentioned assumptions, the computer simulation was initiated by constructing N=350 data sets, each of which consisted of n=5 measurements. The measurements associated with each data set were randomly selected from a normal distribution under the constraint $\mu=0$ and $\sigma=1$. A unique seed was selected for the generation of each data set. In this context, each data set constituted a rational subgroup. Next, the mean and standard deviation of each rational subgroup was computed using Eq. (5-2) and Eq. (5-4), respectively. In addition, the cumulative standard deviation was progressively calculated across all N=350 subgroups.

Nonrandom perturbations in the response mean were created as follows. A uniform random distribution was used to create a series of mean shift vectors, one for each of the 350 subgroups. A positive vector called for a positive shift in the mean and a negative vector called for a negative shift.

The extent of the mean shift for each subgroup was determined by a random normal number. Each of these numbers was multiplied by the corresponding vector, as previously mentioned. Essentially, this had the effect of simulating a "random walk" between two limits. The intent here was to generate a random normal distribution of vectored "mean shift" values given as standard normal deviates.

To simulate nonrandom dynamic mean behavior, a ten-point moving average of the vectored mean shifts was employed. The resulting pattern of mean behavior is displayed in Figure G-1.

Each of the N=350 mean shift values, as given in Figure G-1, was added to each value of the respective subgroup. As before, the mean and standard deviation were calculated for each of the shifted subgroups. In addition, the cumulative standard deviation was progressively calculated across all 350 subgroups. Finally, a ratio was calculated of the cumulative standard deviations for each shifted subgroup to that of the respective unshifted subgroup. Figure G-2 shows a plot of these ratios as the number of subgroups increases.

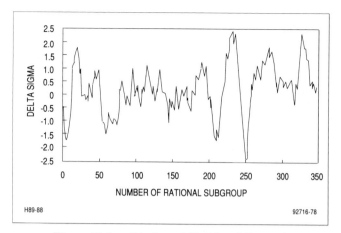

H89-88

92716-78

Figure G-1.   Display of Simulated Dynamic Mean Behavior Used to Interject Nonrandom Pertubations Across the N = 350 Subgroups

The ratios in Figure G-2 are equivalent to the value of c, the inflation factor given in Eq. (6-9) in the text.

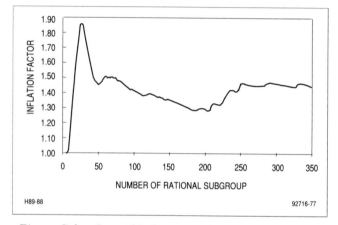

H89-88

92716-77

Figure G-2.   Rate of Inflation in the Standard Deviation Due to Simulated Dynamic Mean Behavior

Repeated simulations tend to verify that the value of c does fall in the range 1.4 to 1.6, as stated in paragraph 6.2. From Figure G-2 it can be seen that the result of nonrandom causal variables perturbing the system over time, has the effect of inflating the standard deviation. In this case the inflation factor is 1.45. It should be noted that many runs were necessary to achieve convergence of the inflation factor. In the case of this example, over 250 runs were needed before a stable value of the inflation factor became evident. The implications of this for "real world" problems should be self-evident to the experienced practitioner.

A final point should be made here. In an environment of continual improvement, there is the possibility that, for long periods of time, those variables contributing to the nonrandom behavior of the mean may be brought under better control. In such a case, one might expect the extent of variance inflation to decrease over time. However, one could also postulate that further improvements might have a positive effect on the random or short-term variation. In this latter case, the inflation factor might remain the same due to concurrent reductions in both the long- and short-term variances. Though the inflation factor might stay the same, the overall affect is one of improvement, because both the short- and long-term variations have been reduced.

GLOSSARY OF TERMS

Term	Definition
ABSCISSA	The horizontal axis of a graph.
ACCEPTANCE REGION	The region of values for which the null hypothesis is accepted.
ALPHA RISK	The probability of accepting the alternate hypothesis when, in reality, the null hypothesis is true.
ALTERNATE HYPOTHESIS	A tentative explanation which indicates that an event does not follow a chance distribution; a contrast to the null hypothesis.
ASSIGNABLE CAUSE	A source of variation which is non-random; a change in the source ("VITAL FEW" variables) will produce a significant change of some magnitude in the response (dependent variable), e.g., a correlation exists; the change may be due to an intermittent in-phase effect or a constant cause system which may or may not be highly predictable; an assignable cause is often signaled by an excessive number of data points outside a control limit and/or a non-random pattern within the control limits; an unnatural source of variation; most often economical to eliminate.
ASSIGNABLE VARIATIONS	Variations in data which can be attributed to specific causes.
ATTRIBUTE	A characteristic that may take on only one value, e.g. 0 or 1.
ATTRIBUTE DATA	Numerical information at the nominal level; subdivision is not conceptually meaningful; data which represents the frequency of occurrence within some discrete category, e.g., 42 solder shorts.
BACKGROUND VARIABLES	Variables which are of no experimental interest and are not held constant. Their effects are often assumed insignificant or negligible, or they are randomized to ensure that contamination of the primary response does not occur.
BETA RISK	The probability of accepting the null hypothesis when, in reality, the alternate hypothesis is true.
BLOCKING VARIABLES	A relatively homogenous set of conditions within which different conditions of the primary variables are compared. Used to ensure that background variables do not contaminate the evaluation of primary variables.
CAUSALITY	The principle that every change implies the operation of a cause.
CAUSATIVE	Effective as a cause.
CAUSE	That which produces an effect or brings about a change.
C CHARTS	Charts which display the number of defects per sample.
CHARACTERISTIC	A definable or measurable feature of a process, product, or variable.
CENTRAL TENDENCY	Numerical average, e.g., mean, median, and mode; center line on a statistical process control chart.

Term	Definition
CENTER LINE	The line on a statistical process control chart which represents the characteristic's central tendency.
CLASSIFICATION	Differentiation of variables.
COMMON CAUSE	See RANDOM CAUSE.
CONFIDENCE LEVEL	The probability that a random variable x lies between the interval $(x - C_{\alpha/2})$ to $(x + C_{\alpha/2})$.
CONFIDENCE LIMITS	The two values that define the confidence interval $(x - C_{\alpha/2})$ to $(x + C_{\alpha/2})$.
CONFOUNDING	Allowing two or more variables to vary together so that it is impossible to separate their unique effects.
CONSUMERS RISK	Probability of accepting a lot when, in fact, the lot should have been rejected (see BETA RISK).
CONTINUOUS DATA	Numerical information at the interval of ratio level; subdivision is conceptually meaningful; can assume any number within an interval, e.g., 14.652 amps.
CONTINUOUS RANDOM VARIABLE	A random variable which can assume any value continuously in some specified interval.
CONTROL CHART	A graphical rendition of a characteristic's performance across time in relation to its natural limits and central tendency.
CONTROL SPECIFICATIONS	Specifications called for by the product being manufactured.
CUTOFF POINT	The point which partitions the acceptance region from the reject region.
DATA	Factual information used as a basis for reasoning, discussion, or calculation; often refers to quantitative information.
DEGREES OF FREEDOM	The number of independent measurements available for estimating a population parameter.
DENSITY FUNCTION	The function which yields the probability that a particular random variable takes on any one of its possible values.
DEPENDENT VARIABLE	A Response Variable; e.g., y is the dependent or "Response" variable where $Y = f(X_1 \ldots X_N)$ variable.
DISCRETE RANDOM VARIABLE	A random variable which can assume values only from a definite number of discrete values.
DISTRIBUTIONS	Tendency of large numbers of observations to group themselves around some central value with a certain amount of variation or "scatter" on either side.
EFFECT	That which was produced by a cause.
EXPERIMENT	A test under defined conditions to determine an unknown effect; to illustrate or verify a known law; to test or establish a hypothesis.

Term	Definition
EXPERIMENTAL ERROR	Variation in observations made under identical test conditions. Also called residual error. The amount of variation which cannot be attributed to the variables included in the experiment.
FACTORS	Independent variables.
FIXED EFFECTS MODEL	Experimental treatments are specifically selected by the researcher. Conclusions only apply to the factor levels considered in the analysis. Inferences are restricted to the experimental levels.
FLUCTUATIONS	Variances in data which are caused by a large number of minute variations or differences.
FREQUENCY DISTRIBUTION	The pattern or shape formed by the group of measurements in a distribution.
HISTOGRAM	Vertical display of a population distribution in terms of frequencies; a formal method of plotting a frequency distribution.
HOMOGENEITY OF VARIANCE	The variances of the groups being contrasted are equal (as defined by statistical test of significant difference), e.g., $\sigma^2_A = \sigma^2_B$.
INDEPENDENT VARIABLE	A controlled variable; a variable whose value is independent of the value of another variable.
INTERACTION	When the effects of a factor A are not the same at all levels of another factor B.
INSTABILITY	Unnaturally large fluctuations in a pattern.
INTERACTION	The tendency of two or more variables to produce an effect in combination which neither variable would produce if acting alone.
INTERVAL	Numeric categories with equal units of measure but no absolute zero point, i.e., quality scale or index.
LINE CHARTS	Charts used to track the performance without relationship to process capability or control limits.
LOWER CONTROL LIMIT	A horizontal dotted line plotted on a control chart which represents the lower process limit capabilities of a process.
MIXED EFFECTS MODEL	Contains elements of both the fixed and random effects models.
NOMINAL	Unordered categories which indicate membership or nonmembership with no implication of quantity, i.e., assembly area number one, part numbers, etc.
NONCONFORMING UNIT	A unit which does not conform to one or more specifications, standards, and/or requirements.
NONCONFORMITY	A condition within a unit which does not conform to some specific specification, standard, and/or requirement; often referred to as a defect; any given nonconforming unit can have the potential for more than one nonconformity.

Term	Definition
NORMAL DISTRIBUTION	A continuous, symmetrical density function characterized by a bell-shaped curve, e.g., distribution of sampling averages.
NULL HYPOTHESIS	A tentative explanation which indicates that a chance distribution is operating; a contrast to the null hypothesis.
ONE-SIDED ALTERNATIVE	The value of a parameter which has an upper bound or a lower bound, but not both.
ORDINAL	Ordered categories (ranking) with no information about distance between each category, i.e., rank ordering of several measurements of an output parameter.
ORDINATE	The vertical axis of a graph.
PARAMETER	A constant defining a particular property of the density function of a variable.
PARETO DIAGRAM	A chart which ranks, or places in order, common occurrences.
P CHARTS	Charts used to plot percent defectives in a sample.
PERTURBATION	A nonrandom disturbance.
POPULATION	A group of similar items from which a sample is drawn. Often referred to as the universe.
POWER OF AN EXPERIMENT	The probability of rejecting the null hypothesis when it is false and accepting the alternate hypothesis when it is true.
PREVENTION	The practice of eliminating unwanted variation a priori (before the fact), e.g., predicting a future condition from a control chart and then applying corrective action before the predicted event transpires.
PRIMARY CONTROL VARIABLES	The major independent variables used in the experiment.
PROBABILITY	The chance of something happening; the percent or number of occurrences over a large number of trials.
PROBABILITY OF AN EVENT	The number of successful events divided by the total number of trials.
PROBLEM	A deviation from a specified standard.
PROBLEM SOLVING	The process of solving problems; the isolation and control of those conditions which generate or facilitate the creation of undesirable symptoms.
PROCESS	A particular method of doing something, generally involving a number of steps or operations.
PROCESS AVERAGE	The central tendency of a given process characteristic across a given amount of time or at a specific point in time.
PROCESS CONTROL	See STATISTICAL PROCESS CONTROL.
PROCESS CONTROL CHART	Any of a number of various types of graphs upon which data are plotted against specific control limits.

Term	Definition
PROCESS SPREAD	The range of values which a given process characteristic displays; this particular term most often applies to the range but may also encompass the variance. The spread may be based on a set of data collected at a specific point in time or may reflect the variability across a given amount of time.
PRODUCERS RISK	Probability of rejecting a lot when, in fact, the lot should have been accepted (see ALPHA RISK).
PROJECT	A problem, usually calling for planned action.
R CHARTS	Plot of the difference between the highest and lowest in a sample. Range control chart.
RANDOM	Selecting a sample so each item in the population has an equal chance of being selected; lack of predictability; without pattern.
RANDOM CAUSE	A source of variation which is random; a change in the source ("trivial many" variables) will not produce a highly predictable change in the response (dependent variable), e.g., a correlation does not exist; any individual source of variation results in a small amount of variation in the response; cannot be economically eliminated from a process; an inherent natural source of variation.
RANDOM EFFECTS MODEL	Experimental treatments are a random sample from a larger population of treatments. Conclusions can be extended to the population. interferences are not restricted to the experimental levels.
RANDOMNESS	A condition in which any individual event in a set of events has the same mathematical probability of occurrence as all other events within the specified set, i.e., individual events are not predictable even though they may collectively belong to a definable distribution.
RANDOM SAMPLE	One or more samples randomly selected from the universe (population).
RANDOM VARIABLE	A variable which can assume any value from a set of possible values.
RANDOM VARIATIONS	Variations in data which result from causes which cannot be pinpointed or controlled.
RANGE	The difference between the highest and lowest values in a set of values or "subgroup."
RANKS	Values assigned to items in a sample to determine their relative occurrence in a population.
RATIO	Numeric scale which has an absolute zero point and equal units of measure throughout, i.e., measurements of an output parameter, i.e., amps.
REJECT REGION	The region of values for which the alternate hypothesis is accepted.
REPLICATION	Observations made under identical test conditions.
ROBUST	The condition or state in which a response parameter exhibits hermeticity to external cause of a nonrandom nature; i.e., impervious to perturbing influence.

Term	Definition
REPRESENTATIVE SAMPLE	A sample which accurately reflects a specific condition or set of conditions within the universe.
RESEARCH	Critical and exhaustive investigation or experimentation having for its aim the revision of accepted conclusions in the light of newly discovered facts.
RESIDUAL ERROR	See EXPERIMENTAL ERROR.
SAMPLE	One or more observations drawn from a larger collection of observations or universe (population).
SCATTER DIAGRAMS	Charts which allow the study of correlation, e.g., the relationship between two variables.
SPECIAL CAUSE	See ASSIGNABLE CAUSE.
STABLE PROCESS	A process which is free of assignable causes, e.g., in statistical control.
STANDARD DEVIATION	A statistical index of variability which describes the spread.
STATISTICAL CONTROL	A quantitative condition which describes a process that is free of assignable/special causes of variation, e.g., variation in the central tendency and variance. Such a condition is most often evidenced on a control chart, i.e., a control chart which displays an absence of nonrandom variation.
STATISTICAL PROCESS CONTROL	The application of statistical methods and procedures relative to a process and a given set of standards.
SUBGROUP	A logical grouping of objects or events which displays only random event-to-event variations, e.g., the objects or events are grouped to create homogenous groups free of assignable or special causes. By virtue of the minimum within group variability, any change in the central tendency or variance of the universe will be reflected in the "subgroup-to-subgroup" variability.
SYMPTOM	That which serves as evidence of something not seen.
SYSTEM	That which is connected according to a scheme.
SYSTEMATIC VARIABLES	A pattern which displays predictable tendencies.
THEORY	A plausible or scientifically acceptable general principle offered to explain phenomena.
TEST OF SIGNIFICANCE	A procedure to determine whether a quantity subjected to random variation differs from a postulated value by an amount greater than that due to random variation alone.
TWO-SIDED ALTERNATIVE	The values of a parameter which designate an upper and lower bound.
TYPE I ERROR	See ALPHA RISK.
TYPE II ERROR	See BETA RISK.

Term	Definition
UNNATURAL PATTERN	Any pattern in which a significant number of the measurements do not group themselves around a center line; when the pattern is unnatural, it means that outside disturbances are present and are affecting the process.
UPPER CONTROL LIMIT	A horizontal line on a control chart (usually dotted) which represents the upper limits of process capability.
VARIABLE	A characteristic that may take on different values.
VARIABLES DATA	Numerical measurements made at the interval or ratio level; quantitative data, e.g., ohms, voltage, diameter; subdivisions of the measurement scale are conceptually meaningful, e.g., 1.6478 volts.
VARIATION	Any quantifiable difference between individual measurements; such differences can be classified as being due to common causes (random) or special causes (assignable).
VARIATION RESEARCH	Procedures, techniques, and methods used to isolate one type of variation from another (for example, separating product variation from test variation).
$\overline{X}$ & R CHARTS	A control chart which is a representation of process capability over time; displays the variability in the process average and range across time.

INDEX

M (cont)

Multi-vari analysis, 8-10

Mutually exclusive events, 2-2

N

Nominal
    pool, 6-17
    specification, 6-13, 6-15

Nonconformance, 1-3, 3-4, 5-7, 5-11, 6-18, 7-13, 8-2, 8-7, 8-8, 8-14
    to standard, 2-1, 2-4

Nonconformities, 5-10

Nonrandom
    error, 6-4, 6-5, 7-2
    influences, 3-5, 5-7, 5-12, 6-7
    perturbing influences, 6-1
    variations, 7-12

Normal
    curve, 5-10
    density function, 5-9
    distribution, 5-4, 5-6, 5-10, 5-13, 5-14
    limiting distribution, 5-9

Normalized
    rolled-throughput, 2-3
    rolled-throughput yield, 2-4, 2-9

Null condition, 8-7

O

Observed defects, 2-4

Occurrences, 2-6

Optimization study, 8-14

Out-of-spec, 2-8

P

Poisson, 5-9
    distribution, 2-5, 5-9
    model, 5-9

Parameter
    analysis, 4-2
    capability, 4-3, 7-7, 7-10
    capability data, 3-4
    capability ratio, 7-6, 7-7, 7-8
    characterization, 5-1, 6-1, 8-1
    control, 4-2, 8-18
    definition, 4-2

optimization, 4-2
robustness, 6-12, 8-9
statistics, 5-2

Pareto, 3-6, 8-2
    analysis, 8-2
    principle, 6-3, 6-4

Performance
    characteristic, 6-3
    index, 5-11
    standards, 8-7

Perturbing
    nonrandom errors, 6-4
    nonrandom influences, 8-8, 8-9

Point estimate, 6-20

Poisson, 2-7, 3-4, 6-19, 6-20
    equation, 2-6
    model, 2-8
    relation, 2-6
    law, 2-6

Population, 5-1

Probabilistic certainty, 6-4

Probability, 2-2, 5-6
    density, 5-8
    distribution, 5-8
    of nonconformance, 6-9
    of occurrence, 2-6

Problem solving, 4-8

Process, 4-1
    characterization, 7-1
    capability, 6-5
    capability ratio, 6-12
    capability ratios, 8-8
    characterization, 4-1, 4-2, 4-3, 4-10, 6-8, 6-17, 7-4, 8-3
    characterization metrics, 6-1, 7-1
    characterization study, 4-7, 8-4
    mean, 6-17
    parameter control, 4-2
    parameter optimization, 4-2
    performance, 4-1
    standardization, 6-1

Producibility, 1-2, 1-3, 1-5, 2-1, 2-8, 3-4, 3-5, 3-6, 4-3, 6-1, 6-7, 6-17, 7-8, 8-18
    metrics, 2-4, 3-6
    optimization, 3-6

Product
    characteristic, 7-1
    parameter analysis, 4-2
    parameter definition, 4-2
    performance, 6-17
    response characteristics, 4-1
    variation, 1-3